T0305109

Women in Leadership and Management

NEW HORIZONS IN MANAGEMENT

Series Editor: Cary L. Cooper, CBE, *Professor of Organizational Psychology and Health, Lancaster University Management School, Lancaster University, UK.*

This important series makes a significant contribution to the development of management thought. This field has expanded dramatically in recent years and the series provides an invaluable forum for the publication of high quality work in management science, human resource management, organizational behaviour, marketing, management information systems, operations management, business ethics, strategic management and international management.

The main emphasis of the series is on the development and application of new original ideas. International in its approach, it will include some of the best theoretical and empirical work from both well-established researchers and the new generation of scholars.

Women in Leadership and Management

Edited by

Duncan McTavish
Senior Lecturer, Glasgow Caledonian University, UK

Karen Miller
Senior Lecturer, Glasgow Caledonian University, UK

NEW HORIZONS IN MANAGEMENT

Edward Elgar
Cheltenham, UK • Northampton, MA, USA

Published by
Edward Elgar Publishing Limited
Glensanda House
Montpellier Parade
Cheltenham
Glos GL50 1UA
UK

Edward Elgar Publishing, Inc.
William Pratt House
9 Dewey Court
Northampton
Massachusetts 01060
USA

A catalogue record for this book
is available from the British Library

Library of Congress Cataloguing in Publication Data

Women in leadership and management / edited by Duncan McTavish, Karen Miller.
        p. cm. — (New horizons in management)
    Includes bibliographical references and index.
    1. Women executives. I. McTavish, Duncan. II. Miller, Karen, 1971- III. Series.
    HD6054.3.W638 2006
    658.4'092082—dc22

                                                                    2006011710

ISBN-13: 978 1 84542 646 0
ISBN-10: 1 84542 646 0

Printed and bound in Great Britain by MPG Books Ltd, Bodmin, Cornwall

Contents

Contributors

Dr Patricia Bryans is Principal Lecturer in Corporate Development and Programme Director at Newcastle Business School, Northumbria University. She is based in the Corporate and Management Development Centre which specializes in developing bespoke management awards and management development interventions for organizations. Patricia's research is concerned with individual and organizational learning, and management development, especially women in management, and she publishes, presents and reviews journals and conferences in this area.

James Collins is a doctoral student at Cranfield School of Management conducting research in public sector leadership. He holds undergraduate and postgraduate qualifications in psychology from Sunderland University and the University of Kent. He has presented papers on the meanings of leadership and on discourse and leadership at a number of international management and leadership conferences.

Dr Sandra Fielden is a Senior Lecturer in Organizational Psychology in the Manchester Business School, University of Manchester and is Co-Director of the Centre for Diversity and Work Psychology where she researches issues of diversity, equal opportunities, female small business owners, women in management, organizational politics, and organizational change. Sandra is a charted psychologist and an Associate Fellow of the British Psychological Society, and is joint director of the 'Innovations in Coaching and Mentoring' programme. Sandra is also editor of *Women In Management Review* and has been chair of the 'Gender and Management' track of the British Academy of Management. She is well published with numerous journal papers and book chapters and is co-editor of the recently published books *Individual Diversity and Psychology in Organisations*, and *International Handbook of Women and Small Entrepreneurship* (with M.J. Davidson).

Dr Caroline Gatrell, at Lancaster University's Management School, conducts research in the area of family practices, motherhood and paid and unpaid work. Her research has received acclaim with the publication of her recent book, *Hard Labour: The Sociology of Parenthood* (Open University Press, 2005). She has been a keynote speaker at DTI and British Academy seminar series. Dr Gatrell continues her research interest in theoretical approaches to the management of reproduction and parenting, cultural practices and lived experience at the Institute for Cultural Research by developing a research cluster on Hard Labour: The Cultural Politics of Reproduction and Parenting.

Carrianne Hunt is a doctoral student as the Centre for Diversity and Work Psychology, Manchester Business School, and is currently working on an ESF-funded project to develop and design an evidence-based e-coaching programme, specifically for female entrepreneurs. Carrie holds a Masters in Health Research at the Institute for Health Research, Lancaster University, and previously worked as a Programme Manager at the NHS National Nursing Leadership Programme.

Prof. Roger Levy is Director of the Graduate Academy of Business at Glasgow Caledonian University and holds degrees from the University of Leicester, the University of Glasgow and McGill University. His main research interests lie in the field of the management of EU programmes and the ongoing reform of the management systems of the European Commission. In this context he is a member of the University Association for Contemporary European Studies and has published and presented papers extensively, acted as an expert adviser to the Commission on its evaluation capacities, and organized conferences and seminars. Prof. Levy's publications include *Managing, Monitoring and Evaluating the EU Budget; Internal and External Perspectives* (EIPA, 1999) and *Implementing European Union Public Policy* (Edward Elgar, 2000).

Dr Sharon Mavin is Associate Dean in Newcastle Business School, Northumbria University. Her research and consultancy expertise concerns organizational behaviour, management development, social architecture, individual and organizational learning, and women in management. Her research concerning female misogyny and senior women has received national media attention. Sharon is European Editor of the Learning Organization, and active referee for international journals and conferences primarily exploring gender in organization and women in management.

Gillian A. Maxwell is a Senior Lecturer at Glasgow Caledonian University. Her research interest is human resource management issues and developments, in particular managing diversity, ethics in HRM, work-life balance and human resource development. Recent publications include *Human Resource Management: International Perspectives in Hospitality and Tourism* (2002), *Take the Time* (2003) publication of the Equality Exchange, Fair Play Scotland and Department of Trade and Industry, and various journal articles.

Dr Duncan McTavish is Senior Lecturer in Management at Glasgow Caledonian University and Director of the Centre for Public Policy and Management. He holds degrees from Strathclyde and Glasgow Universities and at the latter was holder of the prestigious Alexander Stone scholarship. His research interest is public and private management with publications in the areas of the historical development of business and public sector management; the relationship between strategy, policy making and service management in the further education and health care sectors; partnership and the delivery of public services; gender and management in public and private sectors. He has secured funding from the EU, Scottish Executive, Leadership Foundation for Higher Education to manage a number of research projects analysing gender in the management of the small to medium size enterprise, larger business, further and higher education sectors. He has published extensively.

Dr Karen Miller is a Senior Lecturer in Public Management at Glasgow Caledonian University and member of the Centre for Public Policy and Management. She holds degrees from South Africa and the United States of America, and has worked for a number of public, non-governmental and academic institutions, and as a consultant. Her research interest lies in public sector reform, civil service leadership and women in public life. She has developed programmes to improve women's participation in public life in various countries. Her other accomplishments include awards and scholarships such the Edmund Muskie Fellowship. Karen is part of a successful ESF and Scottish Executive funded gender and management project. Her publications include *Public Sector Reform: Governance in South Africa* (Ashgate, 2005), and various journal and conference papers.

Dr Susan M. Ogden is a Senior Lecturer in Management at Glasgow Caledonian University, and has led research and published in the field of compulsory competitive tendering, best value and employee flexibility across public, private and not-for-profit sectors. Her current research interest lies in gender balance in management in the small to medium-sized enterprise sector, and to this regard is part of an ESF and Scottish Executive funded gender in management research project.

Prof. Robert Pyper is Professor of Government and Public Management, and Head of the Globalization and Public Policy Group at Glasgow Caledonian University. His main research interests lie in the areas of UK civil service management and policy, systems of official and political accountability, and accountability in the devolved polities. His work has been published in a range of books, book chapters and journal articles such as *The New Public Administration in Britain* (with John Greenwood and David Wilson;

Routledge, 2001), *The New Public Management in Britain* (with Andrew Massey; Palgrave, 2003), and *Public Management and Modernization in Britain* (with Andrew Massey; Palgrave, 2005). Prof. Pyper is also editor of the journal *Public Policy and Administration* and is a regular commentator on aspects of government and politics for the media.

Dr Val Singh is senior research fellow in organizational behaviour, working in the Centre for Developing Women Business Leaders at Cranfield School of Management, where she undertook her PhD following a portfolio career as civil service executive, English teacher and manager in higher education. Her current research focuses on gender diversity on top UK company boards; ethnic diversity; diversity management across Europe; women's corporate networks; the social construction of leadership; work/life balance, and role modelling. Her Female FTSE Index research with the Centre director, Professor Susan Vinnicombe OBE, has been widely published and discussed, including in Downing Street, the House of Lords and in 15 countries. She is Gender Editor of *The Journal of Business Ethics* and has published and refereed many journal articles. Her consultancy assignments include conference speaking, lecturing and workshops, research and writing. She is a regular judge of the UK National Business Awards, and advises on other awards.

Prof. Ann Stevens is Professor of European Studies at Aston University where she researches and publishes on French and European Union government. She has degrees in History (Cambridge University), MSc (Econ) in European Studies and a PhD in Government (London School of Economics). She held a career in the civil service and has taught at the universities of Sussex and Kent, and as a visiting Professor at Paris I, Paris II and the Institute of Political Studies in Lille. She is the author of *The Government and Politics of France* (Palgrave, 2003) and *Brussels Bureaucrats? The administrative services of the European Union* (with Handley Stevens; Palgrave, 2001) and editor (with Richard Sakwa) of *Contemporary Europe* (Palgrave, 2005). She is currently working on a book on *Women Power and Politics* for Palgrave.

Dr Elaine Swan is a senior teaching fellow at Lancaster University Management School, where she directs The Health Foundation's Leaders for Change Programme and teaches on gender, race and organization studies on the School's Executive MBA. Her research interests are in the sociology of therapeutic cultures; the psycho-social effects of diversity work; and gender and emotions in the workplace. She is currently co-directing two major in-depth qualitative studies funded by the DfES. Recent publications include *On Bodies, Rhinestones and Pleasures: Women Teaching Managers in*

Management Learning; Thinking with Feeling and she is co-editing a special issue on diversity work in the journal *Policy Futures in Education* (with Sara Ahmed).

Prof. Susan Vinnicombe OBE has an MA in Marketing (Lancaster University) and a PhD in Organizational Behaviour (Manchester Business School). She has held positions in Thomas De La Rue International, British Airways and Imperial College of Technology, London. She was appointed as Director of the Leadership and Organization Development Community at Cranfield School of Management, and sits on the School's Executive Committee. She teaches on a variety of programmes and directs the executive programme for senior women managers/directors. Her research interests are women's leadership styles, the issues involved in women developing their managerial careers and gender diversity on corporate boards. Her Research Centre is unique in the UK with its focus on women leaders and the annual Female FTSE 100 Index is regarded as the UK's premier research resource on women directors. Susan has numerous books and articles, including *Working in Organizations* (with A. Kakabadse and J. Bank; Gower, 2004) and *Women with Attitude: Lessons for Career Management* (with John Bank; Routledge, 2003). She is on the editorial board of *Group and Organization Management* and *Women in Management Review* and is a consultant for various organizations across the globe. She is regularly interviewed by the media for her expert views on women directors, and is frequently asked to speak at conferences.

Dr Teresa Waring is Associate Dean of Business and Management at the University of Sunderland Business School. She has been Director of Quality and Learning at Newcastle University Business School and previously worked at Northumbria University. Dr Waring has a PhD in Information Systems and has published widely in this area. She recently completed a research project based in a UK National Health Service Primary Care Trust and currently has a funded two year research project with a private sector healthcare organiz-ation. Along with Information Systems she also publishes in the areas of research methods and gender issues in organizations.

Zoë van Zwanenberg is Chief Executive of the Scottish Leadership Foundation. She has had a successful career in the civil service and had held a range of management posts from Deputy General Manager at a large District General Hospital, to Police Force Personnel Officer, to NHS Director of Personnel and Training for a Community Unit, and Management and Employee Development Manager at InterCity business. She was appointed as Director of HR for Anglia Railways, helping them to prepare for franchise and the move into the private sector. Zoë then moved to the Environment Agency, England and Wales, as their Organisation and Management Development Adviser, working through the issues involved in a complex merger and restructuring process. She is a specialist in human resources and people development, holds a number of positions on various boards and is a vocal advocate for women in management and leadership.

Preface

There is no shortage of evidence outlining the low levels of women in leadership and management, relative to men. This represents not only unequal opportunity – unacceptable in modern societies – but also a loss of talent to business and public organizations. This book analyses the issues behind this and gets behind the headline figures.

All the chapters are new, based on original research, never previously published. The volume has contributions from well established researchers and writers in the field and introduces new research and 'new blood' into a lively area of research and debate. Some chapters are the result of collaborative work between academic researchers, some between academics and other organizations, for example the Scottish Leadership Foundation. Contributions cover a broad range of sectors: public sector; large FTSE 100 businesses; small and medium size enterprises; entrepreneurial businesses; and international comparisons with the European Union. The theoretical and thematic approach also addresses issues like: gendered business and management education; female misogyny; female managerial identity in the workplace; gender and professional mistake making; the impact of modernization and new public management. Authors are from a wide range of universities and individual chapters show a British and broader European perspective.

Women in Leadership and Management is a major contribution to an important area of concern. There are also clear directions which the book signposts: business practices which facilitate the advance of women in management and leadership; societal attitudes and assumptions which inhibit progress; the context and importance of political and policy commitment to make things happen.

I strongly commend this book to the academic audience, but also to a much wider readership in the practitioner, business and policy communities.

Zoë van Zwanenberg
Chief Executive
Scottish Leadership Foundation

Introduction   Women in leadership and management: progress thus far?

Karen Miller

Social, demographic and economic changes have profoundly altered the status of women during the twentieth century. Many more women are now engaged in paid employment, but pay and conditions are often inferior to those of men doing comparable work. Women are excluded from some jobs and professions, and their progress in others is restricted (Home Office, 1974).

Women, by the 1960s and 1970s, were increasingly entering the workplace and calling for equal rights. In Britain this was answered in the 1970s by a policy entitled Equality of Women (1974), the preamble to legislation which outlawed gender discrimination and disparities in pay. The legislation, introduced over 30 years ago, attempted to address the equal rights for women and included the Sex Discrimination Act (1975) and the Equal Pay Act (1970). The legislation also saw the establishment of the Equal Opportunities Commission (EOC) in the hope of achieving equality of treatment and opportunities for men and women in the workplace. The legislation, although applicable to both sexes, was more relevant and welcomed by women as it is mostly women who face discrimination and exclusion from the workplace. In the intervening years amendments to the legislation were made (for example the Equal Pay for Work of Equal Value Amendment in 1984 and the Sex Discrimination Act amended in 1999) to further enhance the legislation. The UK government introduced a number of policies to further underpin the ethos of the legislation such as Fairness for All (2004). In the international arena the issue of gender discrimination and the rights of women had also gained momentum with many countries introducing similar legislation to the UK. The European Commission introduced the Equal Treatment Directive (1976) and the United Nations Organization highlighted the importance of women in society with the first World Conference of Women in Mexico (1975).

The publication of this book is opportune given the 30 year anniversary of legislation in the UK and recognition of women's rights internationally. Moreover, the auspicious timing of this book has seen the introduction of new legislative and policy initiatives in the UK; the Equality Act (2006), the Gender Duty, and the release of the Women and Work Commission's report (2006). In marking these momentous occasions for women's rights (and equality opportunities in general), and with the publication of this book, it is worth asking how much progress has been made in addressing gender discrimination in the workplace. According to the EOC (2006: 8–9) women's representation, on average, in:

- political life is 28 per cent (members of parliament, assemblies, local councils, Cabinet and the House of Lords);
- business leadership is 12 per cent (Directors of FTSE 100 and small businesses);
- media is 17 per cent; and
- public and the voluntary sector is 23 per cent.

In 1974 2 per cent of women were managers and less than 1 per cent were directors (EOC, 2006: 10). In 2005 women overall constituted 33.1 per cent of managers and 14.4 per cent of directors (Women and Work Commission, 2006). Thus, in 30 years women's representation to directorship level has increased at most by 14 per cent; an average increase of 4.6 per cent per decade. The increased representation of women to senior positions has at most been slow.

It is acknowledged by the Women and Work Commission (2006: 1) that women who work full-time earn 13 per cent less than their male counterparts, and that women still constitute only a third of senior managerial and leadership positions in the UK (Women and Work Commission, 2006: 35). Women continue to be relegated to low-paying, part-time employment with their earnings over a life time and in a pensionable age lower than men (Women and Work Commission, 2006: 4–5). In addition to these negative effects of inequalities, the continual discriminatory practices and exclusion of women from the workplace has implications for the UK economy. For example, it is estimated that women's increased participation in the labour market could be worth 1.3 to 2 per cent of GDP (Women and Work Commission, 2006: vii). Moreover the gainful employment and enabling workplace environment for women would have productivity benefits for UK businesses such as attracting and retaining employees, improving commitment, reducing absenteeism and staff turnover costs, and enhancing decision making and innovation (Women and Work Commission, 2006: 7). On the whole increased female participation in the workplace and in public life can have benefits for society and the economy with positive female role models – being examples for future generations of potential employees, public officials, professionals and entrepreneurs.

There are so many opportunities for women now, I want to show [my daughter] what she can do ... I want to say to [her] 'look at mummy, she goes to work, she has an interesting job, she has a balanced life ...' (extract from Chapter 5)

As is evident from the Women and Work Commission and Equal Opportunities Commission reports as well as this book, women still face discrimination, pay inequality, and frustrated access to senior positions in the workplace and from professions. After 30 years of legislation and policies the representation of women in the workplace and in public life, particularly at senior echelons, has been slow and inconsistent. The Equality for Women White Paper (1974) stated that; 'The unequal status of women cannot be dealt with by legislation alone ...' The authors of the policy document called upon government to ensure equality of opportunity for women (Equality for Women, 1974). But in 30 years there has been a gap between policy and practice, which is evident in a persistent gap in pay and female representation in management and leadership. Why does this gap exist?

The UK government established a commission, the Women and Work Commission, to investigate this gap and provide recommendations for addressing it. The authors of this book welcome the Commission's findings and hope that many of the recommendations are adopted and implemented. The Commission's report focuses on the gender pay gap, engaging girls and women in careers, addressing stereotypical attitudes, balancing work and family, and the 'glass ceiling' – most of which is similarly explored by this publication. Much of the findings of the Commission's report is already known, and has been researched and reported upon by many scholars for many decades (for example Kanter, Rappoport, Burke, Brass, Eagly, Davidson, Cooper, Schein, Rosener and the contributory authors of this book). It is hoped that in the decades to come the authors of this book and another Commission will not be asking; why has progress been so slow?

This book answers this question, but goes further by providing explanations and analysis for continued gender discrimination and the 'glass ceiling'. The book, based on primary empirical research, raises interesting debates and discussions on gender discrimination and frustrated female career progression. In some cases the book is reflective and has debates between contributing authors such as the idea of female role models and stereotypical feminine skills as 'women's special contribution'. Chapter 1 provides perspectives of the gendered nature of leadership and management by presenting the debates between the differences between male and female leadership as opposed to no differences. Furthermore, Chapter 1 provides an organizational perspective of women in public life and the masculine organizational culture in which they lead and manage. Chapter 2 discusses how this masculine organizational culture and masculine way of managing and leading is reinforced through education and development of managers in postgraduate management programmes. Moreover, Chapter 2 provides an interesting perspective of the gendered nature of the education environment and academia. Chapter 2 argues for gender awareness in education, research and teaching practice. Similarly, Chapter 3 discusses the training and development of managers and leaders. It argues that management and leadership development encompasses stereotypical feminine skills such as 'emotional intelligence'. However, these skills are often within a masculine organizational culture or used to bolster the culture, which places contradictory demands on managers and leaders, both male and female. Chapter 4 presents an interesting perspective of female leadership and role models – the idea of female misogyny and that there is not always solidarity behaviour between women in the workplace. Moreover, Chapter 4 highlights the contradictory demands and expectations women often face in leadership positions – they are expected to behave in a feminine manner, but have also to assimilate with a dominant male organizational culture. The 'maternal wall' is discussed in Chapter 5 and how women are still regarded as an organizational liability because of their reproductive status and the traditional view of motherhood being incompatible with paid employment. Within an organizational context there will always be errors or mistakes which take place. But is the way in which mistakes are perceived and managed, gendered? Chapter 6 provides some evidence for this and interesting perspectives of how mistakes are viewed and organizationally managed.

The first part of the book is a theoretical discussion, presenting various debates of gender discrimination and the 'glass ceiling' while the second part of the book provides a sectoral and organizational perspective of the theoretical discussion. Chapter 7 explores the issue of the slow progress of women to the senior echelons of corporate business. Chapter 7 outlines the debates explaining the slow progress, but also discusses where women have succeeded, providing some best practice examples. It also argues for the business case for women in management and leadership and provides some critical factors for sustained female inclusion and career progression. The focus of Chapter 8 is the small business environment and explains women's experience in this sector – a sector that sometimes offers flexibility, opportunities for work-life balance, and a supportive organizational environment. Chapter 9 focuses on entrepreneurs and shows that for female entrepreneurs there is often frustrated access to developing a business. Based on research in this area, the authors of Chapter 9 provide some suggestions such as on-line coaching to assist female small business development and their entrepreneurial ambitions. Chapter 10 concerns the sector which has the highest proportion of female employment – the public sector – specifically in the education and health sectors. Chapter 10 also shows that despite some progress of women into management, the progress is slow with most women still at lower ranks of public organizations. Like many of the preceding chapters, Chapter 10 argues that there is a masculine organizational culture and management practices which partly explains the low levels of female representation in management and leadership. This is also evident in Chapter 11 which provides a European perspective by exploring the issue of gender inequality in the European Commission – an international body which prides itself on promoting the equality and human rights agenda. The concluding chapter ties the strands of various debates and argues not so much how far we have come, but what we need to do in order to address the gap between policy and practice.

EXPLANATIONS FOR GENDER DISCRIMINATION AND THE 'GLASS CEILING'

The Women and Work Commission's (2006) comprehensive study explains the causes for pay discrimination as:

> Few organisations have gender inequality deliberately built into their pay structures, but such discrimination does exist and can stem from a range of causes. It is most likely where there are different pay structures for different groups of staff ... Or it may arise where employers seek to match pay to market rate.

This somewhat innocuous explanation ameliorates the fact that for some employers there were profitability gains to be made from paying female employees less than their male counterparts. The Commission recommends promoting career development opportunities and encouraging girls and women to embark upon non-stereotypical careers in order to increase the number of women in the workplace and in professions. Although as mentioned the report and its recommendations are welcome, there is perhaps an oversight with the overemphasis by the report on issues of pay discrimination, and engaging girls and women in non-stereotypical careers. The oversight lies in ignoring masculine organizational leadership and culture.

This book argues that there exists a male-dominated leadership echelon and masculine organizational culture in UK and European organizations, which knowing that undervaluing female employees is illegal, continued to do so for more than 30 years. Furthermore, an organizational culture and leadership, which despite the numbers of women entering professions and organizations, continue to frustrate their career development and progression. What exists in some UK and European organizations amounts to institutional sexism.

Leaders and managers will often argue that there are insufficient women in the profession or in the organizational ranks, and therefore they cannot be held accountable for the low levels of female representation in their organization, that is there are insufficient women in the 'pipeline' argument. Perhaps this is true with an air of complacency, but in many fields and professions (for example business, academia and health professions) there are many women. But despite 30 years of legislation and the growing numbers of women in the workplace, they continue to face the 'glass ceiling' and often experience direct and/or indirect discrimination.

ORGANIZATIONAL CULTURAL BARRIERS

Leadership and management continue to be the domain of men, that is 'think manager, think male' (see Chapters 1, 2 and 7). This has implications for women and the gendered organizational context in which they work. Men and women, rightly or wrongly, are perceived in a particular way in society, which permeates organizations. They are assigned gender roles, which are 'shared beliefs that apply to individuals on the basis of their socially identified sex' (Eagly and Johannesen-Schmidt 2001: 783). These socially defined roles are assumed behaviours for men and women, that is stereotypical behaviours, which are present in the gendered workplace and organizational culture (ibid). These stereotypical gender roles are manifest in agentic and communal behaviours (ibid). Agentic behaviours are characterized by assertive-ness, controlling, confidence, aggressiveness, dominance, forceful and competitiveness (ibid: 783). Communal behaviours are characterized by affection, kindness, sympathy, interpersonal sensitivity, supportiveness and helpfulness (ibid). Agentic behaviours are stereotypically associated with men and communal behaviour stereotypically associated with women (ibid). In an organizational context agentic behaviours may involve speaking assertively, having a competitive drive, influencing other, directing people to complete tasks, and so on, while communal behaviours may involve supporting colleagues, using interpersonal and relational skills, accepting direction, and so on (ibid). In an organizational context and culture it is often the agentic behaviours which are valued – 'think manager, think male' (Eagly and Johannesen-Schmidt 2001; also see Chapters 1, 2, 4 and 7). However, increasingly communal skills are being valued and leaders and managers are receiving training on effective interpersonal communication, coaching, team building, emotional intelligence, and so on (see Chapters 3 and 9). But these communal skills – stereotypically associated with female behaviours – are often underpinning a masculine organizational culture. Organizations are increasingly requiring male and female employees to be competitive and aggressive yet have excellent communal skills to engage with various stakeholders in an increasingly dynamic and global economy. Are organizations requiring employees, male and female, to have a 'multiple personality' approach to management and leadership?

What are the implications for employees, in particular women, when assigned these stereotypical, dichotomous gender roles?

Chapter 1 presents an interesting debate on transformational (often associated with feminine, communal styles of leadership) and transactional leadership (often associated with male, agentic leadership styles) (Yoder, 2001). These contradictory demands often manifest themselves in the manner in which women are perceived and stereotyped because management and leadership is gendered (Carli and Eagly 2001; Ridgeway 2001; Yoder 2001; Eagly and Johannesen-Schmidt 2001). If women behave in a communal style then it is what is expected and regarded as their 'special contribution' to management and leadership, and therefore do not receive recognition as it is what is expected of women. However, when men behave in this manner their communal style of leading and managing is recognized (for example developing an effective team) and often rewarded. When men behave in an agentic manner there is no sanction, rather stereotypically it is accepted and rewarded (for example aggressively seeking a promotion). However, when women take on agentic styles of leading and managing there is a sanction – often criticized as the 'more male than the men'. Women are therefore in a no win situation with contradictory demands placed upon them. Thus, if they assimilate to a dominant male organizational culture they may 'fit' in but are excluded by others (see Chapter 4). Is it no wonder when women in the 'pipeline' look up they ask themselves:

> When jobs or promotion do come up people now consider do they really want it, do they really want to go there! Is it worth the extra hours, money or work? (extract from Chapter 10)

The masculine organizational culture manifests itself in managerial practices. Chapters 2, 3 and 10 highlight how managerial practices place more job demands on employees, male and female, to meet performance targets, work long hours, take on more work to show initiative, and so on – often to the sacrifice of a work-life balance. Paradoxically, these managerial practices, in an attempt to increase organizational productivity, are in fact discouraging employees from seeking career advancement (as illustrated by the above extract). The sacrifice therefore is not only a work-life balance for individual employees, but for the organization it is the sacrifice of future managers and leaders. Staff turnover and poor rates of retention and succession invariably affect organizational productivity.

Employees, male and female, want a positive working environment, conducive to the demands of their lifestyle but allowing them at the same time to work and develop a career – all part of the self-identity. However, it is often the perception of employers and an institutionally sexist organization to view women as an organizational liability due to their reproductive and motherhood status. As Chapter 5 explains motherhood and paid employment are part of many women's self-identity, which should be supported. The idea of women as mothers (or potential mothers) being an organizational liability is an anachronistic and erroneous assumption to the disadvantage of women's career ambitions and also to organizational productivity. It should also be borne in mind that many men increasingly desire to be more involved in the raising of children and domestic life. So then do organizations penalize all employees who desire a work-life balance?

Institutional sexism, masculine organizational culture and practices compound to frustrate women's progress in careers and professions. Organizations will have to reflect on the type of work environment which they want to provide for employees; one which provides job and career satisfaction and at the same time produce organizational productivities. This does not have to be a dichotomous effort. As is evidenced from the chapters in this book, attitudes, organizational culture and managerial practices need to change, because if we do not support women's progress we do not capitalize on the talents and potential of over half of the population – to the detriment of society.

REFERENCES

Carli, L.L. and Eagly, A.H. (2001), 'Gender, Hierarchy, and Leadership: An Introduction', *Journal of Social Issues*, **57**(4), 629–36.

Eagly, A.H. and Johannesen-Schmidt, M.C. (2001), 'The Leadership Styles of Women and Men', *Journal of Social Issues*, **57**(4), 781–97.

Equal Opportunity Commission (2006), *Who Runs Britain?*

Home Office (1974), Equality of Women White Paper, Cmnd.5724, London: HMSO.

Ridgeway, C.L. (2001), 'Gender, Status and Leadership', *Journal of Social Issues*, **75**(4), 637–55.

Women and Work Commission (2006), *Shaping a Fairer Future*, London.

Yoder, J.D. (2001), 'Making Leadership Work more Effectively for Women', *Journal of Social Issues*, **57**(4), 815–28.

PART I

Issues, debates and perspectives

1. Exploring gendered leadership

James Collins and Val Singh

INTRODUCTION

The Equal Opportunities Commission (EOC) in commemorating the 30th anniversary of its foundation and equality legislation, reported that between 1975 and 2005 the number of women entering the workforce increased by a third and the number of female managers increased from less than 2 per cent to approximately one third in 2005 (EOC, 2005). Higher education has also seen a substantial increase in the proportion of female students. This has increased from 33 per cent to 57 per cent. However, despite these positive steps the proportion of women holding senior managerial or leadership positions in their organizations remains extremely low (Powell 2000; Singh and Vinnicombe 2005; EOC 2005). For more detailed analysis of female company board members refer to Chapter 7. Similarly, in the public sector women struggle to achieve leadership positions as research by the EOC and UK government show that although more women have attained middle management positions, they continued to be under-represented at senior level (for example EOC 2006; IDeA and LRDL 2004; see also Chapter 10).

It is clear that there are still few women in leadership positions in the business world, and that this is a concern for both public and private sectors in the UK. So what is it about leadership that makes it so difficult for women to achieve the senior-most positions in the business world? What are the characteristics of successful leaders? Are women less suited to leadership positions, or are there structural barriers that do not allow women to progress to the top? What does leadership mean, and how do men and women experience being successful leaders?

Explanations of why so few women attain top positions are frequently discussed in the context of gender differences between male and female managers, or in terms of the organizational barriers faced by women in the workplace. The gender differences discussion focuses on themes such as early socialization processes and the development of different behaviours or traits in childhood and whether this results in gendered leadership behaviour styles. The explanation that women are faced by workplace barriers frequently employs the 'glass ceiling' as a metaphor for the hurdles faced by working women (Morrison *et al.* 1987; Davidson and Cooper 1992). Organizational cultural barriers built on biases or gendered stereotypes work to prevent women from attaining senior positions, as indicated by the 'think manager, think male' syndrome (Schein *et al.* 1996). What both perspectives have in common is the theme that women face prejudice and are disadvantaged in the workplace.

In this chapter, we first explore research into leadership styles and whether these differ by gender. We review the barriers to women gaining leadership positions, and in particular, consider the 'think manager, think male' syndrome that persists in the construction of successful leadership as masculine. We will also explore the social construction of successful leadership and personal meanings of 'successful leadership' drawing upon research with chief executives of Scottish public bodies. Our empirical research, carried out by in-depth interviews, shows that for these chief executives, personal meanings of 'successful leadership' relate to concerns and needs that can be reflected by three themes. These we describe as profile, relationships and performance. We found that CEOs perceived these themes to be important not only to their organization, but to themselves. Exploring gender differences, we describe how some women leaders perceive women to have a more consensual style of leadership. This supports a body of evidence emerging from researchers into transformational leadership (for example Bass *et al.* 1996; Eagly *et al.* 2003). However, other women leaders do not believe that there are any differences in the ways women lead at chief executive level. The chapter concludes with a consideration of the implications for practice and recommendations for further research.

GENDER DIFFERENCES: DO MALE AND FEMALE LEADERS ADOPT DIFFERENT STYLES?

The 'Yes to Differences' Position

One of the major themes in gendered research concerns the question of the degree to which women and men are different, and whether this influences their behaviour or ways of working and leading (Rosener 1990; Butterfield and Grinnell 1999; Eagly *et al.* 2003). These authors suggest that societal norms promote a general stereotype of gender roles which have been cultured through a process of social learning. These socialization practices encourage the development of skills, traits and behaviours that are different between men and women, which in the eyes of many men and women are perceived as contrary to those required in the higher echelons of management.

Gilligan's (1982) seminal work describes how early life experiences of women lead them to desire connection and to place greater importance than men on certain aspects of responsibility, morality and justice. Women place value on working in a humanistic, social and inclusive way for the common good, whereas men take an approach which places a greater emphasis on independence and individual rights. Where men have regard for individualism, women tend to believe that inclusivity and communitarianism are more important. Helgesen (1990) similarly suggests that women have a different management style which can bring benefits to the organization. In her view, women are more inclined to take a fresh perspective, identify what is not working and develop new solutions. Compared with their male peers, women leaders are more willing to share power, make decisions and solve problems based on shared ideas and information, and encourage participation and expression. Women prefer organizational structures that enable consensual working rather the traditional hierarchical structures favoured by men. Helgesen describes this as 'the female advantage'.

Rosener (1990) identified that the leadership styles adopted by women have changed over time. Examining the style of leadership employed by women compared with their male counterparts, she suggests that many of the pioneer female executives adopted and emulated the methods, style, rules and conduct employed by successful men. These women, who in terms of personal achievement were breaking new ground, utilized traditional leadership methods associated with male leaders in large organizations. These were authoritarian, command, control and rule based approaches to leadership; a stereotypical masculine style. However, referring to a second generation of senior women managers, who have more recently achieved positions at the top level of management, Rosener comments that these women do not adopt a stereotypical masculine style of corporate behaviour; rather they attribute their leadership power to the interpersonal skills, attitudes, expertise and skills that are developed by women's shared life experiences outside of the positions of power.

Rosener describes the style adopted by women as an 'interactive leadership style' consisting of behaviours that represent power-sharing, energizing, encouraging participation, mutual trust and respect, and enhancing self-worth. She states that the women 'described themselves in ways that characterize "transformational" leadership – getting subordinates to transform their own self-interest into the interest of the group through concern for a broader goal' (Rosener, 1990: 120). Conversely male managers were more likely to use their position as a source of power and employ methods based on formal authority. In short, men are more likely to adopt 'transactional leadership' methods. Rosener suggests that women's traditional role in society is to offer a supportive and cooperative environment and that this influences their leadership style. Bass and colleagues (for example Bass 1990; 1998; Bass *et al.* 1996) have similarly reported women's leadership style to be more transformational than their male counterparts.

These authors have found that women seem to be less inclined to self-interest, preferring to consider communal goals, as Gilligan (1982) described. Women leaders prefer to encourage participative decision making rather than giving directive orders. Summarizing the findings of a series of studies in a number of diverse private and public sector organizations, Bass *et al.* (1996) state that in terms of gendered leadership, female leaders are 'rated no less, and generally more, transformational than their male counterparts while also being rated less on passive leadership styles' (Bass *et al.* 1996: 26). Yoder (2001) has suggested that although transformational leadership is no more effective if employed by women or men, female managers may have the advantage that transformational behaviours are similar to the supportive and caring behaviours associated with their gender role. Bass (1990) explains that although transformational leadership can be learned by anyone, through their gendered experiences women have been socialized towards this approach.

Examining transformational leadership in the UK public sector, Alimo-Metcalfe and Alban-Metcalfe (2001) describe a model which places importance on the leader as a partner rather than as the charismatic hero. They found significant gender differences across most dimensions of transformational leadership. For example, women leaders were found to be more likely to work together in a consensual style and to strengthen connections between groups and individuals both within and outside the organization.

Eagly and colleagues have carried out a number of meta-analyses reviewing gender and leadership style (for example Eagly and Johnson 1990; Eagly *et al.* 2003). Although gender differences have been found to be small, women tend to be more likely to share information, and employ consensual, participative and empowering methods that are inclusive and team based. Women's interpersonal communication and listening skills are based on empathy, mutual trust and respect; the skills necessary for conflict handling and negotiation. In contrast, men are more likely to be more directive, autocratic and task orientated, use formal authority, and exchange reward for good performance whilst punishing under-achievement. These are the behaviours that characterize transactional leadership.

The 'No Differences' Position

Although evidence of behavioural and personality differences between male and female managers is a consistent finding across a number of studies as indicated above, other authors have reported no significant gender differences. Examining gender and transformational leadership, Komives (1991) reported male and female managers to be generally equally transformational, with both groups stating that a collaborative style built on consensual relationships was important to effective leadership.

In his meta-analysis of the literature relating to gendered characteristics and leadership behaviours, Powell (1990) reported that he could find no support for the view that there are differences in the traits of male and female leaders. Similarly, in her review of the gendered leadership literature, Ferrario (1994) states that although research examining explanations of women's failure to attain leadership positions has frequently focused on gender differences, she could find no evidence that men and women lead in different ways. When leaders' ratings provided by subordinates are examined, there is again no evidence of significant gender differences in the perceptions of whether male or female leaders utilize greater levels of transformational behaviour (for example Komives 1991; Carless 1998; van Engen *et al.* 2001). Carless (1998) found that although women leaders reported greater levels of transformational behaviour, analysis of their subordinate ratings revealed no differences in the transformational behaviour exhibited by their male and female bosses.

Summary of Gendered Differences in Leadership Style

Although the evidence may be mixed, many authors do describe a gendered leadership style in which male managers are more likely to be autocratic and employ a command and control style of leadership, whereas women prefer to lead in ways that are consensual, empowering, encourage participation and team-work. In short, women are more likely to employ a transformational leadership style that can be described, as Gilligan (1982) suggests, as 'connected'. This is the style of leadership that is considered to be effective in the current environment of continual change, increased labour market participation of women and other excluded groups, and rapid globalization. However, other authors suggest that there is little evidence of gender differentiated leadership traits or characteristics, or of subordinates' perceptions of male and female leaders. The proponents of both perspectives agree that women continue to fail to attain top leadership positions.

ORGANIZATIONAL BARRIERS

A further set of explanations are those that describe the difficulties faced by women in terms of the organizational context or environment. These have been variously described as organizational barriers (Indvik 2004), situation-centred explanations (Powell 2000) or structural and systematic practices (Burke and McKeen 1992). As we briefly described above, a number of authors have put forward an explanation that a 'glass ceiling' holds women back and that organizational cultural barriers built on the biases or stereotypes held by men prevents women attaining senior positions. Regardless of competency, women tend to remain in a 'stuck group' of under-achievers (for example Morrison and Von Glinow 1990; Davidson and Cooper 1992; Powell 1999; Heilman 2001; Gherardi 1994; Meyerson and Fletcher 2000; van Vianen and Fischer 2002). Morrison and Von Glinow (1990: 200) describe this 'glass ceiling' as 'a barrier so subtle that it is transparent, yet so strong that it prevents women and minorities moving up the management hierarchy'.

The traditional business workplace has been described as inherently patriarchal, dominated by a masculine culture, where power and authority largely rest with men (for example Marshall 1995). As men hold the large majority of top positions, they are able to control the workforce and maintain masculine values and norms (for example Kanter 1977; Fagenson 1990). Thus prejudice is maintained by these institutionalized systems. Recognising that male organizational cultures are dominant, Meyerson and Fletcher (2000: 126) state:

> Most organizations have been created by and for men and are based on male experiences. Even though women have entered the workforce in droves in the past generation, and it is generally agreed that they add enormous value, organizational definitions of competence and leadership are still predicated on traits stereotypically associated with men: tough, aggressive, decisive.

In addition to culturally based organizational prejudices, Ferrario (1994) describes a number of formal barriers that hinder women's progress. She outlines how in an era of dual-earner households, women still bear the brunt of responsibility for child care. However, the provision of flexible working and family friendly policies is poor, and this serves to aggravate the problems faced by women. Similarly researchers have found that women are not provided with the same opportunities as their male counterparts. Ohlott *et al.* (1994) found gender differences in gaining developmental assignments, with women having fewer opportunities to stretch and develop in readiness for more senior roles, eventually leading to selection of the males with the crucial portfolio of experiences. Harris (1997) for example found that women were less likely to be offered overseas assignments. Ragins *et al.* (1998) suggest that, in the quest for opportunity and high roles, women have the burden of having to actively seek out and obtain key posts, whereas men are approached and encouraged to take up senior positions. Vinnicombe and Singh (2003) found that whilst male directors reported actively seeking out influential people earlier in their careers, female directors reported making it clear to potential mentors and sponsors that they really would like to be helped, so the actions were fairly similar for both sexes.

Powell (2000) suggests that where women have broken through the 'glass ceiling', the presence of women in senior positions is a challenge to existing cultures and norms. However masculine cultures continue to dominate, sustained by sex-type stereotyping of workplace gender roles; the traits and behaviour of successful people are those considered to be stereotypically masculine.

STEREOTYPING LEADERSHIP

It would seem that 30 years after legislation to improve workplace gender equality, women do not appear to have equal access to leadership positions in either private or public sector organizations. The workplace is dominated by a masculine culture. This is in part maintained by gendered perceptions of a 'successful' leader/manager. Thus workplace discrimination is maintained by institutionalized systems based on subjective assessments of promotability and leadership capability. In a series of studies over a period of four decades, a consistent finding is that that the 'successful leader' is perceived to behave and act in ways associated with masculine traits. Although women now make up approximately 30 per cent of middle manager positions, the 'think manager, think male' phenomenon prevails. This, as discussed in the introductory chapter of this book, presents a hurdle for women as they strive to achieve senior positions.

Women's 'special contribution' to leadership, as discussed above, is precisely the leadership style called for and encouraged by management development programmes (see Chapter 2). However, this 'contribution' of stereotyped female skills is at odds with the dominant masculine culture.

PERSONAL CONCEPTIONS OF SUCCESSFUL LEADERSHIP

To provide more insight from the practitioner world, we draw upon a new study of leadership in the Scottish public sector. This provides personal conceptions of successful leadership held by both men and women chief executives, in a devolved governance context that might have offered increased opportunities for women to succeed as organizational leaders.

We present the findings of our research which explored the personal meanings of 'successful leadership' held by chief executives of Scottish public bodies. For these leaders, 'successful leadership' relates to concerns and needs that can be reflected by three themes. These we describe as profile, relationships and performance. In this section we discuss these themes and explore differences in the conceptions of 'successful leadership' held by women and men CEOs.

We carried out in-depth interviews with 21 male and female current and former CEOs of Scottish public bodies. They are responsible for the provision of a range of public services such as health, culture, sport, education, environment and community welfare, and are accountable to ministers and the Scottish Parliament. Scotland presents an interesting case as devolution was said to represent new opportunities and a 'dawn of new hope' as evidenced in pre- and post-devolution documents. For example; the Scottish Constitutional Convention (1995) and the Scotland Act (1998) both of which had equality as a founding principle.

Senior Women's Representation in Scotland

From a perspective of gender equality, supported by the positive language described above, devolution appears to offer improved opportunities for women in public life. The electoral system led to a significantly larger number of women parliamentarians in the Scottish Parliament (37 per cent compared with 19 per cent at Westminster). This was largely achieved by a policy of affirmative action by New Labour in Scotland that implemented a system of candidate selection by 'twinning' winnable seats (an affirmative action policy which has subsequently been legally challenged). Female and male candidates were allocated equally to constituencies deemed to be winnable at the election, resulting in an equal number of male and female Labour members of the Scottish Parliament. Given that prior to devolution, Scottish women represented only 7 per cent of the Scottish parliamentarians in Westminster, the proportion of women in the Scottish Parliament represents a major turnaround for women in Scottish politics.

Although the statistics present a positive picture in terms of women leaders of Scottish political representation, there is evidence that, despite promises 'to appoint more people from under-represented sections of society to public office' (Scottish Executive, 2000), relatively few women are promoted to senior posts. In 2000 the Scottish Executive promised to 'increase by 2002 the proportion of bodies chaired by women from the 1998 level of 22 per cent to 35 per cent'. However, updated statistics in December 2005 show that women held only 19 per cent of the chairs to Scottish public bodies, even less than the 1998 level (Scottish Executive, 2005). Moreover, an examination of statistics for women holding senior management positions in December 2005 shows that only three of the possible chief executive posts in the 32 Scottish Non-Departmental Public Bodies (NDPBs) are held by women.

In addition to the statistics described above, the EOC (2005) data for women's representation in senior public positions in Scotland shows that women represent only 12.5 per cent of the senior judiciary and 10.3 per cent of senior police officers. In local government, only 20 per cent of councillors are women, and only 12.5 per cent of local authority CEOs are female.

Women Poorly Represented in Leadership Positions

The women CEOs in our study recognized that they were members of a minority group and that women were poorly represented in leadership not only in Scotland but also in the rest of Britain. The female CEOs talked about the many public promises to address workplace gender inequality, but felt that little had changed in the five or six years since devolution. They commented that although very positive messages had emerged following increased parliamentary equality in the Scottish Parliament, there were still few women achieving the senior and top positions across most public bodies and at government cabinet level.

A further concern was the very public way that some female CEOs (and women government ministers) had left their posts. Media stories relating to their departure and resignations painted a negative picture about the treatment of these senior women. For example, the news stories surrounding the departure of a female CEO reported that the chair of the organization had described her as 'not macho enough'. Most of the women CEOs stated that these kinds of experiences were evidence that ambitious women not only faced a difficult path to reach the top, but sometimes still faced prejudice even when they had achieved the most senior positions. However, a minority of the women CEOs held the view that women did have the opportunity to progress through all levels of the organization, to break through the 'glass ceiling' to take up the most senior posts. Their view was that although women may be faced with some prejudice, the ability of a candidate will prevail over this hurdle.

Discussing the problems of prejudice and the evidence of female turnover at both CEO and ministerial level, most of the women CEOs reported a continued sense of gender-related disadvantage. Similar findings have been reported by Broussine and Fox (2002) in the context of UK local government. Examining the experience of female CEOs, they found that despite attempts to introduce policies to challenge and change the traditional cultures within this sector, little had actually been achieved. Broussine and Fox suggest that biases in CEO selection processes and a macho culture perpetuated by the predominance of men in senior positions serve to reinforce gender prejudice in local government. In summary, they state: 'Local Authority leadership appears to be stuck in the mould of operational management rather than transformational leadership' (Broussine and Fox, 2002: 89).

Women Leaders' Views on Affirmative Action

Although the women CEOS in our study held a somewhat pessimistic view about the gender imbalance being actively addressed, most did not believe that women should be favoured through affirmative action plans. Their negative attitude to affirmative action mostly reflected a concern of how beneficiaries are perceived by others and how they would personally feel about benefiting in this way. They were concerned that they might be less valued by their subordinates and peers and feel less qualified to take up their CEO role. For these CEOs, the ability of the individual was of prime importance and being perceived to have benefited from affirmative action almost automatically would erode the beneficiary's real talents or skills in the eyes of others.

Their concerns largely mirror those which have been widely reported elsewhere. For example, Heilman and Alcott (2001) found that participants reported negative self-evaluation in the knowledge that others viewed them as having been preferentially selected. Heilman *et al.* (1992) found that beneficiaries were perceived as less competent and work active, and Summers (1991) found that women discounted the qualifications of others whose promotion was perceived to have come about through affirmative action. Interestingly, Summers also reported that male participants generally discounted the qualifications of all women in management positions – evidence indeed of gender stereotyping of leadership as masculine.

The Importance of Context for Successful Leadership

The context within which the leadership takes place has a major impact on the notions of 'successful leadership' held by these CEOs. Many CEOs described the difficulties of working in an environment in which a large number of stakeholders hold particular and sometimes different interests. Within the political domain, CEOs and their organizations need to work with civil servants, politicians, ministers and with local government. They frequently work in cooperation and partnership with other private and public service providers, and of course most of these organizations provide services to the public and therefore service users and their interest groups are also major stakeholders.

A large number of CEOs reported that the public services are dominated by a blame culture and that some politicians and CEOs tend to be risk averse. Similar findings have been reported by the UK government's Performance and Innovation Unit (PIU 2001). Describing the difficulties of working in a blame culture, many of the male and female CEOs stated that their tenure was fragile because they knew that regardless of responsibility, they would be held accountable for problems or failures associated with their organization. These

CEOs described themselves as 'scapegoats' who have to 'carry the can' for failure. They saw their position as one which protected ministers from responsibility for the poor performance of public bodies. Although they largely accepted that this was the way that CEOs in the public sector were treated, they believed that a culture which promoted joint responsibility would be perceived by service users as a learning environment in which improvements could come about through learning from mistakes.

PERSONAL CONCEPTIONS OF SUCCESSFUL LEADERSHIP

Within this environment, CEOs stated that in order to be successful leaders, they require support or endorsement from important stakeholders. Support is dependent on stakeholder perceptions regarding the CEO and their organization. Positive stakeholder perceptions depend on the character and ability of CEOs and their organizations. These perceptions are built through CEOs' attention to relationships, profile and ensuring good performance. This provides CEOs and the organization they lead with the credibility and legitimacy necessary for successful leadership.

Leadership and Performance

As our study examined CEOs' perceptions of 'successful leadership', it is perhaps not surprising that these CEOs described success in terms of performance and delivery. Both the male and female CEOs interviewed said that performance was not simply a matter of achieving targets. For example, they were concerned that their organizations delivered 'real' improvements to service users, that their staff worked in an environment in which job satisfaction is important, and that their organization functioned in ways that ensured a beneficial impact on society or the environment as a whole.

As the link between success and performance can be considered a given, in this chapter we have elected to place more emphasis on the themes of relationships and profile. This is not to suggest that the link between success and performance is not a substantial subject in its own right.

Leadership and Relationships

As we have described above, good working relationships with various key stakeholder are crucial to successful leadership. CEOs described how these relationships were built around stakeholders' perceptions concerning issues such as competence, influence, trust, honesty and teamworking. Good stakeholder perceptions about the organization and its CEO provided the credibility necessary for successful leadership, in their view.

Some CEOs described this relationship in terms of the 'fit' between themselves and key stakeholders. For example, discussing her relationship with the chair of her organization, one of the female CEOs who had resigned her position stated that 'my style probably just didn't fit'. Another male CEO stated 'from the very first time I met the chair, I recognized that there was a problem'. The importance of fit has been explored by a number of authors (for example Heilman 1983; Rynes and Gerhart 1990; Nelson 2005).

In her model, Nelson (2005) describes three important conceptions of fit. Person–organization fit (P–O) concerns the congruence between the individual and the organization in which they work, for example, the match between an employee's personal values and beliefs and those espoused by the organization. Person–job fit (P–J) concerns the match of the skills and abilities of employees to their work requirements. Finally, and of interest in our study is person–decision maker fit (P–D) which relates to the way that the two senior people, such as the CEO and the chair, are able to work together. Discussing the notion of P–D fit, Nelson describes how the expectation of a strong working relationship between the leader of the council and the local government CEO is assessed when the prospective CEO attends the final interview and at the time the final decision is made. In her work on CEOs, Nelson mainly considers the P–D relationship at the time of a candidate's selection. However an interesting aspect in our study is that of poor person–decision-maker fit which occurred after CEOs had been in their posts for some time, which sometimes resulted in CEO departure.

Having described the relationship between themselves and the chair of their organization as one of the most important in terms of successful leadership outcomes, the CEOs in our study said that difficulties in the relationship mainly came about when their existing chair retired and a new individual was appointed. They talked of how they had to completely rebuild a relationship with the new incumbent and that this sometimes proved difficult. Given the important and usually powerful role of the chair of an organization, a breakdown of this relationship is likely to lead to less successful leadership outcomes for the CEO.

Examining fit in terms of gender prejudice, Heilman (1983) presents a lack of fit model as an explanation of workplace discrimination. This describes the poor fit between an individual woman's position and a perception that the position is a masculine sex-typed role. Heilman suggests that this lack of fit serves to sanction continued workplace sex bias and prejudice. Thus in our study, the description of a CEO as 'not macho enough' by the new chair of the organization is evidence of not only a poor person–decision maker relationship, but also evidence of a gender bias in the fit between the two most senior people in the organization.

Leadership and Profile

All CEOs talked of how managing both their personal and organization profile is a necessary part of successful leadership. They described how profile contributes to improved awareness of both the organization and the leader. Outlining the need to engage in strategies that enhance profile, CEOs described proactive self-presentation actions such as self-promotion, networking and improving visibility, all of which help to increase positive perceptions about the organization and the leader. By utilizing such strategies, CEOs are engaging in small 'p' politics and impression management (for example Goffman 1959; Schlenker 1980; Rosenfeld *et al.* 2002). As Schlenker (1980) describes, impression management involves the action that individuals take to create and maintain the desired views or impression that others hold about them. Impression management and raising one's profile through visibility becomes important for both personal and organizational longevity. Similarly, a Catalyst (2002) study reported that lack of visibility is one of the barriers to women in their efforts to break through the 'glass ceiling'.

LEADERSHIP, NETWORKS AND POLITICAL SKILLS

Most of the female CEOs said that their careers had progressed in an environment mainly dominated by men. Although some had worked in organizations such as social care or health which engaged a high proportion of women, males were mostly employed in the upper tiers of management in these organizations (see Chapter 10). The women CEOs' view therefore was that male managers still dominated even in organizations in which higher numbers of women were employed.

The female CEOs who had progressed through a male dominated route talked of the interpersonal networks which they had established during their career. The importance of interpersonal networks to career progression has been widely discussed (for example Burt 1997; Brass 1985; Ibarra 1993; Mainiero 1994; Ragins and Sundstrom 1989). For example, examining women's progress through the 'glass ceiling', Mainiero (1994) interviewed women at vice-president level or above in Fortune 500 companies. She describes the stages of the path through the 'glass ceiling' and found that to attain these senior positions, women first 'developed an awareness of corporate culture', and then 'built credibility through alliances and networks'.

This provided women with the ability to 'utilize their personal skills to influence and overcome obstacles'.

It is consistently reported that men have more developed informal networks, particularly with other men, and that these networks are central to career progress. In contrast, women are less aware of the importance of informal networks at senior levels, and tend to have poor access to the powerful male-dominated networks (Ibarra 1992; Ragins and Sundstrom 1989). This serves to exclude women from resources, information, the opportunity to establish allies and to create mentoring relationships with the males in senior positions.

In our study, we found that some female CEOs believed that as their careers had progressed, they had been able to break into and use what were mostly male-dominated networks. Indeed, they believed that their networks were as fully developed as those of their male counterparts. However, consistent with most research, some women CEOs in our study said that because of the traditionally high number of male CEOs in the public sector, senior men do have networks which are more developed than those of their female peers. Some women CEOs believe that women are frequently excluded from men's networks and they perceived this to be a deliberate policy, which disadvantaged women as they sought promotion to senior positions in their organization. The 'old boys' network was said to still dominate the public services particularly in the higher reaches of the civil service.

Whether these female CEOs had managed to gain membership of the male dominated networks or not, they all believed that developing informal connections with other women in similar senior roles was a useful and important means of social support for female CEOs in the public sector. However, they also noted a paradox; in that although the networks developed by senior women were intended to assist younger women to break through into top positions, these networks could not function fully in the same way as the male networks (with access to powerful people, information and resources) until the numbers of senior women reach a critical mass.

WOMEN'S WAYS OF LEADING

Most female and male CEOs described their own conceptions of successful leadership in terms of transformational qualities, characteristics or behaviours. For example, they talked of empowering staff and providing a consultative and collaborative environment which encouraged team-working. However, although both male and female CEOs described themselves in this manner, some women leaders appeared to consider themselves as more transformational than their male counterparts. For example, whilst a few women considered that individual differences rather than gender characteristics accounted for different leadership behaviour, most expressed their belief that they and their female peers were more likely to work in a collaborative and less authoritarian style than their male counterparts. These female leaders said they wanted the best qualities of their employees to emerge, so that the employees would have a feeling of personal self-worth as well as value the work they were doing. This finding is consistent with authors who have described women managers as engaging in a greater level of transformational behaviour compared with male managers, that is the 'yes to differences' position (for example Rosener 1990; Helgesen 1990; Bass and Avolio 1994; Carless 1998; Eagly *et al*. 2003).

Some women CEOs believed that a new generation of male leaders is emerging in both the civil service and at CEO level in the public sector. Male leaders who are less autocratic are more likely to engage in the collaborative and inclusive style associated with the ways that women lead. Fondas (1997) describes the shift in organizational cultures away from a stereotypical masculine task-oriented, directive, autocratic and hierarchical model of leadership towards an empowering and interactive style as the 'feminization of management'. However both male and female CEOs who said that they personally employed typically transformational behaviours added that where necessary, they could take hard-nosed and directive decisions. This is recognition that effective leaders are required to employ both transformational and transactional behaviour, as indicated by previous studies (Bass 1985; Bass and Avolio 1994; Alimo-Metcalfe and Alban-Metcalfe 2001). This may support the arguments made by proponents of the 'no differences' position.

WOMEN LEADERS AS ROLE MODELS AND MENTORS

As described earlier, both male and female CEOs executives in our study described the problems of working in a blame culture and in environments in which masculine cultures were still frequently found. Although these negative cultures flourish, women CEOs said that the presence of women in top positions provides a message to ambitious women that although there are few women in the most senior positions, it is possible for women to achieve their full potential and attain leadership roles. Having attained senior positions, the women CEOs saw themselves as role models to the next generation of female middle managers who aspire to reach the top. Some also acted as mentors to women promoted to top team positions in their organization. They therefore saw the negative media news stories surrounding the departure of women CEOs as an erosion of the positive message surrounding women's achievements. One female former CEO described her resignation as a 'double loss'. The first loss was that the departure of a senior women leader reduced the already small number of available role models. Second, when leaders leave following a breakdown of the relationship with their chair or minister, the public nature of their departure is apparent to male and female middle managers and provides a poor image of the way that 'non-macho' or 'failing' CEOs are treated.

The importance of role models and establishing and maintaining mentoring relationships rather than diluting them should not be underestimated (for an alternative perspective of female role models see Chapter 4). Apfelbaum and Hadley (1986) comment that an absence of mentors and female workplace role models or reference groups serves to reinforce and maintain gender biases. Catalyst (2000) reported that while gender stereotyping was the principal barrier to women's carrier advancement, the lack of role models and mentors was one of the major barriers to women in their efforts to break through the 'glass ceiling'. The symbolic value of senior women role models is also emphasized by Sealy and Singh (2006) as important for women's perceptions that the barriers to their progression within their organization are permeable, if they are good enough.

CONCLUSION

This chapter has introduced the issue of leadership and gender and shown that women have struggled to achieve leadership positions. Through an overview of the research literature, this chapter has identified that some studies, particularly a meta-analysis by Eagly and her colleagues, indicate no differences between men and women leaders in terms of traits considered necessary for leadership. Some authors take the position that women and men are essentially different in terms of their psychological development, with men valuing individualism. Other studies have revealed similar traits but gendered preferences for particular styles of leadership, with men preferring a command and control transactional style, and women taking a more inclusive and collaborative approach.

In the latter half of this chapter, findings from a new study have revealed the meanings of successful leadership held by leaders of Scottish public sector organizations, where there are few women in the most senior roles, despite the optimism and transformational language of the transition into devolution. Only in politics did women take a major share of new positions. The findings show that for Scottish public sector CEOs, there were three key factors that need to be managed. Not only is good performance essential for successful leadership, but considerable attention has to be given to managing relationships and personal and organizational profile with a number of different stakeholders, both within and outside their organization. Women leaders did express preferences for more transformational leadership, but so also did most of the male CEOs. They also reported a shift towards a more androgynous style, using both transactional and transformational leadership as necessary. The women CEOs in this study held the view that sex-role stereotyping of leadership as masculine is still a major barrier for women. They saw themselves as role models of leadership for aspiring women, and were proactive in engaging in women's career development activities such as networks. These findings have implications for those preparing themselves for CEO positions, and for those responsible for the identification and development of future leaders.

A better understanding is needed of the contexts of leadership and the capability of men and women to adapt their preferred leadership style to new circumstances. Further research is needed into leadership and gender, particularly in contrasting contexts such as sector and country, in the changing environment of global economy. Without excellent leaders drawn from the best talent of both men and women, organizations will not be able to achieve the best results possible. 'Think manager, think male' needs to be translated into think leader, think the best person possible; male or female.

REFERENCES

Alimo-Metcalfe, B. and Alban-Metcalfe, R.J. (2001), 'The Development of a New Transformational Leadership Questionnaire', *Journal of Occupational and Organizational Psychology*, **74**(1), 1–27.

Antal, A.B. and Izraeli, D.N. (1993), 'A Global Comparison of Women in Management: Women Managers in their Homelands and as Expatriates', in E.A. Fagenson (ed.), *Women in Management: Trends Issues and Challenges in Managerial Diversity*, Newbury Park: Sage.

Apfelbaum, E. and Hadley, M. (1986), 'Leadership Ms- Qualified: II. Reflections on, and Initial Case Study Investigations of Contemporary Women Leaders', in C.F. Graumann and S. Moscovici (eds), *Changing Conceptions of Leadership*, New York: Springer-Verlag.

Bass, B.M. (1985), *Leadership and Performance Beyond Expectations*, New York: The Free Press.

Bass, B.M. (1990), 'From Transactional to Transformational Leadership: Learning to Share the Vision', *Organizational Dynamics*, **18**(3), 19–31.

Bass, B.M. (1998), *Transformational Leadership: Industry, Military and Educational Impact*, Mahwah, NJ: Erlbaum.

Bass, B.M. and Avolio, B.J. (1994), *Improving Organizational Effectiveness through Transformational Leadership*, Thousand Oaks, CA: Sage.

Bass, B., Avolio, B. and Atwater, L. (1996), 'The Transformational and Transactional Leadership of Men and Women', *Applied Psychology: An International Review*, **45**(1), 5–34.

Brass, D.J. (1985), 'Men's and Women's Networks: a Study of Interaction Patterns and Influence in an Organization', *Academy of Management Journal*, **28**(2), 327–43.

Broussine, M. and Fox, P. (2002), 'Rethinking Leadership in Local Government – the Place of "Feminine" Styles in the Modernised Council', *Local Government Studies*, **28**(4), 28–102.

Burke, R.J. and McKeen, C.A. (1992), 'Women in Management', in C.L. Cooper and I.T. Robertson (eds), *International Review of Industrial and Organizational Psychology*, New York, NY: Wiley, pp. 245–84.

Burt, R.S. (1992), *Structural Holes: The Social Structure of Competition*, Cambridge, MA: Harvard University Press.

Butterfield, D.A. and Grinnell, J.P. (1999), '"Reviewing" Gender, Leadership and Managerial Behaviour: Do Three Decades of Research Tell Us Anything?' in G.N. Powell (ed.), *Handbook of Gender and Work*, Thousand Oaks, CA: Sage, pp. 223–38.

Carless, S.A. (1998), 'Gender Differences in Transformational Leadership: An Examination of Superior, Leader and Subordinate Perspectives', *Sex Roles*, **39**(11 12), 887–902.

Catalyst and Opportunity Now (2000), *Breaking the Barriers: Women in Senior Management in the UK*, London: Opportunity Now.

Catalyst and Conference Board Europe (2002), *Women in Leadership: A European Business Imperative*, New York, NY: Catalyst.

Davidson, M.J. and Cooper, C.L. (1992), *Shattering the 'Glass Ceiling': The Woman Manager*, London: Paul Chapman.

Eagly, A.H. and Johnson, B.T. (1990), 'Gender and Leadership Style: A Meta-analysis', *Psychological Bulletin*, **108**(2), 223–56.

Eagly, A.H., Johannesen-Schmidt, M.C. and van Engen, M.L. (2003), 'Transformational, Transactional and Laissez-faire Leadership Styles: A Meta-analysis Comparing Women and Men', *Psychological Bulletin*, **129**(4), 569–91.

Equal Opportunities Commission (2005), *Then and Now: 30 Years of the Sex Discrimination Act*, Manchester: EOC.

Equal Opportunities Commission (2006), *Sex and Power: Who Runs Britain 2006?*, Manchester: EOC.

Equal Opportunities Commission (2006), *Who Runs Scotland 2006?*, Glasgow: EOC Scotland.

Fagenson, E.A. (1990), 'Perceived Masculine and Feminine Attributes Examined as a Function of Individuals' Sex and Level in the Organizational Power Hierarchy: a Test of Our Theoretical Perspectives', *Journal of Applied Psychology*, **75**(2), 204–11.

Fagenson, E.A. and Jackson, J.J. (1993), 'The Status of Women Managers in the United States', *International Studies of Management and Organization*, **23**(1), 93–112.

Ferrario, M. (1994), 'Women as Managerial Leaders', in M.J. Davidson and R.J. Burke (eds), *Women in Management: Current Research Issues*, London: Chapman Publishing.

Fondas, N. (1997), 'Feminization Unveiled: Management Qualities in Contemporary Writings', *Academy of Management Review*, **22** (2), 257–82.

Gherardi, S. (1994), 'The Gender We Think, the Gender We Do in our Everyday Organizational Lives', *Human Relations*, **47**(5), 591–610.

Gilligan, C. (1982), *In a Different Voice: Psychological Theory and Women's Development*, Cambridge, MA: Harvard University Press.

Goffman, E. (1959), *The Presentation of Self in Everyday Life*, London: Penguin.

Harris, H. (1997), 'Women in International Management: an Examination of the Role of Home Country Selection Processes in Influencing the Number of Women in

International Management Positions', PhD Thesis: Cranfield School of Management.

Heilman, M.E. (1983), 'Sex Bias in Work Settings: The Lack of Fit Model', in B.M. Staw and L.L. Cummings (eds), *Research in Organizational Behaviour*, Greenwich, CT: JAI Press, pp. 195–214.

Heilman, M.E. (2001), 'Description and Prescription: How Gender Stereotypes Prevent Women's Ascent up the Organizational Ladder', *Journal of Social Issues*, **57**(4), 657–74.

Heilman, M.E. and Alcott, V.B. (2001), 'What I Think you Think of Me: Women's Reactions to Being Viewed as Beneficiaries of Preferential Selection', *Journal of Applied Psychology*, **86**(4), 574–82.

Heilman, M.E., Block, C.J. and Lucas, J.A. (1992), 'Presumed Incompetent? Stigmatization and Affirmative Action Efforts', *Journal of Applied Psychology*, **77**(4), 536–44.

Heilman, M.E., Block, C.J., Martell, R.F. and Simon, M.C. (1989), 'Has Anything Changed? Current Characterizations of Men, Women and Managers', *Journal of Applied Psychology*, **74**, 935–42.

Helgesen, S. (1990), '*The Female Advantage: Women's Way of Leadership*', New York: Doubleday.

Ibarra, H. (1992), 'Homophily and Differential Returns: Sex Differences in Network Structure and Access in an Advertising Firm', *Administrative Science Quarterly*, **37**(4), 422–47.

Ibarra, H. (1993), 'Personal Networks of Women and Minorities in Management: A Conceptual Framework', *Academy of Management Review*, **18**(1), 56–87.

IDeA and LRDL (2004), *Prospects: Diversity and the Career Progression of Managers in Local Government*, London: Improvement and Development Agency.

Indvik, J. (2004), 'Women and Leadership', in P.G. Northouse (ed.), *Leadership Theory and Practice*, Thousand Oaks, CA: Sage, pp 265–99.

Kanter, R.M. (1977), *Men and Women of the Corporation*, New York: Basic Books.

Komives, S.R. (1991), 'The Relationship of Same and Cross Gender Work Pairs to Staff Performance and Supervisor Leadership in Residence Hall Units', *Sex Roles*, **24**(5–6), 355–63.

Mainiero, L.A. (1994), 'On Breaking the Glass Ceiling: The Political Seasoning of Powerful Women Executives', *Organizational Dynamics*, **22**(1), 5–20.

Marshall, J. (1995), *Women Managers: Moving On*, London: Routledge.

Meyerson, D. and Fletcher, J.K. (2000), 'A Modest Manifesto for Shattering the Glass Ceiling', *Harvard Business Review*, **78**, 126–37.

Morrison, A.M. and Von Glinow, M.A. (1990), 'Women and Minorities in Management', *American Psychologist*, **45**(2), 200–208.

Morrison, A., White, R. and Van Velson, E. (1987), *Breaking the Glass Ceiling*, Reading, MA: Addison-Wesley.

Nelson, D. (2005), 'An Examination of the Cognitive Construction of Fit among Chief Executives and Senior Elected Members in Local Authorities in England and Wales: Is it Gendered?', PhD Thesis: Cranfield School of Management.

Ohlott, P.J., Ruderman, M.N. and McCauley, C.D. (1994), 'Gender Differences in Managers' Developmental Job Experiences', *Academy of Management Journal*, **37**(1), 46–67.

Performance and Innovation Unit (2001), *Strengthening Leadership in the Public Sector: A Research Study by the PIU*, London: HMSO.

Powell, G.N (1990), 'One More Time: Do Female and Male Managers Differ?', *Academy of Management Executive*, **4**(1), 68–75.

Powell, G.N. (1999), *Handbook of Gender and Work*, Thousand Oaks, CA: Sage.

Powell, G.N. (2000), 'The Glass Ceiling: Explaining the Good and Bad News', in M.J. Davidson and R. Burke (eds), *Women in Management: Current Research Issues*, London: Sage, pp. 236–50.

Ragins, B.R. and Sundstrom, E. (1989), 'Gender and Power in Organization: A Longitudinal Perspective', *Psychological Bulletin*, **105**(1), 51–88.

Ragins, B., Townsend, B. and Mattis, M. (1998), 'Gender Gap in the Executive Suite: CEOs and Female Executives Report on Breaking the Glass Ceiling', *Academy of Management Executive*, **12**(1), 28–42.

Rosener, J.B. (1990), 'Ways women lead', *Harvard Business Review*, **November–December**, 119–25.

Rosenfeld, P., Giacalone, R.A. and Riordan, C.A. (2002), *Impression Management in Organizations*, London: Routledge.

Rynes, S. and Gerhart, B. (1990), 'Interviewer Assessments of Applicant "Fit": an Exploratory Investigation', *Personnel Psychology*, **43**(1), 13–34.

Schein, V.E. (1973), 'The Relationship of Sex Role Stereotypes and Requisite Management Characteristics', *Journal of Applied Psychology*, **57**(1), 95–100.

Schein, V.E. (1975), 'The Relationship Between Sex Role Stereotypes and Requisite Management Characteristics Among Female Managers', *Journal of Applied Psychology*, **60**(3), 340–44.

Schein V.E. (2001), 'A Global Look at Psychological Barriers to Women's Progress in Management', *Journal of Social Issues*, **57**(4), 675–88.

Schein, V.E., Mueller, R., Lituchy, T. and Liu, J. (1996), 'Think Manager – Think Male: a Global Phenomenon?', *Journal of Organizational Behavior*, **17**(1), 33–41.

Schlenker, B.R. (1980), *Impression Management: The Self-concept, Social Identity and Interpersonal Relations*, Monterey, CA: Brooks-Cole.

Scottish Constitutional Convention (1995), *Scotland's Parliament, Scotland's Right: Report to the People of Scotland*, Edinburgh: Scottish Constitutional Convention.

Scottish Executive (2000), *Appointments to Public Bodies in Scotland: Modernising the System: Consultation Paper*, Edinburgh: The Scottish Executive.

Scottish Executive (2005), *Public Bodies and Public Appointments*, www.scotland.gov.uk/Topics/Government/public-bodies/public-appointments, January 2006.

Sealy, R. and Singh, V. (2006), 'Role Models, Work Identity and Senior Women's Career Progression – Why are Role Models Important?', unpublished working paper, Cranfield: Cranfield School of Management.

Singh, V. and Vinnicombe, S. (2005), *The Female FTSE 200*, Cranfield: Cranfield School of Management.

Summers, R.J. (1991), 'The Influence of Affirmative Action on Perceptions on a Beneficiary's Qualifications', *Journal of Applied Social Psychology*, **21**, 1265–76.

van Engen, M.L., van der Leeden, R. and Willemsen, T.M. (2001), 'Gender, Context and Leadership Styles: a Field Study', *Journal of Occupational and Organizational Psychology*, **74**(5), 581–98.

Van Vianen, A.E.M. and Fischer, A.H. (2002), 'Illuminating the Glass Ceiling: the Role of Organizational Culture Preferences', *Journal of Occupational and Organizational Psychology*, **75**(3), 315–37.

Vinnicombe, S. and Singh, V. (2002), 'Sex Role Stereotyping and Requisites of Successful Top Managers', *Women in Management Review*, **17**(3–4), 120–30.

Vinnicombe, S. and V. Singh (2003), 'Locks and Keys to the Boardroom: A Comparison of UK Male and Female Directors' Careers', *Women in Management Review*, **18**(6), 325–33.
Yoder, J.D. (2001), 'Making Leadership Work More Effectively for Women', *Journal of Social Issues*, **57**(4), 815–28.

2. Challenging gendered leadership and management education

Sharon Mavin, Patricia Bryans and Teresa Waring

INTRODUCTION

In this chapter we argue that UK business and management schools continue to operate a gender blind approach (or at best gender neutral) to management education, management research and the development of management theory. This echoes a pattern repeated in the practice of management. The issue of whether this gender blindness results from 'not seeing', 'being unaware', 'suppressing gender' or 'gender defensiveness' (Linstead 2000: 298) remains problematic.

Reflecting on our experiences within two UK business schools and on our ongoing empirical research carried out over six years, we provide substantive arguments relating to the masculine nature of management, the place of academic women in management, the male dominated processes of management education and research, and the need to re-engage with gender in management education. We conclude with a call for an 'unlearning' and a 'rethinking' of gender blind management education and provide some examples of how this might be achieved.

It has been reported by Mathur-Helm (2005) that within the Fortune 500 companies only one in eight corporate officers are women and very few occupy positions of CEO, president, director, or executive vice president (see Chapter 7). Thus it would appear that there is continued need to explore barriers to women's advancement in management and leadership, as only a few women are able to negotiate persistent obstacles to senior positions (Nelson and Burke 2000).

Women are not indifferent to their own career development. Simpson *et al.* (2004a) note that many women in the UK prepare themselves for a career in management by taking a Master of Business Administration (MBA) (Bickerstaff 1992), with the MBA often seen as a means of breaking through the 'glass ceiling' into senior management positions (Baruch *et al.* 2004). However, once they begin their MBA programmes it would appear that management research, theory and management education may be failing women due to the gendered nature of the academic curricula and the perpetuation of the manager as male status quo (Schein and Davidson 1993).

The widespread suggestion that mainstream management theory is more accurately labelled 'male stream', in so much as it fails to recognize the relationship between management and gender, is known as 'gender blindness' (Wilson 1996). Universities are uniquely placed to play a crucial role in enabling individuals, organizations and professional bodies to critically challenge their ways of working and thinking. The danger with ignoring this role is that it leads to 'impoverished learning', an anathema to the knowledge society. By ignoring the concept of gender, business and management schools (BMSs) reinforce the collusion with the status quo, simply repeating existing management theory and practice. BMSs cannot continue to replicate this practice as organizations of the future require people who can think beyond the traditional paradigm.

It is our contention that BMSs should rethink management in terms of the role of men and women as well as valuing both. We argue, based on our longitudinal research, that there should be a greater degree of reflexivity in approaches to management. First there is the need to 'unlearn' traditional approaches to management theory, education and management practice. This should be accompanied by a 'rethinking' and a scrutiny of this academic base. To 'rethink' requires imagination and wisdom. It requires reflections upon or endeavours to put aside conventional ways of knowing … 'It requires a reflexive ability that does not simply challenge our assumptions in the sparring and reductionist mode of much academic debate, but rather exhibits a sensitive awareness to subtlety and nuance' (Hughes and Kerfoot 2002: 473).

Our aim in this chapter is therefore to critically scrutinize and enable a consciousness raising in our audiences by highlighting what we understand as gender blindness within management, management research and management education. However, UK BMSs may continue to be gender blind but the issue of whether this gender blindness results from not seeing, being unaware, 'suppressing gender' or 'gender defensiveness' (Linstead 2000: 298) remains problematic.

UNLEARNING GENDER BLINDNESS

Wilson (1996) in her discussion of gender blindness accuses management theory of being male stream; first because it provides little room for any analysis of those actual individuals who occupy the role, treating management as an abstract set of functions, principles or processes; second because it fails to recognize gender as a significant variable, even in the face of overwhelming empirical evidence.

Linstead (2000: 297) views this gender blindness as an inculcated way of not seeing or being unaware and argues that the 'founding fathers' of management theory were very gender aware but they actively worked to 'suppress gender' in their theories. In terms of the 'founding fathers', Linstead (2000) cites Matteson and Ivancevich's (1989) claim that Maslow's Hierarchy of Needs theory is built on flawed primate research, even more flawed sexuality research and is distinctly gender biased. Yet it has been so influential in management theory as to become a 'classic among classics'.

Linstead (2000) argues that this suppression within the work of the 'founding fathers' results from an epistemological stance that reduces all difference, including gender, to either an epiphenomenal or interferential status. It was either an unwanted effect of practical variabilities or a deviant source pattern that needed to be smoothed out by the system. The question is to which system is Linstead referring? Is it the positivistic, scientific male system? As authors we are able to accept the argument that issues of gender are perceived by some as actively interfering with the status quo, as deviant and which need smoothing out. Indeed these are often used as arguments to post-rationalize specific practices and theories. However, Linstead (2000: 302) argues that while there may still be genuine pockets of gender blindness, far more reactive 'gender defensiveness' and 'suppression' are present where there is resistance to taking gender seriously.

THE MASCULINE NATURE OF MANAGEMENT AND LEADERSHIP

Patriarchy is commonly used to describe the context and process through which men and male dominated institutions promote male supremacy. This can be through both control of access to hierarchical power or characteristics of knowledge claims (Nicolson 1996: 22). However, Wacjman (1998) argues that while the legitimacy of patriarchy has been eroded it is far from being rendered obsolete and the material and institutional structure of patriarchy are still largely intact. Patriarchy organizes material and linguistic practices around a primary signifier that might be expressed as 'male authority' and within this context the social category 'woman' is subordinated to the category of 'man' (Katila and Merilainen 1999: 165). While patriarchy itself changes historically, due to its systematic nature, patriarchy is not optional. At the interpersonal level patriarchy is not a conspiracy among men that they impose on women; it is a complementary social process between men and women (Smith 1997). Women cannot escape patriarchy, they can only be liberated through a struggle to change the system and for men likewise patriarchy is not optional (Cockburn 1991: 8).

Burke and Davidson (1994) argue that managerial and professional women live and work in a larger society that is patriarchal, a society in which men have historically had greater access to power, privilege and wealth than women. In patriarchal organizations dominated by men, the informal rules and masculine discourse of management establish the requirements of conformity to the dominant culture (Ledwith and Colgan 1996). Patriarchy forms a backdrop within organizations to dominant and traditional forms of management which have developed within a general male-dominated social context, characteristically performed or assumed to be performed, by men (Hearn 1994). Collinson and Hearn's (1994) argument that what we call management both as the actual practice of managers and as theory, can be understood as 'what men do'.

The 'management as male' paradigm within management theory is evident from the 1960s when McGregor (1967) commented that the model of a successful manager was aggressive, competitive, firm and just, and argued that he is not feminine or intuitive in a womanly sense. Here the very expression of emotion was widely viewed as a feminine weakness that would interfere with the business process. This lack of gender awareness is evident in Weber's (1968) ideal-typical forms of authority, in Taylor's (1947) scientific approach to management and in conventional organizational psychology where the major contribution to the prescriptive study of leadership has emerged.

Bartram (2005) argues that in the 1970s and in particular through the work of Mintzberg (1975) the construct of management was male. 'Men are managers and managers are men: the two constructs conflate to mean the same thing' (Bartram, 2000: 108). 'Mintzberg (1975) based his research on men occupying a range of management roles from foremen to chief executives; women did not figure at all in the level of management according to his research' (Bartram, 2000: 9). MBA programmes have been historically grounded in courses underpinned by Mintzberg's work which continue to influence their development. His recent call for management education to shift paradigms to focus upon management practice and associated leadership, interpersonal and communication skills is now impacting on the redesign of a number of MBAs and equivalents (Mintzberg and Gosling 2002). It is clear that Mintzberg's theories, that create subject positions which neglect women, will continue to be central to management curricula and to impact on management education.

In the 1990s Collinson and Hearn (1994) pointed to a historical neglect of gender in the study of leadership and the psychological literature persisted. Thus as theories of management have been based historically on the ways men do things it then follows that management education and management development, as underpinned by these theories, perpetuate such biases and as Bartram (2005) argues, they maintain women in subject positions that are other.

Without acknowledging the historical specificity of management theories and the gender neutral or defensive context in which they were developed, then management theory can be presented as universalized, maintaining the management as male status quo and continuing to hide women's perspectives and experiences. Management education which is not gender aware continues to silence women's voices and provides little or no space for women to be managers (Bartram 2005).

As the model of the successful manager continues to be a masculine one, the male managerial perspective operates against aspiring women as it represents a curious absence, in fact a blackout of images of women being in senior management and performing as leaders (Ferrario 1991). The very language of management is resolutely masculine. Organizations are then a crucial site for the ordering of gender and for the establishment and preservation of male power (Wajcman 1998: 7). Hearn (1994) argues that it is generally taken for granted that it is men who are managers, or who are at least the dominant group, both socially and numerically in management, and so it may be taken for granted that women are in second place in management (Mavin 2001a).

Management itself has traditionally implied maleness and maleness has often carried with it managerial and leadership qualities, that women are assumed sometimes by men to inherently lack (Hearn, 1994: 196). Therefore the social construction of management is one in which managerial competence is intrinsically linked to qualities attached to men.

These persistent male stereotypes of management serve to make natural and thereby help to generate a close identification between men and management. According to this view, men are more independent, objective, competitive and better suited to handle responsible leadership positions than the typical, gentle, sensitive, passive, stereotyped woman. One example of this is the report of Sir Alan Sheppard of Grand Metropolitan speaking at the 1992 Confederation of British Industry Corporate Governance meeting that 'he would dearly love to appoint a woman with the qualities of Sir John Harvey-Jones or Sir Dick Giordano' (two of his most famous non-executives), 'but any women seeking to match them would have to have an operation'.

In general those holding this type of stereotypical view are likely to perceive women as ineffective leaders in jobs incongruent with the traditional female passive sex role (Ferrario 1991). Ambitious women who aspire to leadership are still subject to derogatory comments such as 'dragons', 'battle-axes', 'barracudas' and perceived as more male than men (Still 1994;

Mavin 2001a; see Chapter 4). Whilst the debate concerning transactional (traditionally associated with male characteristics) and transformational (associated with female characteristics) leadership continues (see Chapter 1), Korabik *et al.* (2001) argue that such research has been developed primarily by studying male leaders. Recently as more transformational styles and the concept of 'emotional intelligence' are viewed as important in organization, we argue that whilst gaining in popularity, they are a call for men to 'feminize' their styles and skills rather than encouraging and including more women into management and leadership (see Chapter 3).

As a consequence of the continued domination of the management as male paradigm, women managers are 'out of place' (Mavin 2001a) in 'foreign territory', 'travellers in a male world' (Marshall 1984; Wajcman 1998: 50). Coates (1998) also argues that the suppression of femininity is a prerequisite to joining the corporate crusade and comments 'the corporate crusade, its strategy and mechanisms, are more subtle than anything experienced earlier in the management of organizations, as a result individuality and femininity have been sacrificed' (Coates 1998: 9).

Whilst Wacjman (1998: 7–8) notes 'women's presence in the world of men is conditional on them being willing to modify their behaviour to become more like men or to be perceived as more male than men' and Maier (1999: 89) argues 'men and women recruited into dominance within organizations tend to internalize the requirements of the position becoming like men'. In this context it is clear that women cannot win and they face the contradictory demands of being feminine and business-like (Wacjman 1998: 7–8). They cannot join as a woman and once they start to behave like a man, they cannot be a 'proper woman' (Maddock 1999). UK University BMSs have a role to play in challenging this management as male perspective. While the concepts of manager and management remain male or at best gender neutral and uncontested within education, there will be little impact made on management research or management practice.

Gendered Management Knowledge and Theory

Nicolson (1996: 28) argues that the control of knowledge is being preserved by the continued exclusion of women in positions of power in academia. Indeed Belenky *et al.* (1997: 5) argue along with other academic feminists, that conceptions of knowledge and truth, accepted and articulated today have been shaped throughout history by the male dominated majority culture. Acker (1980) argues that men impose their conceptualization of the world on women, whose own experience is regarded as less valid, less convincing and a less scientific basis for understanding. It has long been argued that women have been largely excluded from the work of producing the forms of thought and the images and symbols in which thought is expressed and ordered (Smith, 1975).

The literature on management has tended to treat the managerial function in a peculiarly neutered, asexual way. In 2000, Thomas and Pullen argued that research into management is still almost exclusively from a gender-neutral position but pointed out that criticisms of this lack of gender awareness are not new. This gender neutrality or blindness within management research is evidenced through editorial boards, choice of referees, referee comments, the decision of whether to publish or not and in the choice of journal targeted by the authors, but whether there is gender awareness which is resisted through defensiveness or suppression requires further research.

Gender analyses of management are rarely published in highly rated journal publications and are often omitted from BMSs UK Research Assessment Exercise (RAE) submissions. Subsequently this has significant impact on academic careers and frustration remains with what is accepted as valid management knowledge and research. The RAE compounds gender blindness in management research by the way in which it institutionalizes and financially rewards UK universities on the basis of the quantity and quality of research output. However, this universal system of assessment takes no account of differential academic life chances that are gendered (Knights and Richards, 2001). Knights and Richards (2001: 8) cite research by the Association of University Teachers (AUT) (2000), which shows that 'men are almost twice as likely to be entered in the research assessment exercise, than women'. Moreover, the EOC (2000: 1) provides a guidance note on gender proofing research:

> It is our view that research which is 'gender blind', rather than 'gender aware' may often be bad science or of limited value, particularly if it is used to inform or formulate policy.

The EOC (2000: 1) goes on to advise that a 'gender aware' approach should automatically be adopted within a research project unless there is good reason not to do so.

Gendered Management Education

We have argued that 'the management as male paradigm' is pervasive throughout the cultures of UK BMSs and that the position of academic women within these cultures can be seen to perpetuate the perception that management equals male and reinforces gender blindness. This is supported by research that argues that women lecturers do not make any positive association between the characteristics of managers and those of women. Foster (1994) argues that both men and women lecturers in BMSs stereotype the manager as male and that this is modelled to students of management, who may subsequently perpetuate this stereotype in management practice. This has a direct impact on the student learning experience where in all activities, and regardless of gender, lecturers may perceive management and managers as male or gender neutral.

Hite and McDonald (1995 cited in Smith, 1997) argue that a low level of gender diversity awareness among educators and learners can cause tensions in personal interactions and classroom settings, resulting in embarrassment and discomfort for the individuals affected. This can pejoratively influence the assessment of learner competence by educators. In 2000 Smith reported that women in management education perceive bias arising from gendered attitudes and language of male management educators, resulting in feelings of marginalization and invisibility and the trivialization of female perspectives and experience.

Gender blindness in management education evidences itself through the failure of UK BMSs to evaluate students' current perceptions and experiences of management in organizations on entry to management education. Smith (1997) comments that female and male students of management are likely to have been socialized differently, with different communication styles and that they use language in different ways. Through teaching interventions, management academics may either construct the manager as male or at best gender neutral, and as little evaluation takes place of the student's perceptions of managers on entry, there is a lost opportunity to challenge traditional male constructions and develop alternative views of management and managers.

Simpson *et al.* (2005b) in their study of gender, age and the MBA note that there were difficulties of being female in the context of the MBA course. In their study, women were more critical of the programme and this related mainly to what was perceived to be the 'macho' and competitive culture of the course. Women commented on both the arrogant attitude and the 'bravado' of male students and on the male students' competitive behaviour – referring to the typical MBA graduate (described by one female student as 'mighty big attitude') as in their words, 'aggressive', 'competitive,' 'arrogant' and 'over-confident'. None of the men interviewed commented on the gendered nature of the MBA experience (Simpson *et al.* 2004b: 235).

WOMEN ACADEMICS IN MANAGEMENT EDUCATION

The situation for women academics in the management discipline, whether in business schools or departments of management, often mirrors that of women in business or organizational management, as their knowledge domain and practice is dominated by the male paradigm and their organizational context is patriarchal. The result of this male managerial perspective is that women tend to become sidelined or marginalized (Still 1994), evidenced within management education by the role, status and visibility of women academics and their gendered experiences in this type of environment.

Wilson (1995: 5) argues that UK Higher Education Institutions (HEI) are male institutions with very limited and rigid career patterns and studies show that men have dominated senior places in UK HEI (Bagilhole 1993; Morley 1994; Brooks 1997; Eggins 1997; see Chapter 10 in this volume). The representation of women in top academic jobs is dire (AUT 1999), the salaries of academic women are one fifth less than academic men (Knights and Richards 2001) and there is evidence of endemic sex discrimination in UK universities, which demands action (Wilson 1999). Whitehead (2001) argues that in higher education as well as in business, men and masculine values are dominant. While Priola (2004: 421) comments 'statistics show that men represent the majority of academic staff with 63 percent in the UK and they occupy the most senior academic and managerial positions; Mumford and Rumball (1999) report that only 7 percent of universities world wide are managed by women'.

The number of women academics employed in UK business and management studies has increased steadily, from 2975 in 1999/2000 to 3425 in 2002/03, while men academics have maintained dominance in numbers with 6350 in 1999/2000 rising to 6585 in 2002/2003 (HESA 2004). Significantly, in 2002/03, of the 1060 professors in UK business and management studies, only 145 were women (14 per cent) and only 27 per cent were at senior lecturer grade. However moving down the hierarchical grading scale 37 per cent of women were at the lecturer grade and 50 per cent were researchers in the subject area (HESA 2004). In summary we have invited the reader to reflect with us on the nature and status of management theory and practice and how little has changed over the past 20 years.

THE INVISIBLE ACADEMIC WOMAN

Research exploring the identity of women academics within a post-1992 UK BMS (Mavin, 2001a) illustrates how invisible women can feel and highlights the gender blind nature of management education. The study involved a sample of 149 academic staff, 45 of whom were women with three above the level of senior lecturer (one at principal lecturer, two at head of school), leaving 42 women at senior lecturer or below. The following section includes statements by participants in our research which seeks to illustrate the experiences of women in academia.

Participant A when discussing her experiences as a woman academic within the school comments:

> When I first joined the Business School one or two female colleagues discussed their lack of progression and in particular the sex discrimination case. As a new member of staff I did not think I was being discriminated against or prevented personally from progressing. But as time has gone on I have been on the receiving end of sexist remarks, blatant discrimination, in addition to covert discrimination resulting in a feeling of disempowerment and lack of motivation. (Mavin, 2001a)

Participants were asked 'how are women academics perceived in the School?' Participant B's response is illustrative of many female academics responses: 'Men think that if women are good enough, in male terms, then they will overcome all the obstacles and succeed despite them, but in order to do so they must become "honorary men".' Participant B also described an incident where the Dean of the School, speaking to an almost male audience from the business community, felt comfortable making male macho comments. The story highlighted how women are maginalized, particularly in relation to their status alongside male academics in the external business community.

In particular this research supported the argument of Butler and Landells (1995) that academia is one of the most blatant contexts for women being seen as sex objects by men, while they see themselves professionals, offering judging of women by appearances and sexual partners. In our research into women's experiences within a BMS, the academic women discussed organizational stories concerned with women academics' sexuality and gave examples of academic men assigning them identities based on who they were perceived to be sleeping with. Nicholson (1996) offers the categories of 'loose woman', 'virgin maid', 'whore', 'blue stocking' and 'executive tart', whilst the academic women in this study provide 'dogs', 'sexy chicks', 'dykes' or 'ladette' as ways men had described academic women (Mavin 2001a). The academic women's stories highlight the gendered nature of the organizational culture and the sexualized relations between men and women which serve to continue male supremacy within the professional environment. The stories also explain in some way why challenges to the malestream are sometimes vehemently fought and why management education is gender blind or defensive.

Academia, like business and organizational management, is a male place and women academics continue to be caught in the contradictions of 'bifurcated consciousness', alienated through the lack of fit between the theoretical world and the experiential one (Smith 1975). In UK BMSs, the historically embedded patriarchal cultures continue to assign women academics to second place (Mavin 2001a), paralleling the situation for women managers and leaders in organizations.

Gendered Management Knowledge and Theory

In 1981 Morgan pointed to the 'academic machismo' that often characterized the sociological mode of production and how conferences, seminars and exchanges in scholarly journals seemed to be arenas not only for the practice of academic rationality, but also for the competitive display of masculine skills. This 'academic machismo' is discussed by Höpfl (2000) and can be seen in the processes of PhD programmes completed within business schools. Participant C's experience is illustrative of many students who wish to integrate gender issues into their research. Participant C, a senior lecturer in a business school, wished to use a subjective gendered analysis of organizations for her research but struggled with the power dynamics between herself and her male PhD supervisor (he was senior to her in the school's hierarchy). Participant C faced an all-male panel during the process to approve her PhD proposal, despite her request for a woman to be included. As there were no 'subject experts' in gender in the business school, a male colleague from another school was invited on to the panel. Participant C's supervisor 'accepted' the gendered perspective of her research but rejected her subjectivist stance and insisted upon quantitative enquiry. It was only when he left the institution that she was able to regain her epistemological position and successfully complete the doctorate.

Danieli and Greene's (2003: 2) reflections on gender blind industrial relations research, where there is a lack of gender centrality in theory building as a result of research that has been done by men, on men and for men, we call for a rethinking of management research and the development of management theory. There is also a lack of challenge concerning the gender balance of empirical studies. Seminal, male only American studies based on MBA students remain largely unchallenged and perpetuate the male stream of management research and knowledge, whilst women only populations are criticized as unbalanced and unrepresentative. Similarly Hall-Taylor (1997) argues that academic management journals reinforce the male stream by continuing to publish management research based on the male norm or by presenting this as gender neutral. This silence in the leading journals is important in that they define what is visible, discussible, achievable and identifiable within the discipline of management. Research presented in academic journals is integrated into the learning experience as a support to teaching and development in management education and therefore serves to reinforce existing gendered stereotypes in the learning experience and learning environment.

Gendered Management Education

The gender composition of teaching teams is often an indication of how gender aware, defensive or gender blind BMSs are in management education. In 1995 Sinclair argued for a radical reconstruction of the MBA, and placed gender, sex and sexuality as central to management education. However a student's experience taken from Mavin and Bryans (1999) work on gender on the agenda, highlights that change has been slow:

> As the MBA course progressed, I became more aware of the absence of women. I never had a female lecturer and visiting speakers were always male. Gender issues were never mentioned in the sessions. If I asked questions relating to gender there were three reactions: genuine puzzlement – what did I mean; hostility – did I not understand that this was a business course which was therefore gender neutral; polite interest but no knowledge or suggestions of where I might find such knowledge.

This type of experience sends a strong message to both management students and their organizations. Like 'organizational fit' (Cassell and Walsh 1993), where the numerical distribution of women at different levels of the organization impacts on the experiences of women managers (Simpson 2000a) with women experiencing different degrees of fit depending on their level of comfort or discomfort, within the context of postgraduate management education women can be in the minority as tokens within a cohort and/or struggling to find voice in a masculine programme culture. We argue that their experiences of gender neutral or defensive learning within management education settings result in varying degrees of 'learning fit'.

Whilst using all male academic teams to redesign management education programmes, sends strong messages to the academic faculty and to students who choose the course, perpetuating a lack of diversity and lack of awareness of the impact of gender. Participant D in Mavin and Bryans (2002: 246) illustrates the complexity of gender blindness, awareness or suppression in the development of management education curricula:

> When the new Master of Business Administration course was developed internally, all Divisions had academics represented on this 'prestigious' high status course, but none of the development team were women academics. When the issue was raised by a woman Professor, one senior man commented that if they did so they would have to also consider disabled and ethnic minorities in the composition.

Here a gender aware academic challenges the male norm and is met with a response from another gender aware academic, who interestingly chooses to defend gender blindness so that the gender issue is suppressed and the status quo maintained. Many contributing authors to this book refer to the masculine nature of organizations and 'think manager, think male'. As Vinnicombe and Singh (2002) argue 'over half the women with postgraduate degrees saw the top manager as masculine'. It is evident that postgraduate education has a gender effect. Simpson *et al.* (2005b: 234) noted that on evaluating the MBA four women discussed how they were 'more objective', 'less emotional', 'more detached' and had 'toughened up' as a result of their MBAs. This was seen as useful when difficult decisions had to be made. These results require further research in order to explore the impact of education on the social constructions of women in management.

REFLEXIVITY, MANAGEMENT EDUCATION AND GENDER

The issue of gender needs to be placed on the 'management agenda' and facilitates the 'unlearning' of gender blindness. In terms of the gender conversation, embracing gender or suppressing it within management, Linstead (2000) notes that the motivations behind the choice and the consequences of the suppression should be explicit. However, we argue in order to 'suppress gender' in the practice of management, research and management education, rather than to be 'unaware' or 'gender blind', there has to be a conscious recognition of gender issues. This conscious recognition of the impact of the gendered nature of management and organization should be evident before there can be a conscious choice to 'suppress gender'.

In order to unlearn gender blindness we argue that in general management education is not aware or 'aware enough,' of the gendering processes at work to be able to make a conscious choice to suppress them and therefore may remain gender blind. The more complex issue is establishing whether individuals are gender aware and then choose to resist through gender defensiveness or suppression. A more critical question to explore is why management education and management academics consciously suppress gender?

While the male model of management dominates, it continues to be a struggle against the dominant power and political dynamics in order to challenge institutionalized gender blindness endemic in management education. By challenging the gendered nature of management education, research and theory we can begin the process of 'unlearning' through raising consciousness and challenging the taken for granted assumptions which underpin management education. Rethinking management education requires us to put aside conventional ways of knowing and to explore alternatives.

In order to place gender on the agenda in management education as a means of unlearning and rethinking gender blind management education there are a number of initiatives to challenge the status quo and raise awareness of gender. In our work with a network of academic women (Mavin and Bryans 2002) we discuss experiences of women who have used informal, collective strategies to move on, to challenge existing boundaries of management and their organizations. Some examples include:

- aiming to improve the visibility of women academics in management;
- implicit and explicit challenges were made to the subordination of women academics such as two female academics taking action against a bullying boss;
- as a result of women feeling undervalued and/or facing rejection at promotion, they decided to change the game by building research profiles.

This was explained by Participant E as:

> Rather than continuing to reinforce the stereotype of a female academic, knowing her place and carrying the burden of teaching, administration and student support, in order that the men could build their research CVs, we set ourselves targets for research and publication and regularly monitor our progress. (Mavin and Bryans 2002)

In order to make management theory and research gender aware, academics must critically analyse accepted theory and management practice in terms of gender rather than accepting this as gender neutral or gender blind. As a means of challenging gender blind research there has to be recognition by editorial boards of mainstream management journals that gender is a variable in research and there should be an acceptance into the mainstream of gender analyses of management.

It is suggested, based on the guidance by the EOC (2000) (see discussion above), that research councils stipulate gender aware criteria before allocating monies for management research, as these practical actions impact on management research, students' experience of management education and particularly on what is accepted as management knowledge.

The impact of gender aware management education on women managers is in the interest of BMSs to take on board gender awareness initiatives in order to develop more future satisfied and effective female management graduates (McKeen and Burke 1991) and gender aware male managers, both of which may positively support change in relation to gender issues in organizations. One way to speed up the process of change is to create an awareness and understanding of the processes that support the status quo (Simpson 1995). McKeen and Burke (1991) argue that the most useful activities in preparing women for managerial and professional work are to have women talk candidly about their work, career and life experiences. In the authors' institutions there are initiatives such as supporting the development of women's networks within management courses, introducing and integrating material in courses more reflective and inclusive of women's experiences, and supporting research on women in management. Other interventions to place agenda on the gender include having more women faculty members, enabling their visibility within high profile courses and introducing women managers as central actors in cases and in course materials. Also, placing gender on the agenda explicitly from the beginning of a course identifies what discussions are acceptable and offers students a gender framework for their experiences, learning and development.

Katila and Merilainen (2002: 48) reflecting on their failed attempt to mainstream gender on to the curricula note 'we felt that it was exactly at the beginning of the university studies that teaching of gender issues is needed, not as an optional choice but rather as a compulsory subject'. In one BMS we have enabled gender discussions in a core module at the beginning of a postgraduate programme, including critiquing a working paper 'Management, Men and Women, Leadership and Management Styles' (Mavin 1998b). At the authors' institutions women academics have made changes to elements of their management curricula (Mavin and Bryans 2002), particularly on postgraduate programmes where the study of gender issues impacts on the organizations in which the students are employed; for example, a core teaching module incorporating gender via critiques of 'male stream' management theory, and exploring management careers and development through research on women's careers (Mavin 2001b).

CONCLUSION

There is little sign that trends towards feminization of management have been reflected in the course content or design of the MBAs (Simpson *et al.* 2004b) or in management education in general. Indeed the masculine nature of many management programmes (Mavin and Bryans 1999; Simpson 2000b; Smith 1997) may be largely out of touch with the demands of modern management (Simpson *et al.* 2004b). Management education should be gender aware. It is the responsibility of BMSs and equivalents to place gender high on the agenda (Mavin and Bryans 1999) in order to challenge traditional perceptions of 'manager equals male' (Schein and Davidson 1993). In this chapter we have outlined our critique of gender blind management, research and management education and enabled a critical analysis which illustrates the complexity of gender blindness, defensiveness and gender suppression. As authors and women academics, we call for a critical engagement with traditional management theory and a rethinking of this theory through a gender lens. We have demonstrated the need for gender awareness in the development of new theory and research practice to avoid the continuing gender blind frameworks which become male stream theory and mainstream in management education. It is incumbent upon management journals to recognize and value gendered analysis by becoming critically aware of alternative paradigms; a rethinking of editorial panels may be required.

We have highlighted the experiences of women academics as an indicator of the organizational gender cultures at work; we have raised the issue of gender blind curricula and outlined our own practical strategies to place gender on the agenda in BMSs. Management academics must challenge and rethink their practice and engage in gender conversations with students and colleagues, regardless of how uncomfortable this may be. Those BMSs prepared to actively consider their internal structures, promotion and development practices in terms of the gender of academic staff and consider the course content and delivery methods in terms of gender awareness, can enable a move away from the status quo, become gender aware rather than gender blind, and rethink management education; challenging repeating patterns of management and manager as male. The more complex issue of exploring and challenging those who are aware but who choose to resist and suppress gender requires further research.

This chapter recommends an 'unlearning' and 'rethinking' of gender blind management education, management research and theory. Whilst we can also stand accused of presenting either an unwanted effect of practical variabilities or a deviant source pattern which needs to be smoothed out by the system (Linstead 2000), we have done so in an attempt to provoke uncertainty and provide an opportunity for further reflection and debate.

REFERENCES

Acker, S. (1980), 'Women, the Other Academics', *The British Journal of Sociology of Education*, **1**(1), 81–91.

Association of University Teachers (1999), 'First Steps Toward Gender Audit', *AUT Woman, Supporting Equal Opportunities for All Members of the Higher Education Community*, **47**, Summer.

Association of University Teachers (2000), '*Woman*', **49**, Spring.

Bagilhole, B. (1993), 'Survivors in a Male Preserve: A Study of British Women Academics' Experiences and Perceptions of Discrimination in a UK University', *Journal of Area Studies, Special Issue, Women in Eastern and Western Europe in Transition and Recession*, **6**, 143–56.

Bartram, S. (2005), 'What is Wrong with Current Approaches to Management Development in Relation to Women in Management Roles?', *Women in Management Review*, **20**(2), 107–16.

Belenky, M.F., Clinchy, B.M., Goldberger, N.R. and Tarule, J.M. (1997), *Women's Ways of Knowing: The Development of Self, Voice and Mind*, 10th Anniversary Edition, New York: Basic Books.

Brooks, A. (1997), *Academic Women*, Society for Research into Higher Education, Buckinghamshire: Open University Press.

Bryans, P. and Mavin S. (2003), 'Women Learning to Become Managers: Learning to Fit In or to Play a Different Game?', *Management Learning*, **34**(1), 111–34.

Bryans, P., Gormley, N., Stalker, B. and Williamson, B. (1998), 'From Collusion to Dialogue: Universities and Continuing Professional Development', *Continuing Professional Development*, **1**(4), 135–37.

Burke, R. and Davidson, M. (1994), 'Women in Management Current Research Issues', in M. Davidson and R.J. Burke (eds), *Women in Management Current Research Issues*, London: Paul Chapman Publishing.

Butler, A. and Landells, M. (1995), 'Taking Offence, Research as Resistance to Sexual Harassment in Academia,' in P. Nicolson (1996), *Gender, Power and Organization, A Psychological Approach*, London: Routledge.

Cassell, C. and Walsh, S. (1993), 'Being Seen But Not Heard: Barriers to Women's Equality in the Work Place', *The Psychologist*, March.

Catalyst (2000), '2000 Catalyst Census of Women Corporate Officers and Top Earners', www.catalystwomen.org/research/census.htm.

Coates, G. (1998), 'Integration or Separation: Women and the Appliance of Organizational Culture', *Women in Management Review*, **13**(3), 114–24.

Cockburn, C. (1991), *In the Way of Women: Men's Resistance to Sex Equality in Organizations*, London: Macmillan.

Collinson, D.L. and Hearn, J. (1994), 'Naming Men as Men: Implications for Work Organization and Management', *Gender, Work and Organization*, **1**(1), 2–22.

Danieli, A. and Greene, A. (2003), 'Re-focusing Industrial Relations: Looking Through the Gender Lens', *Third International Gender Work and Organization Conference*, Keele, UK, June.

Davies, C. (1993), 'The Equality Mystique, The Difference Dilemma and the Case of Women Academics', *UGC, Women's Studies Centre Review*, **2**, 53–72.

Davies, C. and Holloway, P. (1995), 'Troubling Transformations: Gender Regimes and Organizational Culture in the Academy', in L. Morley and V. Walsh (eds), *Feminist Academics: Creative Agents for Change*, London: Taylor and Francis.

Eggins, H. (ed.) (1997), *Women as Leaders and Managers in Higher Education*, Buckingham: SRHE and Open University Press.

Equal Opportunities Commission (2000), *A Checklist for Gender Proofing Research*, Manchester: Equal Opportunities Commission.

Ferrario, M. (1991), 'Sex Differences in Leadership Style: Myth or Reality', *Women in Management Review and Abstracts*, **6**(3), 16–21.

Foster, F. (1994), 'Managerial Sex Role Stereotyping among Academic Staff within UK Business Schools', *Women in Management Review*, **9**(3), 17–22.

Hall-Taylor, B. (1997), 'Writing Women into Management or Writing Ourselves Out: A Dilemma for Women as Authors', *Women in Management Review*, **12**(8), 309–19.

Handley, J. (1994), 'Women, Decision Making and Academia', *Women in Management Review*, **9**(3), 11–16.

Harding, S. (1996), 'Gendered Ways of Knowing and the "Epistemological Crisis" of the West', in N. Goldberger, J. Tarule, B. Clinchy and M. Belenkey (eds), *Knowledge, Difference and Power, Essays Inspired by Women's Ways of Knowing*, New York: Basic Books.

Hearn, J. (1994), 'Changing Men and Changing Managements: Social Change, Social Research and Social Action', in M. Davidson, and R.J. Burke (eds), *Women in Management, Current Research Issues*, London: Paul Chapman Publishing.

Höpfl, H. (2000), 'The Suffering Mother and the Miserable Son: Organising Women and Organising Women's Writing', *Gender, Work and Organization*, 7(2), 98–105.

Hughes, D. and Kerfoot, D. (2002), Editorial: 'Rethinking Gender, Work and Organization', *Gender, Work and Organization*, 9(5), 473–81.

Katila, S. and Merilainen, S. (1999), 'A Serious Researcher or Just Another Nice Girl?: Doing Gender in a Male Dominated Scientific Community', *Gender Work and Organization*, 6(2), 163–73.

Katila, S. and Merilainen, S. (2002), 'Metamorphosis: From Nice Girls to Nice Bitches: Resistance Patriarchical Articulations of Professional Identity', *Gender, Work and Organization*, 9(3), 336–54.

Knights, D. and Richards, W. (2001), 'Sex Discrimination in UK Academia', *Rethinking Gender, Work and Organization Conference*, Keele University, 27–29 June.

Korabik, K., Ayman, R., and Purc Stephenson, R. (2001), 'Gender – Role Orientation and Transformational Leadership', presented at the *Rethinking Gender, Work and Organization* conference, Keele, June.

Ledwith, S. and Colgan, F. (1996), *Women in Management: Challenging Gender Politics*, London: Macmillan.

Linstead, S. (2000), 'Comment: Gender Blindness or Gender Suppression? A Comment on Fiona Wilson's Research Note', *Organization Studies*, 1, 297–304.

Maddock, S. (1999), *Challenging Women*, London: Sage.

Maier, M. (1999), 'On the Gendered Substructure of Organization: Dimensions and Dilemmas of Corporate Masculinity', in G. Powell (ed.), *The Handbook of Gender*, California: Sage Publications.

Marshall, J. (1984), *Women Travellers in a Male World*, London: Wiley.

Mathur-Helm, B. (2005), 'Equal Opportunity and Affirmative Action for South African Women: a Benefit or Barrier?' *Women in Management Review*, 20(1), 56–71.

Mavin, S. (1998a), 'Is Organizational Culture the Barrier to Women's Career Advancement?' *The First International Conference of Gender, Work and Organization*, UMIST, 9–10th January.

Mavin, S. (1998b), 'Management, Men and Women, Leadership and Management Style', Working Paper, Newcastle Business School, Northumbria University.

Mavin, S. (2001a), '*The Gender Culture Kaleidoscope: Images of Women's Identity and Place in Organization*', unpublished PhD Thesis, University of Northumbria: Newcastle.

Mavin, S. (2001b), 'Women's Careers in Theory and Practice: Time for Change?', *Women in Management Review*, 16(4), 183–92.

Mavin, S. and Bryans, P. (1999), 'Gender on the Agenda in Management Education', *Women in Management Review*, 14(3), 99–104.

Mavin, S. and Bryans, P. (2002), 'Academic Women in the UK: Mainstreaming Our Experiences and Networking for Action', *Gender and Education*, 14(3), 235–50.

Mavin, S., Bryans, P. and Waring, T. (2004a), 'Unlearning Gender Blindness: New Directions in Management Education', Special Issue of *Management Decision: The Discipline, Study and Practice of Management: A Reflective Enquiry*, 42(3–4), 565–78.

Mavin, S., Bryans, P. and Waring, T. (2004b), 'Gender on the Agenda 2: Unlearning Gender Blindness in Management Education', *Women in Management Review*, 19(6), 293–303.

McGregor, D. (1967), *The Professional Man*, New York: McGraw Hill.

McKeen, C.A. and Burke, R.J. (1991), 'University Initiatives for Preparing Managerial and Professional Women for Work', *Women in Management Review and Abstracts*, **6**(3), 11–15.

Mintzberg, H. and Gosling, J. (2002), 'Reality Programming for MBAs', *Strategy and Business*, **26**(1), 28–31.

Morgan, G. (1981), 'The Schismatic Metaphor and its Implications for Organizational Analysis', *Organization Studies*, **2**, 23–44.

Morley, L. (1994), 'Glass Ceiling or Iron Cage: Women in UK Academia', *Gender, Work and Organization*, **1**(4), 194–204.

Nelson, D.L. and Burke, R.J. (2000), 'Women Executives: Health, Stress and Success', *Academy of Management Executive*, **14**, 107–21.

Nicolson, P. (1996), *Gender, Power and Organization: A Psychological Approach*, London: Routledge.

Priola, V. (2004), 'Gender and Feminine Identities – Women as Managers in a UK Academic Institution', *Women in Management Review*, **19**(8), 421–30.

Schein, V.E. and Davidson, M.J. (1993), 'Think Manager, Think Male', *Management Development Review*, **6**(3), 24–8.

Sheppard, A. (1992), 'Statement at Confederation of British Industry Corporate Governance Meeting', *Financial Times*.

Simpson, R. (1995), 'Is Management Education on the Right Track for Women?', *Women in Management Review*, **10**(6), 3–8.

Simpson, R. (2000a), 'Gender Mix and Organizational Fit: How Gender Imbalance at Different Levels of the Organization Impacts on Women Managers', *Women in Management Review*, **15**(1), 5–19.

Simpson, R. (2000b), 'Winners and Losers: Who Benefits Most from the MBA?', *Management Learning*, **31**(2), 46–54.

Simpson, R., Sturges, R., Woods, A. and Altman, Y. (2004a), 'Career Progress and Career Barriers: Women MBA Graduates in Canada and the UK', *Career Development International*, **9**(5), 459–77.

Simpson, R., Sturges, R., Woods, A. and Altman, Y. (2004b), 'Gender, Age and the MBA: An Analysis of Extrinsic and Intrinsic Career Benefits', *Journal of Management Education*, **29**(2), 218–47.

Sinclair, A. (1995), 'Sex and the MBA', *Organization*, **2**(2), 295–317 in C.R. Smith (2000), 'Notes from the Field: Gender Issues in the Management Curriculum: A Survey of Student Experiences', *Gender, Work and Organization*, **7**(3), 158–67.

Singh, V. and Vinnicombe, S. (2003), 'The 2002 Female FTSE Index and Women Directors', *Women in Management Review*, **18**(7), 349–58.

Smith, C.R. (1997), 'Gender Issues in Management Education: A New Teaching Resource', *Women in Management Review*, **12**(3), 100–104.

Smith, D. (1975), 'Analysis of Ideological Structures and How Woman are Excluded: Considerations for Academic Women', *Canadian Review of Sociology and Anthropology*, **12**, 353–59 in S. Acher (1983), *Contradictions in Terms: Women Academics in British Universities*, in M. Arnot and K. Weiler (1993), *Feminism and Social Justice in Education*, London: Falmer Press.

Stanley, L. and Wise, S. (2000), 'But the Empress has no Clothes! Some Awkward Questions about the "Missing Revolution" in Feminist Theory', *Feminist Theory*, **1**(3), 261–88.

Still, L. (1994), 'Where to From Here? Women in Management, the Cultural Dilemma', *Women in Management Review*, **9**(4), 3–10.

Taylor, F. (1947), *Scientific Management*, Harper and Row, New York in J. Hearn, (1994), *Changing Men and Changing Managements: Social Change, Social Research and Social Action* in M.J. Davidson and R.J. Burke (eds), *Women and Management: Current Research Issues*, London: Paul Chapman Publishing.

Thomas, R. and Pullan, A. (2000), 'What do You Want from Me? A Gendered Analysis of Middle Managers Identities', *British Academy of Management Conference*, 13–15th September, University of Edinburgh.

Vinnicombe, S. and Singh, V. (2002), 'Sex Role Stereotyping and Requisites of Successful Top Managers', *Women in Management Review*, **17**(3/4), 120–30.

Wajcman, J. (1998), *Managing Like a Man*, Oxford: Blackwell Publishers Ltd.

Weber, M. (1968), *Economy and Society*, New York: Bedminster Press.

Whitehead, S. (2001), 'Woman as Manager: A Seductive Ontology'. *Gender, Work and Organizations*, **8**(1), 84–107.

Wilson, F.M. (1995), *Organizational Behaviour and Gender*, UK: McGraw-Hill.

Wilson, F.M. (1996), 'Research Note: Organization Theory: Blind and Deaf to Gender?', *Organization Studies*, **17**(5), 825–42.

Wilson, F. (2004), 'Women in Management in the UK', in L. Davidson and R.J. Burke (eds), *Women in Management Worldwide: Progress and Prospects*, Aldershot: Ashgate Publishing Company.

Wilson, T. (1999), *The Times Higher*, National Association of Teachers and Lecturers, 9th July.

3. Gendered leadership and management development: therapeutic cultures at work[*]

Elaine Swan

INTRODUCTION

The purpose of this chapter is to explore the gendering effects of 'therapeutic cultures' of leadership and management development within the public sector in the UK. By 'therapeutic cultures', I am referring to a congeries of ways of thinking about, and intervening in the 'self' found in many social domains from popular culture, the media, education, healthcare and, significantly for this book, the workplace. The main argument in the growing field that we could call the 'sociology of therapeutic cultures' (Rose 1989; 1996; Nolan 1998; Cloud 1998; Furedi 2003) is that our contemporary era is characterized by an intensification and proliferation of therapeutic ways of thinking. The types of workplace practices I am defining as therapeutic within this expanding field are those such as personal development training, coaching, facilitation, interpersonal skills training, team building and values workshops (Ackers and Preston 1997; Kerfoot 2002; Swan 2003; 2005b; Townley 1994; 1995; Turnbull 1999).

These practices derive from different therapeutic cultures and draw upon very different versions of therapeutic ideas but have in common the belief that the 'self' rather than society is the source of well being and this being the psychological 'self', as opposed to the physical 'self'. The 'self' is seen as the source of its own problems, but also as the main resource for providing potential solutions to these problems. Thus, therapeutic practices offer a range of approaches for thinking about, and intervening in, the 'self', its experiences and its relations with others. These are approaches that focus on the idea that the 'self' can be changed psychologically and behaviourally in order to improve its experiences and goals. The ambit of the therapeutic is now no longer just 'sick' selves but 'healthy' selves. In addition, therapeutic cultures

[*] The views expressed in this chapter do not necessarily represent those of the Centre for Excellence in Leadership.

have generated their own services and products, and with this expansion, critics argue, come new understandings, configurations and moralities of the 'self'. These, it is suggested, bring complex social and political consequences for both individuals and society.

For most commentators such as Christopher Lasch (1980; 1985); Philip Rieff (1966); Richard Sennett (1986); Robert Bellah *et al.* (1985), this proliferation is highly problematic. This denunciative school of thought has permeated more recent accounts such as Frank Furedi (2004), Dana Cloud (1998) and James Nolan (1998) who respond critically to what they see as the more recent colonization of the state, the political arena, education and popular culture by therapeutic idioms. The main concern for them is that therapeutic cultures, by focusing on the 'self', the personal and the subjective, are disregarding the political, social, historical and economic nature of the 'self' and its problems.

There is another much less critical theoretical take on therapeutic cultures. One leading example of this approach is Anthony Giddens (1991; 1992) who argues that traditional sources of guidance on how we should lead our lives, such as religious authorities, local communities and our families have become much less influential. Referring to this process as 'de-traditionalization', he suggests that how we understand who we are, how we should live, and who should help us, is being reconfigured in contemporary society. In essence, for Giddens, this means that the 'self' is no longer given to us, but has to be made. A core concept in his analysis is the notion of 'reflexivity' – the capability of the 'self' to constantly reflect upon, examine and revise who we are, and what we do in the light of new knowledge and the ability to install choice and consciousness into our habitual behaviours so that the present and the future become opened up for decision making. This is where therapeutic cultures can be helpful, according to Giddens, since they provide both solace and resources for reflexivity and self-formation. Therapeutic cultures, in his view, do not destroy the 'self', and its relationships, but make them.

Of significance is that one of the growing sites for the proliferation of therapeutic cultures is within the public sector as a workplace. But in spite of the increasing use of therapeutic ideas and practices within the workplace, very little has been written in management and organizational studies about the effects of this. In particular, there has been very little attention given to the gendered effects of the interface between therapeutic cultures, the workplace and new public management. To start addressing this, in this chapter I will focus on the concept of 'feminization' and its connection with therapeutic cultures in the public sector. This is first because one of the key critiques from the sociology of therapeutic cultures is that many therapeutic practices are feminizing (Furedi 2003; Craib 1994; 1998; Wainwright and Calnan 2002). The second is that feminization as a concept for understanding gendered processes within the workplace is on the increase (Adkins 2001; 2002; Cameron 2000; Leathwood 2005; Deem *et al*. 2000). Third, in some quarters, feminization is taken to mean that women now have it all, if not having gone too far. Feminization, then, as an explanatory framework brings together a number of contemporary debates.

There are of course many debates about how to conceptualize gender in management and organization studies. One dominant model is what Jo Brewis and Stephen Linstead (2004) refer to as the 'gender in management' perspective, and what Nikki Townsley (2003) calls 'gender body counting'. In essence this approach argues for understanding the unique experiences of women, and their so-called natural, or socialized, feminine styles in the workplace. In contrast, this chapter will draw upon what Brewis and Linstead call a 'gendering of management' approach. Drawing upon more discursive and post-structuralist ideas, it will focus in particular on femininities and masculinities as subject positions. Rather than seeing femininities and masculinities as the result of pre-existing essences, such as hormones, types of bodies or socialization, and so on, I will define them as 'ways of being' made available through discourses (Kerfoot and Whitehead 1998). In this view, femininity is not simply the prerogative of women but can be mobilised by men, in different ways, in different contexts and similarly, men 'do not have exclusive property rights on masculinity' (Brewis and Linstead 2004: 78).

The purpose of this is to study what Acker (1992: 251) calls gendering processes, the ways in which 'advantage and disadvantage, exploitation and control, action and emotion, meaning and identity, are patterned through and in terms of a distinction between male and female, masculine and feminine'. Drawing upon an in-depth qualitative case study of coaching in further education colleges in England, I will explore whether therapeutic practices are producing a feminized form of public sector masculinity in line with a neo-human relations approach within some forms of new public management. To start addressing these themes, this chapter begins by discussing definitions of feminization, then proceeds to discuss new public management and masculinities, before moving onto an empirical section focused on feminization within further education.

FEMINIZATION

As mentioned above, the term 'feminization' is used to refer to a number of different gendered and gendering processes and effects in the workplace. As Rosemary Deem *et al*. point out 'feminization is multi-faceted and it may also take different forms in private and public sectors' (Deem *et al*. 2000: 233). To date the concept of feminization has been used to examine where the determinants of gender and gendering processes are to be found: in the social, economic, or the cultural domains (Adkins 2001; 2002; Adkins and Lury 1996; Fondas 1997; Deem *et al.* 2000). Typically, Lisa Adkins (2001; 2002) argues, it is the economic and cultural domains which are most focused on to produce two very different understandings of how gender is constituted. In the first version, it has been used to examine gender in relation to the economic processes and to describe and critique issues such as increasing rates of participation by women in the labour market, women's entry into the vertical and hierarchical divisions of labour previously occupied by men and the differential conditions of different jobs according to whether men or women occupy them. This model, as Deem *et al.* (2000) highlight, should not be taken to argue that feminization is equivalent to the equalization of women in relation to men. This is because, as they and others argue, feminization also leads to reductions in salary, conditions and status when women take up traditional men's positions or replace male workers.

In the second meaning, feminization is used to describe and critique the spread of qualities traditionally associated with women. The types of qualities culturally associated with white middle class stereotypical femininity and seen as part of this trend to feminization may include emotional competences, communication skills, unique skills in empathy and intimacy, and aesthetic strategies (Cameron 2000; Kerfoot 2000; 2002; Leathwood 2005; Clarke and Newman 1997; Newman 2005). In this view, these performances of white middle class femininity have become important new workplace resources for both men and women in producing their jobs, identities and subjectivities. In this version of feminization, the cultural, rather than the economic, is foregrounded as the key determinant of gender (Adkins and Lury 1996; Adkins 2002). There are several recent examples of research on this form of feminization. Thus, in an account of merchant banking in London, Linda McDowell examines a 'new sovereignty of appearance, image and style at work' by men and women, albeit conditioned in gendered ways (cited in Adkins 2002: 15).

Another example is the case study by Deborah Cameron (2002) on the valorization of feminine communication styles within the workplace for example with customers in call centres. She found that communication strategies and qualities associated with traditional white middle class femininity such as emotional expressivity, empathy, warmth, helpfulness, friendly rapport, asking questions, caring and sincerity were used to define good customer service for both male and female staff.

A third example concerns popular management texts. Thus, Nanette Fondas (1997) identified the promotion of white middle class stereotypical feminine characteristics as new techniques of management in a textual analysis of popular management books. The main themes included the suggestion that there should be changes in power relations: the importance of surrendering control, being more egalitarian and sharing responsibility, authority and recognition; the recommendation of replacing command and control leadership styles with a nurturing, helping style that encourages growth, empowerment and learning and finally, the deployment of an emotional style based on being open, empathetic and sensitive, to build emotional connections and fluid networks to replace rigid hierarchies. For Fondas (1997: 270) and others, this feminization is a renewal of the 1930s North American human relations of Mayo in which the texts suggest that 'feminine characteristics admirable in both men and women'.

To summarize, cultural feminization, that is the taking on of white middle class stereotypical feminine qualities, is seen as a new trend in customer and management relations. Key questions are whether this trend is benefiting women and what effects it is having on masculinity in the workplace. Before exploring these questions, I will provide an overview of the development of new public management, and examine the kinds of masculinities seen to be produced through new public management techniques.

PUBLIC TRANSFORMATIONS AND MASCULINITIES

There is a considerable literature on the wide ranging radical changes being undertaken with the public sector in the UK (Barry *et al*. 2003; Clarke and Newman 1997; Dent *et al*. 2004; Dent and Whitehead 2002; Ozga and Walker 1999). One concept used by many of these theorists to conceptualize these changes is that of 'new public management'. Although there are differences in emphases in how theorists employ the term, it is used to describe a number of ideological, political, economic, cultural and operational transformations within the public sector in the past 20 years, both in the UK and internationally. In essence, it denotes a shift – what Yeatman (1994) sees as a paradigm shift – from public administration to management, from rules and regulations to entrepreneurialism, from public good to public service and from 'soft welfare' to the 'harder new realism of market economies' (Metcalf 1985 cited in Mac an Ghaill 1994). As a result, the central tasks and values of public administration have been replaced by management techniques from the private sector and values such as consumer choice, responsibility and accountability from neo-liberalism. In essence, the public sector has been re-structured and re-imagined in terms of marketization, privatization, rationalization, commercialization, flexibility, entrepreneurialism and com-modification (Kerfoot 2000; Dent and Whitehead 2002). In the context of new public management, the emphasis on solving entrenched, complex social, political and cultural and economic problems is reduced to 'technicist explanations and solutions' (Dent and Whitehead 2002: 8). Challenging traditional ways of doing things, professional skills are being replaced by financial, HRM, marketing and strategic management and business management techniques.

Although new public management is not unified, uniform or uncontested (Dent *et al.* 2004), it is underpinned by three overlapping discourses. According to Rosie Cunningham (2000), two of these are scientific management discourses and 'new wave management' discourses such as people-centred human resource management and entrepreneurialism. In light of the proliferation of therapeutic practices and soft human resource management techniques, I want to suggest that we separate out this development of neo-human relations as a discourse in its own right. Scientific management brings with it values of rational control and objectivity, and priorities of financial management, new forms of audit, control and surveillance, monitoring. Neo-human relations brings with it notions of people centredness, the language of mission and values and a focus on affective relations and what is known as soft human resource management (Clarke and Newman 1997). Entrepreneurialism emphasizes the values of neo-liberalism: energy, initiative, self-reliance, personal responsibility and autonomy, and productive self-regulating selves (du Gay 1996). Importantly for Cunningham, these discourses are highly contradictory in terms of values and practices.

This examination of the contradictory values and practices raises questions about how new public management affects people on the ground: a growing number of academics are beginning to explore this (see Chapter 10 for a discussion on new public management and its impact on education and health sectors). Susan Halford and Pauline Leonard (1999: 102) write that we need to understand how the changing content of public service work impacts people in term of their subjectivities – their identities, emotions and sense of 'self'. Building on this argument, several writers have noted how the production of new subjectivities is, in and of itself, one of the key targets for new public management techniques (Linstead and Catlow 2004; Davies and Thomas 2002; Maile 1999; Thomas and Davies 2002; Whitehead and Moodley 1999). Thus, new public management brings with it identities and practices associated with scientific management, neo-human relations and entrepreneurialism rather than those attitudes, priorities and self-conceptualizations associated with professional identities (Davies and Thomas 2002; du Gay 1996). One of the effects of these changes can be the experience and production of new and intensified 'psycho-pathologies' (Swan 2005a; Berg *et al.* 2004). Some academics suggest that it can also bring new opportunities, in particular in relation to gender with its emphasis on feminized skills and values such as building relationships and softer skills (Fondas 1997; Clarke and Newman 1997). Others emphasize the dynamic, contradictory and manifold nature of new public management which means that people respond in different ways. For example, in an analysis of a school where new public management techniques and values were introduced, Mairtin Mac an Ghaill (1994) shows how whilst some teachers held on to their professional identities as teachers, others produced themselves as 'old collectivists', whilst a third group of teachers saw themselves in terms of being 'new entrepreneurs'. New public management then varies across and within sectors and is both contested and uneven in its effects. It can be adopted, resisted, circumvented and mobilized for different ends (Barry *et al*. 2003; Halford and Leonard 1999).

At first blush, this wouldn't seem to have much to do with feminization in either of its terms – economic or cultural. But some feminist theorists have pointed to the gendering effects of new public management in relation to its strategies, practices and identities (Deem *et al*. 2000; Leathwood 2005). One of the most consistent arguments amongst these theorists is that it brings with it new forms of public sector masculinity. There are different types of masculinity within society and within organizations at any one time (Maile 1999). Hence, Collinson and Hearn (1996) identify the following types of masculine cultures within organizations: authoritarianism, paternalism, entrepreneurialism, informalism and careerism, gender blind, feminist pretenders and smart macho. Some, however, are more dominant than others. With the onslaught of new public management, academic commentators suggest that a new entrepreneurial masculinity is challenging or replacing traditional bureaucratic-paternalistic masculinity of public service. There is widespread agreement that this new entrepreneurial masculinity can be defined along the lines of Jenny Ozga's (1994: 106) description of it as 'a "thrusting, competitive, cost-cutting" entrepreneurial masculinity'.

The new performance cultures, intensification of work, shrinking resources and few funding regimes produces machismo in lines with entrepreneurial values of competition, aggression, workaholism, individualism, ruthlessness and competitive presenteeism. In addition to this Darwinist masculinity, scientific management values of new public management with its technologies of performance management bring gendered notions of rationality, analysis, calculation and objectivity.

Producing these masculinities is difficult, even for men. But it presents particular problems for women. As Linstead and Catlow (2004: 478) argue 'images of masculine managerialism contradict cultural scripts of femininity and "being a woman" (see also Thomas and Davies 2002). But it is also argued that it produces spaces for resistance, modification and exploitation by women, even if these spaces are limited and temporary (Halford and Leonard 1999; Thomas and Davies 2002; Deem *at al*. 2000).

Given the variation, and variability of new public management, we need to explore how it manifests itself in particular contexts (see Chapter 10), and how this affects masculinities, feminization and therapeutic cultures. Since 1993 the further education sector experienced a combination of marketization and devolution (Deem *et al.* 2000), which brought with it a number of radical and difficult changes: a new funding regime based on quasi-markets, financial difficulties, redundancies, local pay bargaining, intensification of workloads, under-funding, the employment of contract staff, reduced contacts, new pedagogies, increased student numbers, increasing insecurity and new inspection regimes (Deem *et al.* 2000; Leathwood 2000; 2005; Ozga and Walker 1999; Whitehead and Moodley 1999).

COACHING IN FURTHER EDUCATION

The further education sector (FE) provides a case study of masculinities, feminization and therapeutic cultures in a context of a learning and skills sector. The case study is based on an in-depth qualitative research project on leadership development practices funded by the DfES as part of the Centre for Excellence in Leadership (CEL). Formed in 2003, CEL – a partnership between Lancaster University Management School, the Learning and Skills Development Agency and Ashridge – was created to provide leadership development activities and research for the learning and skills sector, that is FE, Adult and Community Learning and Work Based Learning. This project was part of a broader research programme undertaken by Lancaster University Management School focused on leadership, equality and diversity and learning cultures in the sector.

The study on coaching was conducted by the author and a research associate over a period of two years. It draws on 40 face-to-face interviews with principals, vice principals, assistant principals, middle managers and professional coaches. Documentary evidence and participant observation by the author and research associate was also undertaken in senior management team meetings in three colleges, workshops on coaching, and at meetings and conferences where coaching in the sector was discussed. The interviewees came from a wide cross-section of FE colleges in different parts of England. There were two models of coaching in operation in our study: external, or 'executive coaching' of principals and senior management teams, and internal coaching, or 'workplace coaching', where senior management teams formally coached middle managers.

Executive coaching is a relatively recent phenomenon. There is very little academic research outlining its history or origins. Most sources, academic and popular literature suggest that executive coaching started to emerge in the 1980s in the USA, and slightly later in the UK, with it being referenced in a popular US management text in 1985 by Peters and Austin (Salerno, 2005). A number of reasons are given for its proliferation: increased stress and complexity of people's working and home lives; better transfer of learning than training; ongoing learning; customized learning; solution oriented as opposed to therapies which are problem and past focused. Employed by private sector organizations such as American Express, AT&T, Citibank, Colgate, Levi Strauss, Northern Telecom, NYNEX Corporation, and Procter & Gamble, it is now a rapidly growing industry both in the USA and UK (Olivero *et al.* 1997) and is moving rapidly through parts of the UK public and private sector.

The practice is seen to have developed from consultancy, counselling and management development. Consultants Robert Witherspoon and P. Randall White (1996: 87), writing in a special issue on coaching in the US journal of *Consulting Psychology*, suggest that coaching is a 'repackaging of certain practices that were once subsumed under the more general terms consulting or counselling'. They go on to define it as follows:

> Coaching is individually tailored to the person and the current issue or problem, as opposed to the 'one-size-fits-all' menu provided by many seminars. Instead of stimulating one or two good ideas, coaching is continually focused and relevant. Instead of potentially wasting time and having one's mind wander, the executive can get right to the heart of the matter. The concepts and guidance a person actually needs are presented in ways that the person can immediately apply because they are personalized rather than presented to the group as vague abstractions.

In more popular media, Professor Warren Bennis, a leadership specialist, suggests that the coach 'wears multiple hats. He or she is part consultant, part oracle, part cheerleader, part provider of tough love' (Salerno, 2005). In essence, then, coaching is usually a one-to-one interaction between a client and 'expert' in behavioural, psychological and business techniques.

In spite of my own argument that coaching is part of therapeutic cultures, most practitioners and writers are quite vehement in distinguishing coaching from therapy. Thus, consultant Harry Levinson (1996), again writing in *The Consulting Psychology Journal*, argues that whilst coaching draws upon basic psychological skills and insights, it is more short term and issue focused and therefore cannot attend to more in depth psychological processes such as transference and counter-transference that might be addressed in counselling. Bennis has a different take on this polarization on coaching and therapy. He argues that coaches will ask questions like 'Does this make you happy?' (as cited in Salerno 2005). He suggests that by calling it coaching it makes it more attractive to men and makes it an acceptable form of therapy (ibid). He goes on to argue that 'Even nowadays it's still tough to say, I'm going to see my therapist. It's OK to say, I'm going to get counselling from my coach' (ibid).

My definition of what makes a practice or set of ideas therapeutic is quite broad. In my view, coaching can be described as therapeutic in that it draws upon therapeutic ideas from behaviourism, humanistic psychology, popular psychology, psychoanalysis, new age practices and a diversity of techniques including 360 degree feedback, visioning, role plays, talking, reflection, facilitation techniques. Coaching can also be seen to be therapeutic in its form in that it reproduces the 'talking cure' or confessional between an expert in psychology and client. It can also be defined as therapeutic due to the types of discourses that it draws upon, that is discourses which privilege emotions as special knowledge about the 'self', psychological discourses which draw upon narratives of childhood, the importance of the past and emphasis on agency of the 'self' as opposed to social structures. It can also be seen to be feminizing in that it brings the personal and emotional into the public sphere, and privileges particular stereotypical leadership qualities associated with white middle class femininity as outlined by Fondas (1997) and others (Cameron 2000; Walkerdine 1997).

Having provided an introduction to coaching as a new public management technology, I will now analyse how coaching is imagined with the FE sector, specifically through exploring the webpage produced by CEL on its coaching services, and from interviewees in the study on coaching in the sector. The webpage begins by defining how CEL sees coaching:

> This provides Managers at all levels the essential space to reflect, to identify performance and leadership goals and to take actions to achieve these. Through this process, Managers come to understand themselves and their organization more fully, and are encouraged to challenge existing ways of doing things, and to aim for goals that previously seemed unachievable.

Coaching then is presented as a form of reflexivity which installs a 'derring-do' entrepreneurial masculinity. This echoes theorists such as Giddens (1991) and Beck (1994) who argue that two forms of reflexivity are needed in today's society: 'self-reflexivity' – the ability to reflect on oneself and monitor what we do and are – and 'structural reflexivity' in which we reflect on 'the social conditions of existence and change them accordingly' (Beck 1994: 174). In this quote, this entrepreneurial reflexivity is seen as a form of conscious cognition which leads to innovation and increased agency. For some critics, these ideas of reflexivity reproduce unrealistic ideas about voluntarism in relation to identity and change by assuming that everything within the 'self' and wider organization and society are up for grabs so easily (McNay 1999). Thus, Lois McNay (1999) argues that it underestimates what is preconscious or unconscious in ourselves, and what is firmly entrenched within society. In addition, feminists argue that this understanding of reflexivity requires a form of rational decision maker, linked to ideas about individualism, detachment and self-control that women, because of their cultural association with emotionality and expressivity, are imagined not to be able to perform. The webpage goes on to say:

> Managers work together with a coach whose role is to support, challenge and increase awareness of choice and action through powerful questioning, whilst leaving responsibility for action and success with the individual. Counselling focuses on the individual, consulting on the organization: coaching does both, based on the belief that the key to effective leadership is aligning organizational goals with personal goals, and that this requires space, reflective skills, and critical self and organizational awareness to achieve this. CEL coaches use their expertise in helping managers learn from their own experience.

This quote draws upon key themes which have to be read in the context of wider neo-liberal policies that emphasize choice, responsibility and entrepreneurship. In addition rather than distancing itself from counselling, the webpage claims that coaching incorporates it as well as consulting. The quote also presents a model of leadership in which the private – what used to be seen as separate from work – is not only brought into work but actually lined up with organizational values so that there is no distinction between the personal and organizational. In doing this, the webpage draws upon a number of popular leadership pedagogical discourses such as experiential learning, reflective learning and the notion of awareness. The following quote, from the webpage, provides a more detailed description about this model of leadership:

> Our one-to-one and team coaching options focus on two areas: Leadership and performance. Leadership cannot be simply learned from a textbook or workshop – the ability to engage, empower and motivate others is learnt from experience. Leadership coaching enables managers to develop these qualities grounding them in greater self-knowledge and understanding of others. Performance coaching takes a similar approach, but focuses on specific development areas. CEL also believes that people usually know what is best for them, and at a senior level, possess the internal resources to achieve their personal and leadership goals. The role of the coach is to help them access those resources and to use them appropriately.

In this excerpt, an 'affective' model of leadership is defined. This type of model of leadership draws upon a neo-human relations discourse which defines leadership in social psychology, and in particular, in understandings of affective relationships between leaders and followers as central to effectiveness. As above, particular pedagogies are invoked. In particular, self-experience is seen to provide privileged knowledge for leadership as opposed to external expertise or knowledge. This is in line with certain humanistic therapies in which the 'self' is seen to be a source of goodness and privileged understandings, making it the ultimate reference point and moral arbiter of decisions (Nolan 1998). The last section draws simultaneously on progressivist humanistic psychology and neo-liberalism in which self-knowledge is conceptualized as a possession which can lead to certain forms of mastery of self and others. This is not uncommon in leadership contemporary pedagogies (Swan 2005b) but again reproduces certain masculinized and feminized notions of leadership.

The webpage also describes coaching as an 'intensive development process'. As with much of new public management, a particular kind of tough masculinity is invoked in the notion of intensive. Coaching then is not for wimps: do coaching if you are hard enough! A particular kind of motivation to make coaching work is already embedded in this notion. Finally, the coach is defined as having a particular kind of expertise founded not on leadership expertise more in terms of being able to deploy certain technologies of inducement which install masculinized notions of drive and mastery into the coachee. So rather than the coach providing resources for the leaders to cope or live with the pressure of new public management, this invokes notions of triumph and heroism.

From webpage description, coaching can be seen as one of a growing number of contemporary practices that encourage transformation of the 'self'. In line with current neo-liberal government, the ideal self is one who is entrepreneurial, flexible, innovative, with the capacity to monitor their performance, be reflexive, self-regulate and align their 'selves' with the strategic goals of the organization and considers themselves in terms of a lifelong project of self-improvement (Walkerdine 1997). At the same time, particular feminized qualities are invoked in relation to new styles of leadership being imagined. These themes emerged then from the CEL webpage which raises questions about how these were played out in the interview data from principals and senior managers in FE undertaken as part of our study on leadership development. The following excerpt is taken from an interview with a new principal and is discussing why he found his coach helpful:

> Probably because he's one of the few people who will challenge aspects of my behaviour and thinking, and that's not to say that other people don't but it's always done against a background of strategic decisions that we have to make here ... people won't challenge me about my behaviour or the processes that I adopt basically, whereas my coach will bring it down to quite a personal level.

The new principal presents the focus for coaching within therapeutic terms: emphasising the significance of the 'personal' in contrast to more strategic, organizational, technical issues. In line with the some of the themes taken from the webpage, leadership is conceptualized as a matter of individual behaviour rather than the result of wider social and political issues. Behaviour is seen then as a legitimate focus for change and also, in opposition to some writers such as McNay (1999), imagined as easily amenable to self transformation.

The new principal went on to describe how he dealt with resistance to change by asking himself searching questions: 'Why doesn't he want to go along with you? Does he know what it is you want?' The new principal is extending the notion of therapeutically informed coaching by conceptualizing resistance as a matter of individualized emotions and psychological motivations. The discourse reproduces a model of leadership in which the principal is allowed the right to manage so long as he attends to his own emotions and those of his staff. This focus on emotions as a form of truth about the 'self' is a dominant theme within most therapeutic cultures (Nolan 1998; Furedi 2003; Swan 2003). It also links with an increasing emotionalization of work practices including the emphasis on affective leadership and its associated practices of emotional intelligence, intimacy, trust, informality, introspection – all associated with white middle class femininity (Kerfoot 2002; Clarke and Newman 1997; 2005; Mistzal 2000). As Janet Newman (2005) argues, the new discourse of leadership in the public sector is based on an opposition to the old-fashioned, conservative role of the bureaucrat with their sidelining of personal preferences and emotions. In the new affective leadership model, the emotional individuality of the leader in terms of their enthusiasm, vision, charisma and strong values is critical to developing affective relations between leaders and followers and bringing about transformation in the workplace.

It is not just men though who are subject to these feminizing imperatives as a female vice-principal, in explaining how coaching was transforming her, stated that she now dealt with problems by asking: 'Can I be of any help? Rather than my command and control socialization in this role previously was "right, let's fix a meeting and you get three of them in my office and we'll sort it".' The female vice-principal is seen to have improved because she has left behind the macho masculinity of her former leadership style. The female vice-principal draws upon an understanding of coaching in which it is seen to have installed a new form of feminized leadership in her based on listening, questioning, helping and empowerment instead of a more directive, stereotypical masculinized style. This description echoes many writers' descriptions of the feminization of leadership and work practices and can also be understood as part of the proliferation of neo-human relations within new public management. It exemplifies what Kerfoot (2000: 232) describes as the 'calls to humanise' managers, through company sponsored events designed to reduce status barriers, social skills training packages, or promoting more women into management, point to a perceived need for those in managerial work to engage with rather than dictate to subordinates, in the fullest sense. The notion of the relationship, constructed in terms of interpersonal interactions, has come to be seen as critical to effective leadership as if mutuality and intimacy overcomes status and power (McWilliam 1999). These ideas fit with the development of femininity in terms of emotionality and intimacy as a new technology of leadership that underscores practices of team working (Casey 1995), the focus on relationships (Ozga 1999; McWilliam 1999), emotional openness (Illouz 1997) and what Kerfoot calls 'synthetic sociability' (2002: 191) the development of certain forms of intimacy for instrumental control. In some forms of work it involves the 'emotional proletariat' (Macdonald and Sirianni cited by Fineman 2000: 4). But increasingly organizations across different sectors require the production of feminized emotions and intimacy at a managerial level (Kerfoot 1999; Misztal 2002; Illouz 1997). Thus, managers are being encouraged to develop 'warmer' and more intimate relations with their employees, as well as their customers, with expectations that they will be more open and trusting, and act like a friend, teacher, family member, leader, mentor, facilitator or coach (Ackers and Preston 1997; Casey 1995; 2002; Fondas 1997).

In summary then, this analysis of coaching suggests that we can understand these practices as therapeutic and feminized in the sense that it draws upon psychologized and emotional models of understanding the world. We can understand the increase in these therapeutic practices as part of new public management in a number of ways. First, therapeutic practices, in particular coaching, offer resources and spaces to deal with the demands and difficulties of new public management and its contradictions (Swan 2005). Thus, it can provide spaces in which leaders can reflect on their 'precarious collegiality and extreme isolation' (Kerfoot 2000: 241). Second, it can provide techniques to cope with the potentially damaging and impossible task of producing these different forms of masculinity – entrepreneurial and scientific management. As Brewis and Linstead (2004: 81) argue, scientific management masculinity with its 'emphasis on quantifiability, neutrality and the bottom line require almost inhuman responses to very human problems'. Finally, these practices provide solace and resources for leaders who are required to produce hard nosed masculinities at the same time as performing the contradictory femininities. But what then are the consequences for women? Does this new focus on femininities enable them to accrue economic and cultural value? Does it offer new forms of power and expertise for women?

CONCLUSION

This chapter has outlined some of the ways in which new public management is being reconceptualized as a form of hybrid, drawing upon different masculinities, but at the same time emphasizing certain forms of femininity. Thus a recent CEL brochure advertising master-classes in leadership to FE had one workshop which focused on the 'tough but tender' leadership approach needed for turning around a so-called failing college.

The analysis from this research shows, in line with much recent literature on new public management, therapeutic cultures and FE leadership that discourses on public sector leadership draw upon constructions of white middle class stereotypical feminine emotionalities. This is done, however, in tandem with the performance of different kinds of masculinities: scientific management masculinities, macho masculinities and entrepreneurial masculinities. As Yvonne Due Billing and Mats Alvesson (2000: 149) write, contemporary leaders need to 'care and share as well as to direct and control'. These are being resourced and promoted through therapeutic cultures and their techniques.

Performing femininity could be seen as an advantage to women within the workplace. If stereotypical feminized capabilities such as emotional, communication and interpersonal skills are been seen as new forms of workplace capital, then perhaps women will be able to claim these as special expertise? (See Chapter 1 for a discussion on women's 'special contribution'.) First, Adkins (2002) argues that it is not the feminization of workers that is being prized but the ability to take on both masculinity and femininity. Theorists argue that the ability to take up these hybrid forms is something that men are seen to do in ways that are different from women. In essence, as Wajcman (1998: 77) states, 'men will be advantaged by adding new qualities to those they are already deemed to have'. This is not the case for women for two reasons. First, women are seen as naturally to have these stereotypical feminine skills and therefore are not developing it as a performance or skill – something they can take on or off. Second, women are criticized or punished if they take up entrepreneurial or scientific management masculinities too often or too much (see Chapter 4). Thus, men may 'even exploit and dominate femininities' (Alvesson, 1998: 1000). It is men's reflexivity or mobility in relation to gender which provides new workplace capital for them as men can take up femininities in a way that women cannot take up masculinities. And it is this flexibility which is seen as an important workplace resource. Finally, these femininities are being taken up in ways that bolster masculinity. For example, these approaches can be seen to be advocated as ways to 'balance, civilise, military or enterprising models of management' (Fondas 1997). And as Deem *et al.* (2000) note they can be used instrumentally to 'smooth the transition to new FE'.

REFERENCES

Acker, J. (1992), 'Gendering Organizational Theory', in A.J. Mills and P. Tancred (eds), *Gendering Organizational Analysis*, London: Sage.

Ackers, P. and Preston, D. (1997), 'Born Again? The Ethics and Efficacy of the Experience in Contemporary Management Development', *Journal of Management Studies*, **34**(5), 676–701.

Adkins, L. (2001), 'Cultural Feminization: "Monday, Sex and Power" for Women in Signs', *Journal of Women in Culture and Society*, **26**(3), 669–93.

Adkins, L. (2002), *Revisions: Gender and Sexuality in Late Modernity*, Buckingham: Open University Press.

Adkins, L. and Lury, C. (2000), 'Making Bodies, Making People, Making Work', in L. McKie and N. Watson (eds), *Organizing Bodies: Policy, Institutions and Work*, Basingstoke: Macmillan.

Adkins, L. and Lury, C. (1996), 'The Cultural, the Sexual, and the Gendering of the Labour Market', in L. Adkins and V. Merchant (eds), *Sexualising the Social: Power and the Organization of Sexuality*, Basingstoke: Macmillan.

Alvesson, M. (1998), 'Gender Relations and Identity at Work: A Case Study of Maculinities and Femininities in an Advertising Agency', *Human Relations*, **51**(8), 969–1005.

Barry, J., Dent, M. and O'Neill, M. (eds) (2003), *Gender and the Public Sector: Professionals and Managerial Change*, London: Routledge.

Beck, U. (1994), 'The Reinvention of Politics: Towards a Theory of Reflexive Modernization', in U. Beck, A. Giddens and S. Lash (eds), *Reflexive Modernization: Politics, Tradition and Aesthetics in the Modern Social Order*, Cambridge: Polity Press.

Bellah, R.N., Madsen, R., Sullivan, W.M., Swindler, A. and Tipton, S. (1985), *Habits of the Heart*, Berkeley: University of California Press.

Berg, E., Barry, J. and Chandler, J. (2004), 'The New Public Management and Higher Education: A Human Cost?', in M. Dent, J. Chandler and J. Barry (eds), *Questioning the New Public Management*, Aldershot: Ashgate.

Blackmore, J. (1993), '"In the Shadow of Men": The Historical Construction of Administration as a "Masculinist" Enterprise', in J. Blackmore and J. Kenway (eds), *Gender Matters in Educational Administration and Policy*, London: The Falmer Press.

Brewis, J. and Linstead, S. (2004), 'Gender and Management', in S. Linstead, L. Fulop and L. Simon (eds), *Management and Organization: A Critical Text*, Basingstoke: Palgrave.

Cameron, D. (2000), *Good to Talk*, London: Sage.

Casey, C. (1995), *Work, Self and Society: After Industrialism*, London: Routledge.

Casey, C. (2002), *Critical Analysis of Organizations: Theory, Practice, Revitalization*, London: Sage.

Clarke, J. and Newman, J. (1997), *The Managerial State*, London: Sage.

Cloud, D. (1998), *Control and Consolation in American Culture and Politics: Rhetoric of Therapy*, London: Sage.

Collinson, D.L. and Hearn, J. (1996), 'Breaking the Silence: On Men, Masculinities and Managements', in D. Collinson, and J. Hearn (eds), *Men as Managers, Managers as Men: Critical Perspectives on Men, Masculinities and Managements*, London: Sage.

Craib, I. (1994), *The Importance of Disappointment*, London: Routledge.

Craib, I. (1998), *Experiencing Identity*, London: Sage.

Cunningham, R. (2000), 'From Great Expectations to Hard Times? Managing Equal Opportunities Under New Public Management', *Public Administration*, **78**(3), 699–714.

Davies, A. and Thomas, R. (2002), 'Gendering and Gender in Public Service Organizations: Changing Professional Identities under New Public Management', *Public Management Review*, **4**(4), 461–84.

Deem, R., Ozga, J. and Pritchard, C. (2000), 'Managing Further Education: Is it Still Men's Work Too?', *Journal of Further and Higher Education*, **24**(2), 231–50.

Dent, M. and Whitehead, S. (2002), 'Introduction: Configuring the "New" Professional', in M. Dent and S. Whitehead (eds), *Managing Professional Identities: Knowledge, Performativity and the "New" Professional*, London: Routledge.

Dent, M., Chandler, J. and Barry, J. (eds) (2004), *Questioning the New Public Management*, Aldershot: Ashgate.

Due Billing, Y. and Alvesson, M. (2000), 'Questioning the Notion of Feminine Leadership: a Critical Perspective on the Gender Labelling of Leadership', *Gender, Work & Organization*, **7**(3), 144–57.

du Gay, P. (1996), *Consumption and Identity at Work*, London: Sage.

Fineman, S. (ed.) (2000), *Emotion in Organizations*, 2nd edition, London: Sage.

Fondas, N. (1997), 'Feminization Unveiled: Management Qualities in Contemporary Writings', *Academy of Management Review*, **22**(1), 257–82.

Furedi, F. (2003), *Therapy Culture: Cultivating Vulnerability in an Uncertain Age*, London: Routledge.

Giddens, A. (1991), 'Modernity and Self-Identity: Self and Society', in *Late Modern Age*, Cambridge: Polity Press.

Giddens, A. (1992), *The Transformation of Intimacy: Sexuality, Love and Eroticism in Modern Societies*, Cambridge: Polity.

Halford, S. and Leonard, P. (1999), 'New Identities? Professionalism, Managerialism and the Construction of the Self', in M. Exworthy (ed.), *Professionals and the New Managerialism in the Public Sector*, Buckingham: Open University Press.

Hollway, W. (1996), 'Masters and Men in the Transition from Factory Hands to Sentimental Workers', in D. Collinson and J. Hearn (eds), *Men as Managers, Managers as Men: Critical Perspectives on Men, Masculinities and Managements*, London: Sage.

Illouz, E. (1997), 'Who Will Care for the Caretaker's Daughter: Towards a Sociology of Happiness in the Era of Reflexive Modernity?', *Theory, Culture and Society*, **14**, 31–66.

Kerfoot, D. (1999), 'The Organization of Intimacy: Managerialism, Masculinity and the Masculine Subject', in S. Whitehead and R. Moodley (eds), *Transforming Managers: Gendering Change in the Public Sector*, London: UCL Press.

Kerfoot, D. (2000), 'Body Work: Estrangement, Disembodiment and the Organizational "Other"', in J. Hassard, R. Holliday and H. Wilmott (eds), *Body and Organization*, London: Sage.

Kerfoot, D. (2002), 'Managing the "Professional Man"', in M. Dent and S. Whitehead (eds), *Managing Professional Identities: Knowledge, Performativity and the "New" Professional*, London: Routledge.

Kerfoot, D. and Whitehead, S. (1998), '"Boys Own" Stuff: Masculinity and the Management of Further Education', *The Sociological Review*, **46**(3), 436–57.

Lasch, C. (1980), *The Culture of Narcissism*, London: Abacus.

Lasch, C. (1985), *The Minimal Self: Psychic Survival in Troubled Times*, London: Picador.

Leathwood, C. (2000), 'Happy Families? Pedagogy, Management and Parent Discourses of Control in the Corporatised Further Education College', *Journal of Further and Higher Education*, **24**(2), 163–82.

Leathwood, C. (2005), '"Treat me as a human being – don't look at me as a woman": Femininities and Professional Identities in Further Education', *Gender and Education*, **17**(4), 387–409.

Levinson, H. (1996), 'Executive Coaching', *Consulting Psychology Journal: Practice and Research*, **48**(2), 115–23.

Linstead, A. and Catlow, G. (2004), 'Dilemmas Beyond the Glass Ceiling', in M. Dent, J. Chandler and J. Barry (eds), *Questioning the New Public Management*, Aldershot: Ashgate.

Mac an Ghaill, M. (1994), *The Making of Men: Masculinities, Sexualities and Schooling*, Buckingham: Open University Press.

McNay, L. (1999), 'Gender, Habitus and the Field: Pierre Bourdieu and the Limits of Reflexivity', *Theory, Culture and Society*, **16**(1), 95–117.

McWilliam, E. (1999), *Pedagogical Pleasures*, New York: Peter Lang.

Maile, S. (1999), 'Intermanagerial Rivalries, Organizational Restructuring and the Transformation of Management Masculinities', in S. Whitehead and R. Moodley (eds), *Transforming Managers: Gendering Change in the Public Sector*, London: UCL Press.

Misztal, B. (2002), 'Trusting the Professional: A Managerial Discourse for Uncertain Times', in M. Dent and S. Whitehead (eds), *Managing Professional Identities: Knowledge, Performativity and the 'New' Professional*, London: Routledge.

Morley, L. (1999), *Organising Feminisms: The Micropolitics of the Academy*, New York: St Martins Press.

Newman, J. (2005), 'Enter the Transformational Leader: Network Governance and the Micro-politics of Modernization', *Sociology*, **39**(4), 717–34.

Nolan, J. (1989), *The Therapeutic State*, London: Sage.

Olivero, G., Bane, K.D. and Kopelman, R.E. (1997), 'Executive Coaching as a Transfer Training Tool: Effects on Productivity in a Public Agency', *Public Personal Management*, **26**(4), 461–9.

Ozga, J. and Walker, L. (1999), 'In the Company of Men', in S. Whitehead and R. Moodley (eds), *Transforming Managers: Gendering Change in the Public Sector*, London: UCL Press.

Pritchard, C. (1996), 'Managing Universities: Is it Men's Work?', in D. Collinson and J. Hearn (eds), *Men as Managers, Managers as Men: Critical Perspectives on Men, Masculinities and Managements*, London: Sage.

Puwar, N. (2004), *Space Invaders: Race, Gender and Bodies out of Place*, Oxford: Berg.

Reay, D. (2004), 'Gendering Bourdieu's Concepts of Capitals? Emotional Capital, Women and Social Class', *Sociological Review*, **52**, 58–74.

Rieff, P. (1966), *The Triumph of the Therapeutic: Uses of Faith after Freud*, New York: Harper Torchbooks.

Rose, N. (1989), *Governing the Soul: The Shaping of the Private Self*, London: Routledge.

Rose, N. (1996), *Inventing Ourselves: Psychology, Power and Personhood*, Cambridge: Cambridge University Press.

Salerno, S. (2005), *Shame: How the Gurus of the Self-Help Movement Make Us Helpless*, Nicolas Brearley.

Sennett, R. (1986), *The Fall of Public Man*, London: Faber.

Swan, E. (2003), 'Worked up Selves: Personal Development, Therapeutic Cultures and the Workplace in Contemporary Britain', unpublished PhD Thesis, Lancaster University.

Swan, E. (2005a), 'Leadership Development and the Psychopathologies of New Public Management', CEL working paper.

Swan, E. (2005), 'On Bodies, Rhinestones and Pleasures: Women Teaching Managers', *Journal of Management Learning*, **36**(3), 317–33.

Thomas, R. and Davies, A. (2002), 'Gender and New Public Management: Reconstituting Academic Subjectivities', *Gender, Work and Organization*, **9**(4), 372–97.

Tobias, L.L. (1996), 'Coaching Executives', *Consulting Psychology Journal: Practice and Research*, **48**(2), 87–95.

Townley, B. (1994), *Reframing Human Resource Management: Power, Ethics and the Subject at Work*, London: Sage.

Townley, B. (1995), 'Know Thyself: Self-awareness, Self-formation and Managing', *Organization*, **2**(2), 271–89.

Townsley, N.C. (2003), 'Review Article: Looking Back, Looking Forward. Mapping the Gendered Theories, Voices, and the Politics of Organization', *Organization*, **10**(3), 617–39.

Turnbull, S. (1999), 'Emotional Labour in Corporate Change Programmes', *Human Resource Development International*, **2**(2), 125–46.

Wainwright, D. and Calnan, M. (2002), *Work Stress: The Making of a Modern Epidemic*, Buckingham: Open University Press.

Walkerdine, V. (1997), *Daddy's Girl – Young Girls and Popular Culture*, London: Macmillan.

Whitehead, S. (1999), 'From Paternalism to Entrepreneuralism: The Experience of Men Managers in UK Postcompulsory Education', *Discourse*, **20**(1).

Whitehead, S. and Moodley, R. (eds) (1999), *Transforming Managers: Gendering Change in the Public Sector*, London: Taylor and Francis.

Witherspoon, R. and White, P.R. (1996), 'Executive Coaching: Continuum of Roles', *Consulting Psychology Journal: Practice and Research*, **48**(2), 124–33.

Yeatman, A. (1994), *Postmodern Revisionings of the Political*, London: Routledge.

Yumiko, I. (2005), 'Beyond the Feminization of Masculinity', *Inter Asia Cultural Studies*, **6**(1), 56–74.

4. Expectations of women in leadership and management – advancement through solidarity?

Sharon Mavin

INTRODUCTION

There has been relatively little success in developing a critical mass of women in leadership and management in the UK. Women still earn less than men; gender segregation within management functions still remains (Davidson and Burke 2000) and representation at senior and executive levels remains problematic. Research and interventions which challenge this position to advance women in management are often based on principles and assumptions of sisterhood and solidarity behaviour. Sisterhood and solidarity behaviour assumes that women view other women as their natural allies regardless of hierarchical differences and that senior women view the 'women in management mantle' as their responsibility. However it is argued that solidarity behaviour may set expectations of senior women in management which cannot be fulfilled.

There are tensions in the way that women perceive senior women in management and the expectations that they hold of them. This is highlighted by contradictions in calls for sisterhood and solidarity whilst criticizing senior women as 'Queen Bees' (Staines *et al.* 1973; Abramson 1975) and through assumptions of solidarity behaviour neglecting the complexity of the socially constructed senior woman in management. Incongruity between the managerial and the gender role continues to affect how women in senior management view and are viewed by other women in the organization, often resulting in female misogyny. This chapter challenges the apparent positive and proactive assumptions of solidarity behaviour as a way of advancing women in management and raises the complex issue of negative relations between women in management.

The chapter offers subjective narratives from senior women in the UK housing sector and women management academics to explore senior women's views on leading the 'women in management mantle' and to highlight the complexity of relations between women. In order for women to advance in management, there is a need to refocus research and future action on raising awareness of the impact of female misogyny and to challenge and change overall gendered structures, cultures and systems which continue to impact upon women in management.

SISTERHOOD AND SOLIDARITY BEHAVIOUR

Women are now more prevalent in supervisory and middle management in the UK and as such this should have positively impacted upon the experiences of women in management. However this status quo of second place for women in middle management can become a comfortable place, protected and defended by both men and women in gendered organizations (Mavin 2001). As a woman any move from this comfortable place into senior management becomes problematic. Whilst the presence of women in senior management is perceived as more of a direct challenge to male power in organizations (Davidson and Burke 1994), it can also be portrayed as a beacon of hope for all women in the organization. However it is the crucial point when women aspire to or move into senior management which significantly destabilizes established gendered relations, gendered structures, systems and cultures for both men and women. It is at this juncture that women make the move from the majority of other women, either through ambition or by actual promotion. These processes of separation result in differing expectations and behaviours between women and men.

Considering the presence of women in middle management in the UK, Kanter (1977) argued that as the relative size of a minority group increased then members should begin to experience a reduction in stress and other performance measures while their opportunity to demonstrate competence and managerial potential should increase. Indeed, as the sex ratio becomes more balanced Kanter (1977) noted that minority members can become allies, form coalitions, affect the cultures of the group and develop support networks that enhance the chances of women's career advancement. These elements form the basis of solidarity behaviour.

Kanter's work has been significantly progressed with particular emphasis on networks and coalitions as elements of solidarity behaviour. McKeen and Burke (1991) draw attention to the need for role models so that more feminine ways of managing may be included in the acceptable behaviours for future senior roles. Singh and Vinnicombe (2003b) see women executive directors as role models for women lower down in the organization. Senior women are often recommended to support, develop and work to raise the profile of other women, enabling them to perhaps 'short cut' the otherwise painful journey into management and senior management. Korabik and Abbondanza (2004) argue that solidarity behaviour in the context of women in management is multidimensional. Solidarity behaviour brings together processes of: forming alliances, collaborating, joining together with shared aims, a commitment to changing social structures for women at the collective not just the individual level and behaviours which demonstrate loyalty and gender awareness in managerial practice. They argue that their research contradicts previous 'Queen Bee' approaches of women failing to help one another and questions senior women to determine the extent to which they help and support one another through solidarity behaviour. Korabik and Abbondanza's (2004) preliminary results suggest that women do display solidarity behaviour with mentoring, modifying organizational policies and supporting women's rights for example. They conclude that solidarity behaviour occurs on an individual and group basis, both within and outside organizations, which includes all forms of ties and coalitions that women may form in organizational settings. Korabik and Abbondanza (2004) argue that whilst the total scope of solidarity behaviour has yet to be identified it is enacted by women acting as instruments of social change.

An assumption of sisterhood and solidarity behaviour contends that women will support and align themselves with other women. This assumption is implicit within some research studies which seek to explain the experiences and performance of women in management, recommending that women aspiring to, or progressing, within management should have proactive, visible and high profile senior women as role models and mentors and should belong to women's networks, developing coalitions with other women. What is significant is that by promoting the need for senior women to be involved in such solidarity behaviour as a primary means to advance women in management, then women in management research has, in general, ignored and to some extent perpetuated a 'cover up' of negative relations between women in management. Many studies of women in management have tended to look to senior women in management, either recommending that they do more to help other women (see Mavin and Bryans 2002; McKeen and Burke 1991; Singh *et al.* 2000; Singh and Vinnicombe 2003a) or blame them for becoming honorary men (see Gini 2001), or both. Such research is underpinned by the implicit assumption that women will support and align themselves with other women. The solidarity approach is questioned as the complexity of women's experiences in senior management and negative relations between women are raised and explored.

ARE WOMEN IN MANAGEMENT NATURAL ALLIES?

Negative relations between women in organizations have been highlighted in different arenas since the 1960s (see Abramson 1975; Goldberg 1968; Legge 1987; Nicolson 1996; Staines *et al.* 1973). Legge's (1987) position is that women fail to exploit their potential power in organizations resulting in women failing to build alliances with their natural allies, other women. But do women view other women as their natural allies in management?

There is evidence to suggest that women in organizations find it difficult to relate to women in senior management and that their reactions to senior women perpetuate divisions between them. Nieva and Gutek (1981) argue that the price extracted from women even peripherally included in a predominantly male work group includes a willingness to turn against other women, to ignore disparaging remarks about women and to contribute to the derogation of other women. Also 'women are still more likely than men to be disloyal to their same-sex colleagues' (Greer 2000: 394).

As a context to women's views of senior women in management, O'Leary and Ryan (1994) argue that women in senior management are role-deviant and that when women encounter women at work, their normative expectations of one another illustrate sex role spill-over at its worst. Women do not have consciously articulated norms for boss–subordinate interactions when the boss is a woman and therefore it is not surprising that women at work tend to react to women bosses as women and to men bosses as bosses. For example, 'women subordinates expect their women bosses to be more understanding, more nurturant, more giving and more forgiving than men' (O'Leary and Ryan 1994: 72). Therefore suspicion and equivocation from other women can be used to fuel the belief that women are unsuitable for certain positions because other people, including women, do not want to work for or to deal with women managers or professionals (Marshall 1984: 97). Powell and Butterfield (2003) agree that there is incongruity between the managerial role and senior women's gender role in terms of self-concept:

> If women conform to the gender role by displaying predominately feminine characteristics, they fail to meet the perceived requirements of the managerial role, which calls for mostly masculine characteristics. However if they compete with men for managerial positions and conform to the managerial role by displaying predominately masculine characteristics, they fail to meet the requirements of the female gender role, which calls for deference to the authority of men. (Powell and Butterfield 2003: 92)

The assumption of women as natural allies is particularly problematic once a woman destabilizes the established gendered order by moving into senior management. The nature of senior management for women and the behaviours and actions required to gain entry and remain within this environment do little to sustain notions of sisterhood or solidarity behaviour. Indeed Wacjman (1998) argues that there is not much room at the top for women and that successful women are not so much representatives of, as exiles from, their sex. Senior women are therefore isolated from other women. Wacjman (1998) explains that as organizations are a crucial site for the ordering of gender and for the establishment and preservation of male power then similarities between women and men who have achieved senior management positions far outweigh any differences between women and men as groups.

'Women's presence in the world of men is conditional on them being willing to modify their behaviour to become more like men or to be perceived as more male than men' (Wacjman 1998: 7–8). Maier (1999: 89) agrees, arguing that men and women recruited into dominance within organizations tend to internalise the requirements of the position, becoming like men. Coates (1998: 9) argues 'the corporate crusade, its strategy and mechanisms, are more subtle than anything experienced earlier in the management of organizations. As a result individuality and femininity have been sacrificed.' Women cannot win in this situation. Women managers face the contradictory demands of having to be feminine and business-like (Wacjman, 1998: 7–8). They cannot join as a woman and once they start to behave like a man, they cannot be a 'proper woman' (Maddock 1999). All tokens face the same predicament, how to lose their exaggerated visibility and win the group's acceptance.

'Organizations implicitly, extensively and consistently favour the masculine worldview, whether they realize it or not, rewarding those who conform to it and marginalizing or subordinating those men and women alike who don't (Cheng 1996); men's worldviews mesh neatly with the social order of organization, whereas those of women tend to clash with it' (Maier 1999: 89).

If you are a senior woman and your peer group is men then it is difficult not to develop behaviours and style congruent with 'fitting in' (Bryans and Mavin 2003) and acceptance. This incongruity between the managerial and the gender role affects how women in senior management view and are viewed by other women in the organization. Such incongruity challenges those approaches to advancing women in management which continue to mask this complexity whilst promoting sisterhood and solidarity behaviour.

'QUEEN BEE' OR EACH WOMAN FOR HERSELF?

Assumptions of sisterhood and solidarity behaviour also underpin those studies proposing that women in senior management have not paved the way for other women. Rather than such research challenging the gendered structures and cultures of senior management, women are blamed for becoming more male than the men. Gini (2001) argues that those few women who have broken through the 'glass ceiling' have done so not by embracing feminism but by outperforming men on their own terms: classic careerists who happen to be women. Gini (2001) argues that some of these successful women are more combative and ruthless than their male counterparts because they feel they have to prove they can be rough, tough and resilient. Known as the 'only bra in the room syndrome', characteristics of these types of achievers is their lack of empathy and support of other working women, especially their subordinates. 'Having achieved success by playing hardball and working hard, they expect the same from others' (Gini, 2001: 99).

Such studies present senior women as more 'male than men', for 'pulling up the ladder' or the 'drawbridge' for other women having reached senior levels, therefore creating further barriers to keep women in their place in management. Starr (2001) highlights this and comments on the names used to describe senior women in her research:

> various derogatory names were levelled at these women: the 'honorary blokes', 'the men in skirts', 'traitors to the cause' – the individuals being viewed as having relinquished feminist agendas and 'sisterhood' in the pursuit of masculine policy agendas which, while bestowing personal benefits, exclude women in general. (Starr, 2001: 9)

These perceptions of senior women also perpetuate the use, or misuse, of the term 'Queen Bee' (Abramson 1975) to label senior women in management. Staines *et al.* (1973) offered the label 'Queen Bee' in their early study concerned with women's attitudes towards women's liberation, finding that some women were actively opposed to any changes in traditional sex roles and were anti-feminist. Abramson (1975) used the term 'Queen Bee' to describe women who had already gained prominence in management but who tended to deny that there was systematic discrimination against women. These values were held because if women admitted there was systematic discrimination against other women it would undermine their own level of achievement.

Abramson (1975) argued that while few women were willing to recognize the problem of gender inequality, fewer still were willing to do anything about it, so that 'Queen Bees' would not accept that women who are capable of a management career are unable to progress due to discrimination. The 'Queen Bee' argument has made a comeback as a means of describing senior women's 'bad behaviour' and has done little to foster positive relations between women in management. It perpetuates women in management as a 'one-woman responsibility'. Polarized with solidarity behaviour, 'Queen Bee' approaches ignore the complex gendered processes within organization and the gendered subjectivities of senior women, resulting in the perpetuation of sex role stereotyped expectations of senior women; the assumption that senior women should be representatives of other women in management and responsible for their advancement remains unquestioned.

Kanter (1977) argues that one way to minimize uncertainty in the executive suite is to close top management positions to people who are regarded as 'different'. Thus women have a difficult time in entering top management positions because they are seen as different by male incumbents (Kanter 1977). Indeed 'a woman leader is not viewed as androgynous or as undifferentiated from her male counterparts. She is viewed as a woman who is a leader. In recognizing women leaders as women, we know that they become more visible and enjoy a broader scope to their visibility than do their male counterparts' (Adler 1999: 259). Some women who enter male-dominated fields may try to assimilate (fit in by acting like the men in the in-group), whereas others may experience marginalization (feel isolated and like out-group members). Both of these options can result in a number of undesirable consequences (Korabik 1999: 15). If as a senior woman you do not lead on the women in management mantle, if you do not conform to a feminine model and you develop commonalities with your peer group, who will be mostly men, then you may be vilified for not representing the interests of women and for becoming more male than the men.

However Starr (2001) argues that the 1970s femocrat slogan that you should 'lift as you climb' (to support and mentor other women in their careers) has diminished. 'At the beginning of a new century, organizational restructuring has created a more male dominated and competitive institution which means that "it's each woman for herself"' (Starr 2001: 9).

Significantly whilst there is a wealth of research exploring the gendered nature of organization at senior levels and elsewhere in management, there appears to be difficulty in reconciling senior management as a masculine gendered place where senior women have to continually learn to survive with the expectations of senior women in promoting and progressing women in management issues, whilst not becoming a man or 'Queen Bee'. Sisterhood and solidarity behaviour therefore sets expectations of senior women which cannot be fulfilled.

SENIOR WOMEN AND THE WOMEN IN MANAGEMENT MANTLE

Fundamental to solidarity behaviour is the assumption that senior women should and do view the 'women in management' mantle as their responsibility. However, Mattis (1993) argues that women directors want to be recognized for their talents and abilities, not as representatives of the interests of women, while Rindfleish (2000) in her Australian study of women in senior management argues that as women are heterogeneous they cannot be stereo-typed as 'Queen Bees', but in contrast they do not want the responsibility for leading on the advancement of women in management. Rindfleish (2000) found that the majority of senior women in her study believed that there are barriers to women's progress in management but disagreed as to the nature of the barriers, what their responsibility is to change them and were not keen to be responsible for removing them. These senior women did not view sisterhood and solidarity behaviour as their responsibility and why should they?

Female Misogyny

Previous research has explored women in management by analysing gendered relations between men and women but there is a lack of primary research exploring negative relations between women in management. It is very difficult to uncover and explore these negative relations without falling into yet another 'blame the women' standpoint. However in order to problematize the approach of solidarity behaviour as a means of advancing women in management and to support a refocusing of research to challenge gendered organization, the concept of female misogyny is explored.

In thinking about how men feel about women, the history of misogyny is well known and can be traced back through myths of Western civilization to the first woman (whether she is known as Eve or Pandora) who unleashed evil and misery into the world (Glick *et al.* 1997). Misogyny is generally understood as men's hatred of women and a misogynist as a hater or distruster of women, with the common use referenced to men's behaviours towards women, as intense dislike or enmity and hostility. This hostility can manifest itself in a number of ways, for example, as antagonism, unfriendliness, resentment, aggression, lack of sympathy and opposition. There are varying degrees of misogyny, with male chauvinism understood as prejudiced loyalty to one's cause, group or sex and a male chauvinist as exhibiting prejudiced behaviour against or inconsideration of women.

Applying such understandings to relations between women enables the concept of 'female misogyny' to emerge as a means to describe the manifestations of negative relations between and towards other women. It follows that there are varying degrees of female misogyny, with female chauvinism and female chauvinists interpreted as women who are prejudiced against or inconsiderate of other women. Other manifestations more readily discussed and explicitly enacted, are behaving as a 'bitch' towards other women, being a 'spiteful woman', speaking scathingly, being territorial towards other women, being unfair to other women and intolerant of other women's disloyalty. Female jealousy is also commonly recognized as envy of other women's advantage. In terms of women's behaviour towards women in senior management. Wacjman (1998) argues that many women undermine women's authority and notes that various constructions of femininity which women deploy in relating to men in power, involving being flirtatious, admiring and generally supportive, actively reconstitute heterosexualized forms of dominance and subordination. Therefore women find it difficult to deal with senior women because the strategies they are accustomed to using with men are inappropriate for women. Wacjman (1998) contends that as women have internalized gender hierarchies, it seems almost proper for a man to be in a superior position. In the case of senior men the related power is eroticized and this complex intertwining of power with sexuality means that senior women who are powerful provoke anxieties and ambivalence in women as well as men.

Whilst there is a lack of research concerning how female misogyny manifests and how it relates to women in management, it may provide a means of exploring and explaining relations between women in order to challenge assumptions of solidarity behaviour and refocus action on challenging existing gendered structures, processes and cultures which sustain the status quo. Several issues emerge from these debates. First, the challenge to solidarity behaviour underpinned by the assumption that women align themselves with other women as a means of advancing women in management; second, the expectations of senior women in relation to advancing other women in management and whether these are appropriate and realistic; and third, raising negative relations and processes of female misogyny between women without creating another 'blame the women' perspective.

VIEWS FROM SENIOR MANAGEMENT: THE 'QUEEN BEES?'

Narratives from women at Executive Director level in the UK housing sector from four organizations in the Northeast of England support Gini's (2001) argument that women who have broken through the 'glass ceiling' have done so by outperforming men on their own terms and their responses would historically have fallen within Abramson's (1975) description of a 'Queen Bee'. When asked about women and the 'glass ceiling' interviewee A said:

> What sort of evidence have they got? Have they applied for one job and not got it? Well that's my point about no matter who you are or what level you've got to be resilient. If you want to get to the top you have to be resilient about getting knocked back, I think it's too easy to blame the 'glass ceiling'.

Similarly, interviewee B commented that the 'glass ceiling ... women need to learn there are various ways to crack it ... they need dogged perseverance and persistence'. The women's perceptions of whether they worked harder than those men in similar executive roles, provides a context to their other responses. Interviewee C explained that 'I know I am striving to prove myself all of the time, so yes I have to work harder'. Interviewee B further commented:

> When I was in my previous job I was definitely doing a better job than the men but I always knew I would have to work harder and perform better just to get accepted – which is grossly unfair. Male mediocre performance is OK, female mediocre performance at that level is not OK, if we are mediocre they are onto our case, if it's men they get away with it.

In terms of their management style as senior women, becoming more 'male than men' was recognized as an issue. Interviewee C said:

> I swear more now than I used to. I guess I have sometimes fallen into that ... my temper and raising my voice and swearing. I have bitterly regretted it since and its one of the things I have got a problem with, because it doesn't feel natural to me, I really don't like being like that so then I have gone around and apologized to people.

Interviewee D stated that 'You have to behave more like a man though to be accepted, it's not right and it would be nice to be accepted for what you are rather than what they want you to be'. Similarly, interviewee B highlighted the problems related to fitting in:

> I soon learned that to be accepted I needed to become one of the boys and started swearing and drinking with them. When men cracked sexist jokes, I laughed with them, even though it got right under my skin, I knew to survive I had to play the game ... their game. I even took up golf ... I was known as the honorary man. You also have to play to men's rules otherwise they just won't let you in. People are critical when you assume male traits ... they call you bossy and arrogant, all the negative adjectives, but men who behave this way are seen as strong leaders, etc.

In this study, when the women directors were asked about their perceptions of gender discrimination facing women in management and their views on their responsibility for challenging and changing this. Interviewee C said:

> Getting women to the top is not seen as a priority and that's probably because the decisions are largely men's and they don't see it as a priority! I don't think we will be doing anything proactively to recruit women though, whether we spend more opportunity developing the women we have would be interesting. I wouldn't feel right leading on the issue ... not because I don't believe in it but my priorities lie elsewhere. I don't feel passionately enough about it and I do need to feel passionate about something to lead on something. Having said that I recognize it though and I think there are things that can be done without necessarily going to the barricades ... I hope that's not a cop out?

Interviewee B commented:

> There are not enough women in positions of influence, that's why nothing has changed ... men don't like women at the top they prefer them to be submissive. We at the top have to influence and change things – alter the male resistance ... women have a responsibility to give women more opportunities ... it's about discreet discrimination – its not on not to help women – its not a level playing field and women need a leg up.

Interviewee D responded:

> I think the only way it would be changed is if women were more assertive about it and I don't think we are and I don't think we fight our corner very well. I think as a group we should raise our profile as men won't do it for us. If I was asked to take responsibility for leading gender change within the current management team I would be anxious ... quite anxious ... one woman out of three.

Throughout the interviews the women identified experiences where they were faced with majority male audiences, feeling uncomfortable, exclusion, inadequacy and having to 'psyche' themselves up for occasions, but were reluctant to ascribe this to any form of gendered experience.

They preferred to blame themselves in terms of inadequacy or low self-esteem and identified women's lack of confidence, including their own, as an issue for women in management. They admired male confidence, not competence, and men's self-belief in their own ability. Like Rindfleish's (2000) study, the women described barriers they had faced to varying degrees, and without exception thought the current lack of women at the top to be unacceptable and disappointing but inevitable. Most of the women interviewed thought women had to help themselves by being more confident and persistent and were reluctant to offer women a 'leg up'. The women were not inclined to engage in solidarity behaviours; they wanted to be recognized for their talents, abilities and knowledge and not as representatives of women.

None were prepared to lead on gender issues or to be seen to be visibly supporting women in management. These narratives highlight the difficult 'fitting in' processes of joining senior management and the impact of this on the expectation of solidarity behaviour or sisterhood in relation to other women in management. The senior women do recognize the issue of becoming more male than men but are reluctant to take on the women in management mantle; this is a central dilemma.

Championing women's issues is not a mainstream strategic role valued by most organizations and until it is, why have such expectations of senior women? Men and women label women who hold the women in management mantle as the 'token feminist', enabling a further undermining of women's roles and managerial identities. Simply the threat of being labelled as such leaves senior women feeling uneasy. Assumptions of sisterhood and solidarity behaviour should be revisited to explore the context in which senior women operate and their resulting gendered subjectivities, to make transparent this complexity and to highlight why such expectations of them may be unrealistic.

WOMEN ACADEMICS AND PROCESSES OF FEMALE MISOGYNY

Taken from a research project exploring women's identity and place in organization, narratives from interviews with women who were management academics at principal lecturer grade and below (Mavin 2001) highlight how processes of female misogyny between women manifests within a UK business and management higher education organization. The analysis discussed here centres on the women participants' contradictory behaviours and attitudes towards a particular woman in the organization (for the purposes of this chapter, the woman will be identified hereafter as Martha), who emerged as a predominant character in the women's narratives and towards senior women academics.

Martha was described by women participants as 'the only (woman) legend' in the organization's history, which was the most complimentary description, or as a woman who was 'too sexy for her own good'. Resulting from her overt sexuality, Martha was perceived by the academic women as having done 'a lot of damage' to how women in the organization were viewed. The enactment of female misogyny emerges as stories about Martha are told highlighting a lack of sisterhood or solidarity behaviour. When asked to talk about the heroes, heroines and villains in the organization interviewee E commented:

> There is one female legend, [Martha]. Everybody I met brought her into conversations, talking about the impact she had on the organization. She was too feminine for her own good and people did not know how to handle her and there was some jealousy. Both men and women brought her into the conversation. She is a legend because she networked and used power and influence that was the legend. I heard a lot of stories, people burned to talk about her so she left a kind of mark. To the people this was negative.

When asked what were the important stories in the organization interviewee F answered:

> [Martha] stories, I was able to ridicule her. She used to wear short skirts, skimpy things, short and obscene but the day after she had her interview when she didn't get the job she came into the tea room, and said 'what the fuck do you have to do to get on in this place?' Stories about her sitting with her legs crossed in a mini skirt on the desk in front of students, she had said doesn't it make you feel good when

all your students fancy you. I used to think what a silly cow who does she think she is, she used to do the rounds – she targeted people who were influential and she probably meant 'who the fuck'.

Interviewee G replied:

She [Martha] didn't help the acceptance of women in the organization. She put women back a few years and as she was so prolific and up front they didn't realize that there were serious implications for women. I think she was dangerous and she wasn't popular.

While interviewee H said:

All the men in the organization were sucked into it. She [Martha] was a plausible character, she could make everyone think she could do her job well, you could see her coming a mile off, sitting at the desk with her legs wide open. She got a male student to write her testimonial for her but they didn't renew her contract.

As a woman Martha challenged the dominant masculine culture in a way that had not been evident before, by using her sexuality explicitly. In doing so Martha emerged as the organization's 'executive tart'; she could not be easily understood in terms of the existing constructions of woman or gendered structures and therefore could not be easily managed. In terms of the women's stories about her, these are interpreted as a manifestation of female misogyny demonstrating women's prejudice and antagonism towards other women. Martha destabilized the established sexual order within the organization and was rejected by both men and women; left without a place in the organization.

These narratives evidence the arguments of Starr (2001) and Wacjman (1999), that women and their sexuality destabilize gender stereotypes and organization. When this happens it is clear within this research that it is not sisterhood and solidarity behaviours but processes of female misogyny which come to the fore. Martha was not a senior woman but was attempting to gain a full-time post in a way which challenged the other women's perceptions of their stable gendered order. 'Women express both surprise and disappointment at having to contend with opposition from women as well as men in their roles. It is a statement about women's learnt devaluation of the whole category of woman' (Starr 2001: 10).

Female misogyny is also evident in the perceptions of women academics regarding senior women within the organization. In comparison with their discussions of Martha, the academic women expected solidarity behaviour from senior women in the organization and were disappointed when this was not evident. The women discussed the senior women as 'honorary men' with masculine behaviours and traits and their narratives revealed feelings of being 'let down'. The token senior women were perceived as not being there to support or mentor other women; they were not arguing their cause and had become in some instances, more male than the men (Mavin 2001).

Through their narratives the women demonstrated disappointment with the senior women in that they perceived a lack of what has been described here as sisterhood or solidarity behaviour, from the top down. Holding this view, the token women should have changed the culture and fought their battles for them, as women, retaining their identity as women. For example, Interviewee F talked about what helped and hindered women referring to the two women Heads of Department:

> I don't think we have anybody in position who is prepared to sponsor women ... I have no respect for the AB's [a woman Head of Department] models of management and CD [a woman Principal Lecturer] has now abandoned the people she canvassed to get promoted and I can't do that, its not the way I work.

Commenting on a new woman Principal Lecturer being appointed from outside interviewee K said:

> This is the virtual superwoman coming in. I fully expected her to be a leading academic who I could have a lot of respect for as she would be superior to me ... the reality did not match the expectation. I got the impression that academically she was far superior but if you look at her CV she won't be entered into the RAE [Research Assessment Exercise].

The senior women were perceived in the same way as the senior men, neither group was respected by the women academics. The behaviours of senior women were perceived as male and reinforced the women's ideas of what types of identities are needed when you move into senior management, legitimizing why they did not want to move there in the first place.

Here processes of female misogyny succeed in disassociating women in senior management from other women and perpetuate the gendered order by socially constructing senior management for women. In this research senior management becomes a 'bad place', evidenced not least by the male behaviour and management style required and the superwoman status needed to sustain it, but also because as a woman you become a man and you will be undermined by and face antagonism from women as well as men.

When women experience female misogyny it is worse somehow than male misogyny, as we are put in our place by women who disassociate themselves from us because as women we are in or aspire to senior positions (Mavin 2001). In this research, not only are women in senior management in competition with men and women, but they also have to face antagonism or similar from men and women in the organization. Specifically from those women who feel uncomfortable that senior women have destabilized the established gendered order by moving place, becoming more 'male than the men' and by not using their senior management position to fight the way for other women.

EMERGENT THEMES

Assumptions underpinning sisterhood and solidarity behaviour are problematic both for senior women and other women in organization. The narratives of senior women presented in this chapter support Rindfleish's (2000) study in that they recognize there are barriers facing women in management but they do not feel comfortable in taking responsibility for the women in management mantle. The narratives also highlight that these senior women recognize the taking on of male behaviours in order to fit into senior management. However, developing research and interventions which remain focused upon the role of senior women in advancing women will not challenge or change the organizational structures and gender cultures which socially construct the experiences of women in management.

The narratives of academic women highlight negative relations between women. Reactions to the case of Martha as a woman who wanted to join the organization full-time but who was perceived as using her sexuality too overtly demonstrates how processes of female misogyny undermine assumptions of solidarity behaviour across organizational hierarchies. The same women were then seen to engage in processes of female misogyny, upwards towards senior women for not retaining their femininity and for not taking on the women in management mantle. Therefore expectations of solidarity behaviour from women do not hold across organizational boundaries or up, down and across hierarchical structures.

The different manifestations of female misogyny highlight the contradictory places women take in relation to other women and raise questions about women as 'natural allies' and of the notion of sisterhood and solidarity behaviour for women in management. However it is important to note that these debates should not be interpreted as another 'blame the women' position. 'Queen Bee' characteristics and processes of female misogyny emerge from the complex way in which gender order is embedded, socially constructing everyday experiences for women.

The significant issue which requires further research is the way in which this privileged gendered social order encourages and exacerbates differences between women in order to prevent opposition in the form of an ordered coalition of women's interests. This is not to point to orchestrated behaviours but rather to identify implicit gendered assumptions which foster difference and fragmentation which is, after all, easier to dismiss than joint action.

CONCLUSION

This chapter has explored how less positive relations between women undermine assumptions of sisterhood and solidarity behaviour and has represented narratives from women directors and management academics in the UK to highlight the complexity of female misogyny between women and why expectations of sisterhood and solidarity behaviour are problematic.

The narratives from women directors in the housing sector highlighted why we should refocus future research concerning women in management. There is a need to focus future action on challenging and changing the overall gendered structures and systems in place affecting all women in organization. The narratives from women academics reveal negative relations between women in organization and raise female misogyny as a gendered process which fragments notions of sisterhood and solidarity. Future action research which engages women in senior and other levels in management in consciousness raising to the context in which they are operating and the impact women have on other women, is a way forward and presents a unique challenge to advancing women in management. Enabling such consciousness raising and transparency between women in management is crucial in order to challenge established gender order. The alternative is to maintain the status quo for women in management by continuing with a veneer or pretence of sisterhood and solidarity behaviour whilst as women we continue to 'fight amongst ourselves'.

REFERENCES

Abramson, J. (1975), *The Invincible Woman: Discrimination in the Academic Profession*, London: Jossey-Bass.
Adler, N.J. (1999), 'Global Leaders: Women of Influence' in G. Powell (ed.), *The Handbook of Gender*, California: Sage Publications.
Bryans, P. and Mavin, S. (2003), 'Women Learning to Become Managers: Learning to Fit In or to Play a Different Game?', *Management Learning*, **34**(1), 111–34.
Coates, G. (1998), 'Integration or Separation: Women and the Appliance of Organizational Culture', *Women in Management Review*, **13**(3), 114–24.
Currie, G. and Brown, A.D. (2003), 'A Narratological Approach to Understanding Processes of Organizing in a UK Hospital', *Human Relations*, **56**(5), 563–86.
Davidson, M. and Burke, R.J. (eds) (1994), *Women in Management: Current Research Issues*, London: Paul Chapman Publishing.
Davidson, M. and Burke, R.J. (2000), *Women in Management: Current Research Issues, Volume 11*, London: Paul Chapman Publishing.
Denzin, N.K. (1994), 'The Art and Politics of Interpretation', in N.K. Denzin and Y.S. Lincoln (eds), *Handbook of Qualitative Research*, London: Sage Publications.
Gini, A. (2001), *My Job My Self: Work and the Creation of the Modern Individual*, London: Routledge.

Glick, P., Diebold, J., Bailey-Werner, B. and Zhu, L. (1997), 'The Two Faces of Adam: Ambivalent Sexism and Polarized Attitudes toward Women', *Personality and Social Psychology Bulletin*, **23**(12), 1323–35.

Goldberg, P. (1968), 'Are Women Prejudiced Against Women?', *Trans Action*, **5**, 28–30.

Greer, G. (2000), *The Whole Woman*, London: Anchor.

Griffin, C. (1995), 'Feminism, Social Psychology and Qualitative Research', *The Psychologist*, **8**(3), 119–21.

Kanter (1977), *Men and Women of the Corporation*, New York: Basic Books.

Korabik, K. (1999), 'Sex and Gender in the New Millenium', in G. Powell (ed.), *The Handbook of Gender*, California: Sage Publications.

Korabik, K. and Abbondanza, J. (2004), 'New Theory Supplants "Queen Bee" Notion of Woman in Management', Report by Almina Ali, Office of Research, Ontario Ministry of Education and Training.

Korac-Kakabadse, N. and Kouzmin, A. (1997), 'Maintaining the Rage: From Glass Concrete Ceilings and Metaphorical Sex Changes to Psyschological Audits and Renegotiating Organization Scripts', *Women in Management Review*, **12**(5), 182–221.

Legge, K. (1987), 'Women in Personnel Management: Uphill Struggle or Downhill Slide', in A. Spencer and D. Podmore (eds), *In a Man's World, Essays on Women in Male Dominated Professions*, London: Tavistock Publications Ltd.

Maddock, S. (1999), *Challenging Women*, London: Sage.

Maier, M. (1999), 'On the Gendered Substructure of Organization: Dimensions and Dilemmas of Corporate Masculinity', in G. Powell (ed.), *The Handbook of Gender*, California: Sage Publications.

Marshall, J. (1984), *Women Travellers in a Male World*, London: Wiley.

Mattis, M.C. (1993), 'Women Directors Progress and Opportunities for the Future', *Business and the Contemporary World*, **5**(3), 140–56.

Mavin, S. (2001), 'The Gender Culture Kaleidoscope: Images of Women's Identity and Place in Organization', unpublished PhD Thesis, University of Northumbria at Newcastle.

Mavin, S. and Bryans, P. (2002), 'Academic Women in the UK: Mainstreaming Our Experiences and Networking for Action', *Gender and Education*, **14**(3), 235–50.

Mavin, S. and Lockwood, A. (2004), 'Sisterhood and Solidarity Behaviour vs. Queen Bees and Female Misogyny', full paper presented to British Academy of Management Conference, August, University of St Andrews, UK.

McKeen, C.A. and Burke, R.J. (1991), 'University Initiatives for Preparing Managerial and Professional Women for Work', *Women in Management Review and Abstracts*, **6**(3), 11–15.

Nieva, V.F. and Gutek, B. (1981), *Women and Work: A Psychological Perspective*, New York: Praeger.

Nicolson, P. (1996), *Gender, Power and Organization: A Psychological Approach*, London: Routledge.

O'Leary, V. and Ryan, M.M. (1994), 'Women Bosses: Counting the Changes or Changes that Count', in M. Tanton (ed.), *Women in Management: A Developing Presence*, London: Routledge.

Powell, G.N. and Butterfield, D.A. (2003), 'Gender, Gender Identity and Aspirations to Top Management', *Women in Management Review*, **18**(3–4), 88–96.

Rindfleish, J. (2000), 'Senior Management Women in Australia: Diverse Perspectives', *Women in Management Review*, **15**(4), 172–80.

Singh, V., Vinnicombe, S. and Johnson, P. (2000), 'Women Directors on Top UK Boards', Paper presented to the Annual Conference of the British Academy of Management, September, Edinburgh.

Singh, V. and Vinnicombe, S. (2003a), 'The 2002 Female FTSE Index and Women Directors', *Women in Management Review*, **18**(7), 349–58.

Singh, V. and Vinnicombe, S. (2003b), 'Constructing a Professional Identity: How Young Female Managers Use Role Models', Paper presented to the 2nd Gender, Work and Organization Conference, June, Keele.

Staines, G., Travis, C. and Jayerante, T.E. (1973), 'The Queen Bee Syndrome', *Psychology Today*, **7**(8), 55–60.

Starr, K. (2001), 'What Makes Management Experience Different for Women? Secrets Revealed Through the Structure of Cathexis', Paper presented to the Rethinking Gender, Work and Organization Conference, June, Keele.

Wacjman, J. (1998), *Managing Like a Man*, Oxford: Blackwell Publishers Ltd.

5. Managing maternity

Caroline Gatrell

INTRODUCTION

This chapter explores how professional working mothers manage their responsibilities towards both children and career. I dispute the suggestion that highly qualified women who combine motherhood with management and/or professional roles are not employment-oriented. I assert that mothers who have careers may be highly focused upon both paid work and their children, which may be to the benefit (as opposed to the detriment) of both family and employers. I argue that the way in which such women manage their responsibilities towards jobs and families may be highly complex, and integrated. I propose that the concept of women being either employment- or home-oriented is simplistic. I also challenge the suggestion that mothers with careers are avaricious, as opposed to employment-oriented. I suggest that such women wish to be employed because their job is an important part of their social identity, even if they are living with a male partner who is also employed. Additionally, I argue that the term 'home-orientation' may obfuscate the probability that women who combine motherhood with career differentiate between maternal-orientation (many women value their maternal status) and domestic-orientation (many mothers dislike housework, and resent the gendered assumption that it should be mothers' responsibility).

I begin the chapter by reviewing the literature on the employment-orientation of women managers. In this context I discuss the exclusion of women managers from senior roles and assert that discrimination occurs because of women's actual, or potential, maternity. In relation to social attitudes, an attempt is made to explain (but not to justify) the continuing exclusion of women managers and professionals from senior roles. I then draw upon data from a qualitative study on how highly qualified, employed, heterosexual mothers who are married or co-habiting, manage their responsibilities to children and career (Gatrell 2005). I argue that, while women professionals/managers who are also mothers may invest love and quality time in their children's upbringing, they often remain deeply committed to their employment.

MANAGEMENT, MOTHERHOOD AND DISCRIMINATION

Legislation to protect and encourage women's participation in the workplace has now been in place, both in Britain and in the USA, for over 30 years. Government agencies exist to defend and uphold women's rights in the workplace, and to assist women in seeking legal recourse should they experience discrimination (in the UK, The Equal Opportunities Commission and in the USA, the Department of Labor Women's Bureau). Despite these initiatives, however, women are still conspicuously absent from top level jobs and it is observed that: 'few women break through the "glass ceiling" into [the corporate] elite, despite making inroads into middle management' (Singh and Vinnicombe 2004: 479). The UK EOC notes that, while there is some improvement in the case of public sector appointments, women continue to be excluded from senior roles in business, the judiciary, the military and academia (EOC 2005). In the USA, women account for only 8 per cent of top managers, and female earnings average only 72 per cent of those of equivalent male colleagues (*The Economist*, 2005). And despite the fact that the 'stereotyping of women's career ambition as less than that of men is … untrue' (Singh and Vinnicombe 2004: 480), women continue to be excluded from executive roles because they are (unjustly) perceived to be less employment-oriented than men.

THE 'MATERNAL WALL'

It has been argued women managers and professionals are disadvantaged in the labour market due to their status as potential or actual mothers. Despite anti-discrimination legislation, a negative link continues to be made, by employers, between a woman's reproductive status and her employment-orientation (Williams and Cohen Cooper 2004; Gatrell and Cooper 2006). Every year, 30 000 women in the UK are dismissed from their jobs due to pregnancy, and 200 000 more face discrimination (BBC News 2005). The EOC has stated that this is partly because employers fear that expense and inconvenience may be involved in managing both maternity leave and mothers' subsequent return to work, when women might request flexibility due to their maternal responsibilities. The EOC also argue, however, that such discrimination occurs due to a belief on the part of organizations that mothers are likely to lose their career focus from the moment they become pregnant. Employers thus 'retain a traditional image of motherhood as being incompatible with paid employment' (EOC 2004: 2). As observed by Cockburn (2000: 185), motherhood makes women unattractive in organizational terms because:

maternity provision is (regarded as) a severe nuisance. It makes practical difficulties for managers, increases the proportion of women in the labour force and brings and unwelcome domestic odour, a whiff of the ... nursery into the workplace.

It has been suggested that discrimination in relation to women's maternity occurs because the 'normative' image of womanhood is gendered. While men are seen as employment-oriented economic providers, it is assumed that mothers' chief responsibility and interest is (or ought to be!) embedded within the home (Desmarais and Alksnis 2005). Mothers are therefore constructed as having a lower employment-orientation (and a higher home-orientation) than fathers. Williams (2000: 70) contends that such attitudes affect the progress of all career women, regardless of whether or not they have children, because their reproductive status is in itself sufficient to deter employers: 'The assumption that motherhood does, and should, preclude women from performing as ideal workers affects all women, not just mothers, as employers are wary of employing women on the grounds that women have disappointed them in the past.' Williams' views have been borne out by confidential surveys such as the one undertaken by the UK Institute of Directors (IOD), which revealed that 45 per cent of IOD members would be reluctant to recruit any woman between 16 and 49, due to the possibility that she might have a child (Malthouse, 1997). A more recent survey showed that 80 per cent of human resources professionals would 'think twice before employing a woman of childbearing age' (EOC, 2005b).

Employers' fears that motherhood will reduce a woman's motivation at work are exacerbated if any physical signs of maternity are manifested in the work environment (Malthouse 1997). Thus, women managers/professionals who are pregnant, who take maternity leave or who request flexible working in order to accommodate childcare, are likely to experience discrimination (Blair-Loy 2003). Although this goes against both the spirit and the letter of equal opportunities legislation, employers rationalize such behaviour on the basis that mothers' perceived low employment-orientation provides justification for unfair treatment (Gatrell 2005). Williams (2000) has described this phenomenon as the 'maternal wall'. She suggests that the maternal wall is composed 'of old-fashioned stereotyping of women', the implication being that mothers are not considered 'ideal workers' in the same way that fathers are (Williams 2000: 70). Williams acknowledges that the practices which contribute to the building of the maternal wall are 'often unconscious, as when women's work is scrutinised more closely than men's. Plum assignments and promotions are given to workers who seem able, committed and serious: in the eyes on some beholders, [because of women's maternal status] men fit these images more often than do women' (Williams 2000: 69). In relation to pregnancy and child care, however, women continue to experience open and explicit discrimination and may be demoted, or dismissed from their posts

(Davidson and Cooper 1992; Blair-Loy 2003; Gatrell and Cooper 2006). Williams (2000) has identified three reasons for the exclusion from executive roles of women managers who are also mothers. These are: the marginalization of part-time women managers and professionals (because employers assume that such women are more home- than employment-oriented); the 'executive' (or long-hours) schedule which can be difficult for mothers to accommodate, and the assumption that mothers are unwilling to relocate for career purposes.

THE EXCLUSION OF MOTHERS FROM EXECUTIVE MANAGEMENT ROLES

It has also been argued that the exclusion of women managers from top-level posts is because social attitudes are failing to keep up with changing social trends (Davidson and Cooper 1992; Gatrell and Cooper 2006). It appears that heterosexual women and men are still expected by organizations, policy makers and the media, to fulfil outdated and gendered social roles. Those who fail to do this may be seen as deviant (Stephens *et al.* 2001). In this context, Desmarais and Alksnis (2005) have argued that employed mothers will face criticism in terms of their ability to effectively fulfil either the role of mother or of worker. For this reason, these writers argue that the combination of motherhood with a professional or managerial role is particularly stressful. This is because not only do managing mothers have to contend with the stress factors affecting all senior employees such as 'presenteeism' (Collinson and Collinson 2004; Worrall and Cooper 1999), but because women also have to cope with the additional stresses of discrimination due to their maternal status. Desmarais and Alksnis (2005: 459) further contend that as women become more senior, this situation will 'become progressively worse' because women (and especially mothers) are seen to be 'deviating [even] further from their traditional expectations ... any hierarchical responsibility assumed by female workers exacerbates [the feeling that] all working woman are violating the normative assumptions of the role of women'. These gendered social expectations impact negatively in two ways on the lives of female managers/professionals who are also mothers. In the first place, the employment-orientation of career mothers may be regarded by organizations as deficient. On the other hand, women 'receive the message that if they do perform as an ideal worker, [this] will prove [them] a bad mother' (Williams 2000: 70). In cases where a mother's work orientation is so visible that it becomes undeniable, she is unlikely to be credited with career orientation, but may be accused of greed and an obsession with 'designer lifestyles' (Jackson 2002).

A WOMAN'S PLACE? A SOCIAL AND HISTORICAL UNDERSTANDING

Although the exclusion of women from influential positions in the workplace cannot be justified (either on legal or on social grounds) there is, arguably, a social and an historical explanation for the assumption that the division of labour within heterosexual couples should continue to be gendered. This helps to shed light on why the 'normative' worker continues to be constructed as male; why employed mothers are seen as greedy consumers rather than responsible employees, and why 'good' mothers continue to be regarded as those who eschew paid employment in favour of staying at home (Blair-Loy 2003). It also helps to explain why organizations and the media continue to resist the possibility that career mothers may be equally (or more) employment-oriented, and just as ambitious, as men.

Arguably, the concept of the 'ideal' stay-at-home mother was constructed during the 1950s and 1960s by the American sociologist Talcott Parsons (Parsons and Bales 1956), whose work was influential in both Britain and the USA because it offered policy makers an idealized picture of family life which appeared attractive to governments and organizations both socially and economically. In this vision, most women and men would be married and heterosexual, would produce children and would divide labour along gendered lines, with fathers employed outside the home and mothers focusing their energies on raising children, doing the housework and shopping (Parsons and Bales 1956). Parsons' 'storybook' description of family life has been criticized by later writers, who accuse him of being blind to issues of poverty, race and class (Bernandes 1997). Nevertheless, his image of the family as 'predominantly ... middle class' (Parsons 1971 53) was very influential and (although he may not have intended this himself) helped to ensure that the 1950s picture of mother/homemaker and father/provider became the ideals to which families were encouraged by policy makers to aspire (Gatrell 2005).

MOTHERHOOD: CHANGING SOCIAL TRENDS, CONSTANT SOCIAL ATTITUDES

The 'Parsonian' image of the mother in the home, especially when children were small, was the one that prevailed in popular culture and literature throughout the 1950s, 1960s and even the 1970s. Mothers were usually characterized as white, affluent, able-bodied women who were entirely oriented towards children and housework. For example, in the popular children's reading series produced by 'Ladybird' in the 1960s, the maternal figure is usually depicted in the home with her children by her side 'helping' her with the chores: cooking, cleaning and the laundry (Gagg 1961). Murray (1964) describes the Ladybird reading scheme as 'embrac[ing] ... the natural interests and activities of happy children' (Murray 1964: 2). Arguably, in the 1960s, the image of 'happy children' was integrally bound up with the concept a stay-at-home mother who was entirely home-oriented.

Until the early 1980s, the 'Parsonian' image of motherhood was reflected in labour market trends. The number of mothers who were also employed was low until 1979, with only 24 per cent of mothers returning to work during the first year after childbirth (Pullinger and Summerfield 1998). By the turn of the millennium, however, a major social change had taken place in the labour markets in the UK and the USA (Dex *et al.* 1998; Padavic and Reskin 2002). Partly as a result of the anti-discrimination laws which were passed in the 1970s, and partly due to other changes such as the increasing number of women doing university degrees and that the percentage of women in all occupations who maintained continuous employment after childbirth had risen sharply. However, the opportunity to continue a career was more prevalent among heterosexual mothers who were educated to degree level (or equivalent), and who were occupying professional or managerial roles, than among other groups (Macran *et al.* 1996: 285). At the forefront of this trend were career mothers with pre-school children. This group were likely to have delayed childbearing at least until their 30s and 71 per cent and were likely to be living with the father of the child (Thair and Risdon, 1999). Thus, by 1999, 76 per cent of highly educated, professional mothers of pre-school children were in employment as compared with 27 per cent of women who had no qualifications. Given the rising rate of women's employment and the changes in legislation, which outlawed discrimination on grounds of gender/motherhood and required equality of pay for men and women in equivalent jobs, it might be supposed that the idea of maternal employment would be more acceptable now than it was in the 1950s–1970s. As I have suggested above, however, although social change has occurred rapidly (especially for highly educated women in managerial and professional roles), organizational attitudes and practices have failed to keep pace. The 'maternal wall' is still firmly in place and the majority of organizations have resisted the appointment of women to senior and executive levels (Williams 2000; Blair-Loy 2003; Singh and Vinnicombe 2004; Gatrell and Cooper 2006).

ONLY HERE FOR THE PAY-CHEQUE? CAREER-ORIENTATION, MANAGING MOTHERS AND CONTEMPORARY CULTURAL IMAGES

It is not just among employers that mothers are constructed as having a low employment-orientation. This is also the viewpoint of influential agencies such as of IOD (Roberts 2004) and of some academics such as Catherine Hakim (1996). In her work on preference theory, Hakim (2000) has argued that only 20 per cent of women can be considered to be employment-oriented. The remaining 80 per cent are either home focused (20 per cent) or adaptive (60 per cent), meaning that they are in paid work but regard this as of secondary importance to spousal or maternal roles. Hakim suggests that this applies to highly educated women just as much as it does to those with fewer qualifications. The reason for this, Hakim argues, is because many women who seek a university education do so in order to succeed in 'marriage markets', regarding the labour market as an option to fall back on only if 'the right ... man' fails to materialise (Hakim 2000: 161). Hakim proposes that most employed mothers are predominantly home-oriented. She contends that: 'the main reason for women being less likely than men to attain positions of responsibility is because family responsibilities absorb women's time and energy (Hakim 2000: 90–91). Hakim's views have been strongly refuted by feminist writers (Ginn *et al.* 1996; Crompton 2002; McRae 2003). However, the influence of Hakim's work on policy makers and in the press cannot be underestimated (Gatrell 2005).

For example, Hakim contends that the motivating impetus for maternal employment is because mothers' wish to earn money, rather than job satisfaction, remains paramount (Hakim 2000). Views of this nature are often reflected in cultural and media representations of motherhood, in which employed fathers are constructed as fulfilling their paternal role appropriately while mothers who are successful in their professional capacity are constructed as self-indulgent and materialistic. Such women are presented as purchasing lifestyle goods for their own egotistical ends, or as compensation for children who are deprived of maternal time and care. Company Director Perm Saini, for example, featured in Britain's *Daily Mail*, is portrayed as pursuing a designer lifestyle at the expense of her children. Her achievements as a mother and business women are downplayed. Perm is quoted as saying: 'We have a much higher standard of living than my parents. The boys are at a private school, I drive a Porsche and we live in a lovely house.' In order to emphasize the interpretation of Perm's success as greedy, and selfish, the feature concludes with a comment from Perm's mother Herjinder. Herjinder is presented as a 'good' mother who relinquished career and 'lifestyle' ambitions for the sake of her children. Underlining this point, Herjinder is quoted as saying: 'My grandchildren sometimes miss their mother ... and all the toys in the world don't make up for not having a mother at home' (Courtenay Smith *et al.* 2004). In this way, the *Daily Mail* succeeds in constructing Perm as neither career- nor home-oriented, but as merely avaricious.

THE 'GOOD' STAY-AT-HOME MOTHER

As well as being accused of low career-orientation and greed, employed mothers may also be criticized for fulfilling their maternal obligations inadequately. In 1977, Rich contended that, to be regarded as 'good' mothers, women must 'find their chief gratification in being all day with small children. Their maternal love is, and should be, quite literally selfless' (Rich 1977: 23). Several decades after Rich's comments, research on advertising in women's magazines suggests that the popular and cultural image of the 'good' mother has changed little, and remains embedded in the concept of looking after children in the home (Johnston and Swanson 2003). Furthermore, recent research undertaken by Penelope Leach continues to reproduce dated discourses along the lines that the mothers who 'give their children the best start' are those who remain at home full-time (Leppard and Sanderson 2005). The National Childminding Association, of which Leach is President, states that: 'children up to 36 months need to have a high quality of care ... ideally with their mother. Mother is best' (Leppard and Sanderson 2005). The implications of Leach's research and the press coverage which followed its publication, are that career mothers are irresponsible and selfish, and are failing to 'give their children the best start'.

RESEARCH METHODOLOGY

In the empirical research which I undertook on career mothers, I explored how a sample of well-qualified mothers of pre-schoolers managed their responsibilities to employment and children. The research was qualitative and was not intended to 'represent' the wider population of employed mothers, but rather to enable me to theorize about parents' experiences. Because this chapter focuses on the experiences of mothers, I have not discussed in detail the sampling of men (although fathers were included in the research sample). The fieldwork for the research spanned 2.5 years with 20 mothers and 18 fathers interviewed between 1999 and 2001. It is acknowledged that mothers in the sample were in heterosexual relationships at the time of their interview. Their experiences may therefore differ from those of women in other circumstances such as single parenthood or lesbian partnerships. As observed above, demographic research on career mothers with pre-school children had already identified the characteristics of women most likely to maintain continuous employment after childbirth. The inclusion criteria for mothers was based on the picture provided by the existing quantitative data – all had at least one pre-school child and were married/co-habiting with the father at the time of the interview. They held a first degree as a minimum qualification and were employed in a professional capacity. The definition of 'profession' was taken from the Standard Occupational Classification (Office of Population Censuses and Surveys, 1991).

Couples were located in varying geographical areas across the UK including London, Manchester, Liverpool, Greater Manchester, Durham, Essex and Cheshire. Mothers and fathers interviewed represented a range of financial circumstances. Although all women were employed in a professional and/or managerial capacity, their contribution to family income varied. Seven women worked full-time, and of these, six were 'main breadwinners' within their households and two had partners who were at home full-time with small children. Three women were equal earners and were supposed to be working 80 per cent of a full-time equivalent, but in practice worked long hours which were arranged to fit in with both organizational and children's needs. Of the remaining group, all of whom worked part-time, all were second income earners and three mothers' income was so low in comparison to the cost of childcare that it left household finances in deficit.

MANAGING MOTHERS – HOME OR CAREER ORIENTATION?

Among the professional and managerial women interviewed, all demonstrated a strong career-orientation. The reasons for this were complex and women explained it in a variety of ways which included personal ambition and the belief that their professional status imbued them with high social capital (while motherhood – though they valued this for its own sake – did not). Mothers explained that their job was an important part of their social identity, irrespective of how much they loved their children. In accordance with Marshall and Wetherall's (1989) interpretation of Social Identity Theory, mothers clearly identified themselves with two social groups: 'mothers' and 'career women'. These identifications were so strong that it would have been difficult to separate the characteristics of the individual from her group identity, as most mothers described both their maternity and their paid work as being 'part of who I am'. Many mothers, whether their earning provided the main family income or whether their contribution to household finances was in the negative, regarded both their career and their maternity as a priority, and worked out ways in which they could incorporate both. It was apparent that mothers were motivated to continue paid work following childbirth due to a strong employment-orientation, rather than the desire to purchase 'designer lifestyles'.

Mothers' Employment Orientation – Mothers in Full-time Paid Work

Of the women who worked more than 80 per cent, their employment orientation was very powerful. A senior tax consultant explained how, much as she loved her small son and even though she could probably have afforded to give up or downshift her paid work, she could not have contemplated life without her career:

> It doesn't matter how much I loved my baby and I loved him to the depths of my soul, but I never questioned coming back to work. In my mind, I was definitely coming back. I spent a lot of time trying to figure this out really because we could have managed on [husband's income]. But I've always worked, always, from college, its part of my identity, of who I am and I could never, ever contemplate not working.

For some women, their employment orientation could have been seen as even greater than their maternal orientation. They explained that they loved their children, but that they were nevertheless career-oriented in the way that fathers have traditionally been presumed to be (Lupton and Barclay 1997; Dienhart 1998; Warin *et al.* 1999). A television news producer explained that she loved her daughter dearly, but that her employment-orientation remained powerful and her home-orientation relatively low. She was explicit that her abilities lay principally in her professional life. She found the day-to-day duties of childcare unappealing and was happy to leave her baby in the care of others during the week while she pursued her career. She felt confident that she had made the right decision in remaining in full-time employment and explained:

> All the time I was pregnant, I was sure I wanted to continue work. I never considered having a child meaning the typical thing of motherhood. I never thought it meant me giving up my job, I was absolutely happy to come back full-time because I decided part-time would feel part-time and I didn't actually mind not being with [my baby]. I mean I loved her, I worried about her constantly, but I wasn't particularly interested in her and it was lonely being with her all day [when on maternity leave]. Now she is two, so she is more interesting to be with, but I still see her for only about half an hour in the evening and at the weekends which is very little. But it seems right for me. In truth I probably think the traditional way of doing motherhood is boring and I have no ambition to do it. I don't think I've got any guilt about not wanting it or doing it. I find it strange when I talk to friends who have given up work which is an alien feeling to me. I just think: 'Thank God I don't have to go to coffee mornings, thank God I am at work'.

All mothers (whether employed full-time or part-time) were operating at a senior level, and held management responsibilities. Of these, four women appeared to accept it as inevitable that having children had, if only temporarily, reduced the likelihood that they would progress to (or in some cases retain) very high status roles. Sixteen women, however, demonstrated ambition and a determination to continue up the career ladder. The tax consultant, for example, applied for a more senior role while her baby was only a few weeks old and recounts how she overcame practical difficulties, attending an interview at short notice while on maternity leave, to secure a job that she really wanted:

> I'd interviewed for this job while I was on maternity leave. I've always been very uptight about my jobs, I have always been very determined ... and one of my colleagues from my old firm got a job here. He rang me at home and said 'There's a good job for you here, can you make an interview today?' So the old lady next door pushed [my son] round the park in his pram, and it takes her exactly an hour to do that. So I got a taxi here and got the interview. I interview brilliantly and it's the one thing I can always rely on, if I go for a job I get an offer. So I got the taxi back just as she was coming round which meant that fortunately she didn't have to set off again, which was a good thing. She's very old and I don't know what I was more worried about – the interview or her! Anyway so I got the job, went back to my old job and handed my notice in. That wasn't very popular, but doing well in my career is important to me. And even the maternal instincts couldn't break that.

The experiences of women, as described above, support the argument that gendered assumptions about the division of labour (and mothers' low-career orientation) are simplistic and may depart markedly from the attitudes of some career mothers who work full-time. The descriptions given show the need to continue paid work failed to substantiate the belief that career-mothers are employed in order to fund designer lifestyles. Neither woman talked of wishing to buy expensive consumer items or new cars. Arguably, ambition and employment orientation did not mean that these senior women were failing in 'doing the best' for their children, who were well cared for. For some women, however, full-time employment and a strong employment orientation meant that they interpreted motherhood differently from the traditional, 'Parsonian' model of maternity.

Mothers in Part-time Employment

Most of the mothers in part-time employment were also highly career-oriented. As described above, some women explained that they preferred being at work to being with children when they were very small, because they did not find babies very interesting and were 'bored staying at home'. Others wished to play a lead role in caring for children during their pre-school years, but retained a strong employment-orientation. All mothers employed part-time demonstrated ambition and a strong professional identity and their paid work continued to provide them with a sense of self-worth which they did not feel they could derive from motherhood alone.

Nevertheless, in keeping with Williams' (2000) assertions about the restricted career progress of women managers who work part-time, all of those working less than 80 per cent found that their opportunities for promotion were blocked, due to assumptions on the part of employers that they should be happy to sit in the 'mummy track' (Williams 2000: 73) and let their career take a back seat. In some cases, employers ceased to offer training or pay reviews. In other examples, mothers were allowed to undertake part-time work only if they accepted less favourable terms and conditions than before they had children. Some were given permission to work part-time, but then discovered that there was no provision for them to return to full-time work, or to apply for promotion. Many of the mothers working part-time were unequivocal about the extent of their ambition, and felt resentful if they had been 'blocked' due to their maternal status. A university lecturer and a hospital doctor both experienced discrimination as a result of the assumption that each would (or should) be more home- than career-oriented, given their part-time employ-ment:

> People perceive you as being less 'willing' because you won't allow people to dump extra stuff on your desk that someone else should take. And because you are no longer a soft option, they say: 'There. That proves you are not as committed as before you had children because before, you would have done that work.' The moment I became assertive and said: 'Well, I won't leave any stone unturned in terms of my clinical work, but I won't be available to do unpaid extra', I was perceived as withdrawing my focus from work. So then they sidelined me. And I think that is really unfair. (Hospital doctor)

> As far as the university is concerned they think they have put me where I belong – on the 'mummy track'. They have said I can't even apply for promotion because 'there are no criteria for promoting part-time staff'. They just don't know what to do with ambitious part-time women. They can't understand why I won't be content with just a bit of part-time teaching. (University lecturer)

Some women pointed out that they sought part-time work for only a limited period while children were very small, and still wished to rise up the career ladder. In support of these claims, several were undertaking courses of further study: two were doing PhDs and four others were undertaking professional development. Most had jobs which involved long hours and overnight stays at some point, and all went to great lengths to accommodate the needs of both children and employers. Interestingly, while mothers found organizational discouragement to be in some respects disheartening, this did not necessarily reduce their career-orientation. In some cases it hardened mothers' resolve and made them more determined to succeed. For example a university lecturer who is employed part-time had her contract downgraded when she was eight months pregnant, and she has continued to feel uncertain of her position. Nevertheless, her ambition remains strong, as does her determination to achieve prominence in her field.

Mothers have to prove their commitment and they are constantly being tested out – let's throw this at her and see whether she'll do it. Well, I'm an ambitious person. I always think of my career in the long term, I always have done, and my ambitions haven't gone away.

The unfavourable treatment and uncertain prospects of mothers who were employed part-time accords with Williams' concept of the 'maternal wall', and with Blair-Loy's (2003: 91–92) argument that 'bosses and co-workers ... define part-timers as uncommitted, second class citizens ... Despite this antagonism, these part-timers continue to challenge the ... dictat that professional worthiness can exist only among full-time workers.' They hold fast to their identities as dedicated workers and highly involved mothers, while refusing to abandon either source of meaning in their lives. The tenacity of part-time career mothers did mean that some were not prepared to simply accept what little was on offer from unsupportive organizations. Several – apparently to the surprise of their employers – were prepared to move institutions if this enabled them to obtain promotion, or to negotiate more attractive terms and conditions. These women recognized that they retained highly transferable skills, and sought positions that suited them better, taking their knowledge and expertise with them. An A-level teacher had worked in a senior capacity at the same school for ten years. She recalled how her Head of Department had threatened to dismiss her when she returned to work on a part-time basis. Rather than fight him, or live in a state of perpetual anxiety, she sought alternative employment.

I applied for a job with the school's main competitor. I hadn't had a job interview for ten years, that is how long I had been at my old job, so I was very nervous. So I did a 'mock' interview with my friend and she said 'what are you worried about? You're a gifted and experienced teacher and they are poaching you from the competition. They'll bite your hand off.' And that's what happened and I got the job

Long Hours Cultures and Motherhood

It was evident that, although they might be pressured for time in some areas of their lives, the allocation of quality time to the mother/child relationship was seen by mothers as crucial and no matter how busy they were, all 'ring-fenced' some time to do things with children. Where mothers did have to make compromises this usually involved personal sacrifice rather than disadvantaging either their job or their child. As a public sector manager pointed out:

I can't remember sitting down and buying *Vogue* and relaxing. I can't remember the last time. And I used to love going shopping for clothes. I hardly ever go shopping now.

Whether they worked full-time or part-time, all mothers (except possibly the television producer who was present at work for lengthy and 'unsociable' hours) felt that they attracted disapproval from colleagues because they were not always present at work 'after hours', or at social events. Their experiences, in this respect, are in keeping with the observations of Williams (2005) and Collinson and Collinson (2004) about presenteeism. However, shorter 'official' working times did not mean that these women worked less hard than colleagues. No matter what their formal arrangements with employers, all mothers worked well over and above their contractual hours and most began work again once children were in bed.

Other Reasons for Mothers' Strong Employment Orientation

Mothers' employment orientation has already been discussed in relation to their strong social identification with career. Whether they were working full- or part-time, mothers also gave other, more complex reasons for wishing to maintain their careers. These were bound up with mothers' own definition of 'good mothering' and although some had financial implications, none of them were concerned with designer lifestyles. Instead, mothers focused on love and encouragement as the 'gifts' they wished to offer their children. Mothers considered that their age (all were over 30 and several in their 40s) and their employment experience made them better mothers than if they had had children in their 20s. They considered it to be important to be kind and patient with children, and for children to develop confidence:

> I would like my children to grow up as confident people who can make their own choices in life, and who have the knowledge and confidence to do that. And if I don't do anything else I would hope that that would be my gift to them. I think if I had had children in my 20s I would have been a very different mother from the mother I am now. (Nurse manager)

> I am a better mother now than I would have been then because ... I am now a much more patient and solid person than I would have been then. In the qualities of good motherhood, patience I think has to be absolutely the first one ... I think to treat a child as a person is essential ... one has to be sympathetic to a child's needs and to their frustrations. (Lawyer)

Some mothers felt it was good for children to be aware of their mothers' employed status; for sons to see that women can be successful professionally, and for daughters to understand that a career is available to them. As one female interviewee stated:

> There are so many opportunities for women now, I want to show [my daughter] what she can do ... I want to say to [her] 'look at mummy, she goes to work, she has an interesting job, she has a balanced life'. It's about saying to her 'you can do

it if you want to'. I think there is still this culture of, you know, you marry well and your husband has a good job. Well I wouldn't be happy with that kind of situation for her ... so it's about demonstrating to her: 'it's possible to be independent, women can do this'.

Some women interpreted the concept of 'good mothering' in terms of the provider role previously allocated by Parsons to men. These women wanted to be able to support their children financially should the adult relationship break down, or should their partners die. As a hospital doctor explained:

> There is the aspect of what would happen if I was left having to provide financially for the children. And I feel that to have left work, and to have to pick up the threads as a single parent would be very difficult. I need to keep my hand in so I can support them if need be. So that is another motivation for keeping me at work.

The Integration of Work and Maternal Orientation

Mothers' decisions about professional development and promotion were often, also, integrated with what was 'best' for their children. Arguably, concepts of home and employment-orientation are more complex than has been suggested by, for example, Hakim (1996a; 2000). For instance, a local government officer had relocated when her daughter was two to an area 200 miles away. This was partly for career purposes but also because she felt her daughter would benefit from the change. The officer was the principal earner in her family and she strove to give her utmost to both her career and her daughter, this challenges the organizational assumptions observed by Williams (2000) that career mothers are unpromotable because they are never prepared to relocate. As the officer explained:

> My daughter comes first in every decision. The reason I got my present job was that I want the best for her. She is the reason for me having a push in career terms. I thought about her future, where I want her to be educated, which part of the world would be better. And this job came up and it was fundamentally about motherhood that spurred me on to try for this job because I want the best for her, financially, but also environmentally and culturally.

Other women (both full-time and part-time) managed jobs which involved travel and overnight stays. For example, a doctor regularly slept at the hospital when on call. A lawyer was often required to be away from home, and she shared the responsibility for childcare with her husband.

'Maternal' and 'Home' Orientation – an Understanding

In accordance with the assertions of Desmarais and Alksnis (2005), most of the career women in the sample were regarded by colleagues, friends and family as lacking in home-orientation. They were treated as unusual (or even deviant), due to their employed status. The opprobrium experienced by mothers tended to rise in proportion to their contractual hours. A managing partner in a city law practice, working part-time, explained her concerns that she did not, and could not, conform to the 'standards' achieved by mothers who were not in paid work

> There are certain 'professional' mums who make a point of volunteering for everything and wearing the mantle of the 'perfect mother'. And [my relative] said to me: I can't see the point of you're having children if you palm them off onto other people. That was so upsetting for me.

An NHS Chief Executive Officer who was employed full-time appeared to find the pressures even greater. She said:

> I enjoy, and am dedicated to my job but I still feel the 'guilt' bit about it. But I should be at home. My parents were absolutely horror-struck when I went back to work full-time. A lot of my friends have conformed to the perfect mother role model of staying at home and not working which makes me feel as if I never do anything right. By implication, you're a 'bad mum' if you go back to work [after having children].

> As soon as people know my husband is the main day time carer for the children I get lots of questions about 'Why?' and people push, and they push, and they push. And its downright nosiness, because it's unusual and I find that quite intrusive. And there are comments about me being this pushy woman, you know: 'we know who wears the pants in that relationship don't we', all that kind of stuff, because I am the one that happens to be continuing at work. And I don't actually think you would get that it we were both at work, I don't think you would get the kind of comments that are made, which are horrible.

Defining 'Home-orientation'

In the consideration of career mothers' employment versus home-orientation, the discussion often stops short of defining quite what is meant by 'home-orientation'. Arguably, the term 'home' embraces an assumption that maternity should include the responsibility for (and an interest in!) household management and housework. In my research, in accordance with texts on heterosexual coupledom and housework (Delphy and Leonard 1992; Maushart 2002), it was certainly the case that most mothers found themselves responsible for domestic chores, while male partners either did nothing, or 'helped'. Without exception, mothers resented this. They emphasized how much they disliked housework, and how they saw it as distinct from (and less rewarding than) time spent in direct contact with children. For many women, the management of both professional and maternal roles was challenging, but mostly enjoyable. However, the added and unwelcome responsibility for housework was a 'pressure' which 'got them down'. Mothers used strong emotional adjectives to describe their dislike of housework. While many mothers in the sample might claim both an orientation towards both motherhood and career, the description 'home'-oriented, if we assume that this suggests a love of housework, did not apply. The term maternal-orientation would, therefore, be more appropriate.

CONCLUSION

In this chapter, I have explored how mothers in managerial and professional roles manage both requirements of children and career and I have argued that motherhood is not a predictor of employment-orientation. I have observed that, in keeping with research on maternal employment, career mothers often faced a 'maternal wall' of unfair treatment and discrimination in their paid work. I have contended that this is due to out-dated and gendered social attitudes about what the role of mothers in society should be. I have also suggested that these 'normative' gendered beliefs are at the root of unproven assumptions that mothers' employment-orientation is low, and their home-orientation high. On the basis of my empirical research, I have asserted that the employment-orientation of career mothers may be very powerful, and this is related more to their social identity and to their professional dedication than with a desire to attain a 'designer lifestyle'. I have argued that, although they may not always be 'present' in the workplace, employed mothers often work long hours and will 'go the extra mile' to ensure that jobs are completed to a high standard. I have further contended that the argument that mothers must be either home-oriented or employment-oriented may be simplistic. This is because mothers' employment-orientation is complex, and integrally bound up with their maternal responsibilities.

Finally, I considered the definition of 'home-orientation'. Not only is it inaccurate to assume that mothers are necessarily 'home-oriented' at the expense of the career, but the concept of home orientation – encompassing, as it seems to, a responsibility for housework, as well as for children – is flawed. While many mothers valued their maternal identities, all women disliked housework, and resented the assumption that this should be their responsibility. The term 'maternal orientation' might, therefore, be more accurate.

In conclusion, I suggest that the belief that mothers' employment orientation is low may be highly damaging – not only to the women concerned but to organizations, who risk losing highly qualified and hard working colleagues if they continue to block mothers' career progress. This may prove expensive in terms of organizational recruitment costs, as disenfranchised women leave their employment in search of better conditions, taking their knowledge and expertise with them. It also comes at a cost to the whole economy, if so many highly trained women professionals such as managers, teachers, lawyers and doctors, are systematically excluded from senior roles on the basis of out-dated, inaccurate and unfounded beliefs about mothers' employment-orientation.

REFERENCES

BBC News (2005), 'Pregnant Employees Forced Out', bbc.co.uk, 2 February.

Bernandes, J. (1997), *Family Studies, An Introduction*, London: Routledge.

Blair-Loy, M. (2003), *Competing Devotions: Career and Family among Women Executives*, Cambridge, MA: Harvard University Press.

Cockburn, C. (2002), 'Resisting Equal Opportunities: The Issue of Maternity', in S. Jackson and S. Scott (eds), *Gender: A Sociological Reader*, London: Routledge, pp. 180–91.

Collinson, D. and Collinson, M. (2004), 'The Power of Time: Leadership, Management and Gender', in C.F. Epstein and A.L. Kalleberg (eds), *Fighting for Time: Shifting the Boundaries of Work and Social life*, New York: Russell Sage Foundation, pp. 219–46.

Cooper, C.L. and Davidson, M. (1982), *High Pressure: Working Lives of Women Managers*, Glasgow: Fontana.

Courtenay-Smith, P., Murphy, R. and Appleyard, D. (2005), 'Were our Mums Happier?', *Daily Mail*, 29 April: 49–50.

Crompton, R. (2002), Review of Hakim, C. (2000), 'Work–lifestyle Choices in the 21st Century: Preference Theory', *British Journal of Industrial Relations*, **40**(1), 166.

Davidson, M.J. and Cooper, C.L. (1992), *Shattering the 'Glass Ceiling': The Woman Manager*, London: Paul Chapman Publishing.

Delphy, C. and Leonard, D. (1992), *Familiar Exploitation: A New Analysis of Marriage in Contemporary Western Societies*, Oxford: Polity Press in association with Blackwell Publishers.

Desmarais, S. and Alksnis, C. (2005), 'Gender Issues', in J. Barling, K. Kelloway and M. Frone (eds), *Handbook of Work Stress*, Thousand Oaks: Sage.

Dex, S., Joshi, H., Macran, S. and McCulloch, A. (1998), 'Women's Employment Transitions around Child Bearing', *Oxford Bulletin of Economics and Statistics*, **60**, 79–98.

Dienhart, A. (1998), *Reshaping Fatherhood: The Social Construction of Shared Parenting*, California: Sage.

Economist, The (2005), *Special Report: Women in Business, the Conundrum of the 'Glass Ceiling'*, 23 July: 67–9.

Equal Opportunities Commission (February 2004), *Pregnant and Productive: an Update on Our Investigation*, Equal Opportunities Commission Scotland.

Equal Opportunities Commission (2005a), *Sex and Power, Who Runs Britain, Manchester*, Equal Opportunities Commission.

Equal Opportunities Commission (2005b), 'Press Release: Victims of Pregnancy Discrimination Suffer in Silence', Manchester: Equal Opportunities Commission.

Gagg, M.E. (1961), *Helping at Home, A Ladybird Learning to Read Book* Loughborough: Ladybird.

Gatrell, C. (2005), *Hard Labour, The Sociology of Parenthood*, Maidenhead: Open University Press.

Gatrell, C. and Cooper, C.L. (2006), '(No) Cracks in the Glass Ceiling: Women Managers, Stress and the Barriers to Success', in D. Bilimoria and S. Piderit (eds), *The Handbook of Women in Business and Management*, Cheltenham, UK and Northampton, MA, USA: Edward Elgar.

Ginn, J., Arber, S., Brannen, J., Dale, A., Dex, S., Elias, P., Moss, P., Pahl, J., Roberts, C. and Rubery, J. (1996), 'Feminist Fallacies: A Reply to Hakim on Women's Employment', *British Journal of Sociology*, **47**, 167–74.

Hakim, C. (1996a), *Key Issues in Women's Work*, London: Athlone.

Hakim, C. (1996b), 'The Sexual Division of Labour and Women's Heterogeneity', *British Journal of Sociology*, **47**, 178–88.

Hakim, C. (2000), *Work-Lifestyle Choices in the 21st Century: Preference Theory*, Oxford: Oxford University Press.

Jackson, J. (2002), 'Letter of the Week, Letters', *The Mail on Sunday*, 16 June: 80.

Johnston, D. and Swanson, D. (2003), 'Invisible Mothers: A Content Analysis of Motherhood Ideologies and Myths in Magazines', *Sex Roles*, **40**(1–2), 21–33.

Kahne, H. (1981), 'Women in Paid Work: Some Consequences and Questions for Family Income and Expenditure', *Advances in Consumer Research*, **8**, 585–9.

Leppard, D. and Sanderson, D. (2005), 'Mother Care Gives Children the Best Start', *Sunday Times*, 2 October.

Lupton, D. and Barclay, L. (1997), *Constructing Fatherhood: Discourses and Experiences*, London: Sage.

Macran, S., Joshi, H. and Dex, S. (1996), 'Employment after Childbearing: a Survival Analysis', *Work, Employment and Society*, **10**, 273–96.

Malthouse, T.J. (1997), *Childcare, Business and Social Change*, London: Institute of Directors.

McRae, S. (2003), 'Choice and Constraints in Mothers' Employment Careers: McRae Replies to Hakim', *British Journal of Sociology*, **54**(4), 585–92.

Marshall, H. and Wetherall, M. (1989), 'Talking about Career and Gender Identities: a Discourse Analysis Perspective', in S. Skevington and D. Baker (eds), *The Social Identity of Women*, London: Sage, pp. 106–130.

Maushart, S. (2002), *Wifework: What Marriage Really Means for Women*, London: Bloomsbury.

Murray, W. (1964), *Things We Like, Ladybird Key Words Reading Scheme*, Loughborough: Ladybird.

Office of Population Censuses and Surveys (1990 and 1991), *Standard Occupational Classification*, Volumes 1–3, London: HMSO.

Padavic, I. and Reskin, B. (2002), *Women and Men at Work*, California: Sage.

Parsons, T. (1971), 'The Normal American Family', in B. Adams and T. Weirath (eds), *Readings on the Sociology of the Family*, Chicago: Markham, 53–66.

Parsons, T. and Bales, R. (1956), *Family and Socialization and Interaction Process*, London: Routledge and Kegan Paul.

Pullinger, J. and Summerfield, C. (1998), *Social Focus on Women and Men*, Office for National Statistics, London: The Stationery Office.

Rich, A. (1977), *Of Woman Born: Motherhood as Experience and Institution*, London: Virago.

Roberts, Y. (2004), 'High-fliers Still "Marginalised" by Motherhood', *The Observer* (News), 21 November.

Singh, V. and Vinnicombe, S. (2004), 'Why So Few Women Directors in Top UK Boardrooms? Evidence and Theoretical Explanations', *Corporate Governance*, **12**(4), 479–88.

Stephens, D., Hill, R.P., Commuri, S. and Gentry, J.W. (2001), 'Issues of Control in Two Extreme Household Types', *Asia Pacific Advances in Consumer Research*, **4**, 355–61.

Swan, J. and Cooper, C.L. (2005), *Time, Health and the Family: What Working Families Want*, London: Working Families.

Thair, T. and Risdon, A. (1999), 'Women in the Labour Market, Results from the Spring 1998 Labour Force Survey, *Labour Market Trends*, Office for National Statistics, **107**, 103–28.

Warin, J., Solomon, Y., Lewis, C. and Langford, W. (1999), *Fathers, Work and Family Life*, London: Family Policy Studies Centre.

Williams, J. (2000), *Unbending Gender: Why Family and Work Conflict and What To Do About It*, New York: Oxford University Press.

Williams, J.C. and Cohen Cooper, H. (2005), 'The Public Policy of Motherhood', in M. Biernat, F. Crosby and J.C. Williams (eds), 'The Material Wall: Research and Policy Perspectives on Discrimination Against Mothers', *Journal of Social Issues*, **60**(4), 849–65.

Worrall, L. and Cooper, C.L. (1999), 'Working Patterns and Working Hours: Their Impact on UK Managers', *Leadership and Organization Development Journal*, **20**(1), 6–10.

6. The gendered nature of workplace mistakes

Patricia Bryans

INTRODUCTION

When my manager found out about my mistake he behaved like a mad dog. (Man)

I told my supervisor but he told me not to say anything. (Man)

The Marketing Manager found it out. He laughed when he saw my embarrassment. (Woman)

My manager brushed it off as unimportant. (Woman)

These are some of the responses reported when I asked professionals how their manager or organization had reacted to a mistake they had made at work. The responses represent missed opportunities for individual and organizational learning and are practices which are potentially damaging to employees, organizations and clients.

This chapter explores professional men and women's experience of making a mistake at work, presenting empirical data resulting from a questionnaire and from interviews with men and women from six different professions (teaching, social work, management, human resource management, the police service and health professions). The focus is particularly on the impact of the mistakes on the individuals concerned, discussing their feelings and behaviour both at the time of the mistake and in retrospect, and on the reported reactions and response of their managers. However, the study also concludes with a consideration of the implications for the management and development of people at work. For individuals, making mistakes can be a positive way of learning if we can help to provide a safer environment to support the learner to reflect and share the learning with others. In organizations there are important implications for the management and development of people. For example, anonymous reporting procedures may encourage 'blame-free' cultures and may well reduce error, but may do little to restore the confidence and re-build the professional practice of the mistake-maker. Disciplining people who make serious mistakes may only teach other staff that mistakes should be covered up.

The mistakes of professionals in public services, for example, can result in tragic consequences and high profile criticisms (such as that of cardiac doctors operating on children at the Bristol Royal Infirmary in the 1990s). Fox (2005) reports a survey in the USA in which 80 per cent of doctors and 48 per cent of nurses claimed they had seen colleagues make mistakes, but only 10 per cent had spoken up about them. Recent research by SHL Group (Personneltoday.com 2005) claims that UK employees top the league in covering up mistakes at work, with 72 per cent of the errors they make never coming to light. It reports workers keep quiet about their blunders and managers fail to spot and correct them, with an estimated cost to UK business of £9.8 billion a year. Doherty and Horne (2002) claim that the human cost of even a single error in a public service may be unacceptable.

The professional context is changing rapidly due to developments in technology and advances in knowledge. People expect professionals to be more accountable, leaving professionals more open to criticism than ever before. Although we all make mistakes, we seem to fear or dread making them, despite the opportunities for learning that can arise from them. Popper (1963) claimed that the essays and lectures which comprise his famous book, *Conjectures and Refutation: the Growth of Scientific Knowledge*, are based on one very simple theme – the thesis that we can learn from our mistakes. If we are to learn, it is important that mistakes are not covered up and that individuals are supported in their learning.

LEARNING AT WORK

Boud and Garrick (1999) suggest that learning has recently moved from the periphery to become the lifeblood that sustains organizations, leaving few employment opportunities for those who do not continue to learn and no place for managers who do not appreciate their own vital role in fostering learning. Indeed, research by KPMG Consulting (cited in *People Management*, 2005) estimated that 80 per cent of learning at work occurred informally rather than in formal education and training situations. Matthews and Candy (1999: 49) argue:

> However, rather than being consciously planned, it is now recognised that by far the greatest proportion – perhaps as much as 90 per cent – of organizational learning actually occurs incidentally or adventitiously, including through exposure to the opinions and practices of others working in the same context.

Marsick and Watkins (1990) classified this workplace learning as informal, where learning is mainly experiential and is often planned (such as coaching and mentoring) and incidental, where learning is unintentional, the by-product of another activity. They state: 'We believe that informal and incidental learning, which are difficult to organize and control, represent a neglected, but crucial, area' (Marsick and Watkins, 1990: 3). Billett (1999: 152) sees this learning as 'authentic and rich opportunities to reinforce and extend individuals' knowledge'.

Making a mistake breaks our routine with a jolt and heightens our attention, thus providing a particular opportunity for learning. Marsick and Watkins (1990) see learning from mistakes as an example of 'incidental learning', but what we learn may not be 'inherently correct'. Clients, individual professionals, their organizations and the professions themselves, may have conflicting interests. But if the learning is 'inherently correct' it will avoid the repetition of mistakes, whilst maintaining the confidence of individuals to continue their professional practice.

MAKING MISTAKES

From his studies on error Reason (1990: 9) provides this definition of mistakes:

> Mistakes may be defined as deficiencies or failures in the judgemental and/or inferential processes involved in the selection of an objective or in the specification of the means to achieve it, irrespective of whether or not the actions directed by this decision-scheme run according to plan.

Organizational rather than individual mistakes have been the focus of much of the literature on mistakes. For example, in his case studies of organizations' mistakes and successes Hartley (1994) concluded strongly on the 'desirability of flexibility in an unknown or changing environment'. Perversely, responding to such an environment may well create the conditions where mistakes are more likely. Pearn (1995) sees mistakes as the 'necessary consequence of challenge and experimentation', arguing that organizational intolerance of mistakes will not lead to innovative learning but only to learning 'adaptively' (that is, be able to improve on what they already know and do). Change and uncertainty are characteristic of many organizations. Brooks (1967 cited in Schon, 1995: 15) claims that the professions are faced with an 'unprecedent requirement for adaptability'. Professionals, particularly in the people professions, have to work in what Schon (1995: 42) calls 'a swampy lowland where situations are confusing "messes" incapable of technical solution'. In this swamp are the problems of greatest concern and of crucial importance, yet 'when asked to describe their methods of enquiry, they [professionals] speak of experience, trial and error, intuition and muddling through' (Schon, 1995: 43).

Argyris (1992) and Senge (1991), among others, have written on the need for learning organizations which encourage staff to reflect, develop, think differently and experiment. Yet Pearn and Honey's (1997) analysis shows that the fear of making mistakes or the perceived consequences of being discovered can be so great that efforts are made to try to avoid making mistakes of any kind. They claim that this can have a negative impact on innovation and creativity, promoting individual interests at the expense of the whole organization. But individual interests have a real impact. Hine (2004: 238) noted that managers:

> engage competitively to achieve career success and are concerned to avoid failure. This success–failure duality is a common feature of life generally. We aspire to be good at what we do ... we mostly wish to avoid being regarded as failures.

Success at work may rest on us appearing powerful and infallible. Moore (2000) calls for us to end 'the myth of perfection' and expose our fallibility and praises the courage of those senior doctors who have publicly admitted their past errors in an effort to stop the destructive blaming culture.

In the face of ambiguity most managers react defensively, afraid they will make a mistake (Argyris, 1992). Pearn (1996) found that individuals dislike admitting to mistakes through fear, guilt, blame and possible ill-effects on their personal standing and reputation. Pearn *et al.* (1998: 14) noted that the language used to talk about mistakes is often emotional and highly-charged:

> the language we use to talk about our mistakes is almost always negative ... because we feel threatened and upset by them .... We need words which let us talk about our mistakes in a non-evaluative and neutral way.

Argyris (1992) stresses the importance of breaking the trap of defensive reasoning to start reasoning productively in order to create truly continuous improvement – learning to learn. However, Clutterbuck and Kernaghan's (1990: 55) research into failed companies concluded:

> Less than one in three executives of failed companies learns from the experience. The results of our survey show clearly that people who have presided over the disintegration and collapse of a company usually do not learn from their mistakes.

Clutterbuck and Kernaghan (1990: 57) suggest five main reasons why people ignore the opportunities to learn from mistakes: sheer arrogance (I know this business), fear (let's not upset the apple-cart), overconfidence (we are good at crises), lack of confidence (in own ability to extract the correct lessons), or lack of interest (it's yesterday's problem). Other forms of 'inappropriate learning' are identified by Fineman and Gabriel (1996: 121) who claim that people learn the simple, but demoralizing, lesson that the best thing they can do is protect themselves and that moral principles give way to the practicalities of surviving by blaming someone else or blaming 'the system.' Blaming the system depersonalizes blame and can be a healthy response if it means there is no need for a 'human scapegoat'.

> Instead of orienting the organization's efforts to censuring a single person, it looks at the organization's processes and seeks changes which will prevent similar mistakes happening again. In this way, 'blaming the system' can become a first step towards organizational learning and improvement. Yet, more commonly, blaming the system is the classic excuse for avoiding change and responsibility. It is a failure to recognize and examine a mistake, and therefore a failure to learn from it. (Fineman and Gabriel, 1996: 116)

However, Pearn and Honey (1997) state that all the individuals in their study claimed to have learned from their mistakes, many stating that they could not have learned their lessons in any other way. They emphasize that we must come to terms with the emotions arising from our mistakes to ensure that they do not adversely affect confidence and self-esteem.

Pearn *et al.* (1998: 192–193) present suggestions for managers to follow to help them 'harness the positive powers of mistakes.' Managers should provide a supportive framework to harness the learning potential, as mistakes can play a critical role in learning. They should not deal with mistakes destructively, but use coaching, counselling, feedback and dialogue skills. In order to do this, managers have to deal with their own emotions as well as those of their staff.

Learning from Mistakes – Tensions

Two ideas emerge from the literature as being particularly relevant to this study. They can be described as tensions which embody the difficulties of dealing with mistakes. The first was raised by Kotter (1995) who comments on an underlying tension in the literature between the potentially catastrophic effects of even simple mistakes and of the need to make them in order to learn. In high-risk industries where catastrophic results may occur, simulation training is regularly used to allow novices the opportunity to experiment and learn safely. Such approaches are often used also in the development, supervision and assessment of practising professionals. Away from the relative safety of simulation situations, people wish to avoid failure and feeling embarrassed, threatened, vulnerable and foolish and unfortunately these are all associated with making mistakes.

The second tension concerns the accountability of the mistake-maker. Doherty and Horne (2002) claim managers must manage the tension between the need to learn from mistakes and the need for employees to accept that they are accountable for the consequences of the mistakes they make. Accountability and organizational systems of reward and punishment may not be conducive to learning. Morgan (1997: 89) claims that systems of accountability foster defensive behaviours like covering up mistakes and hiding problems that will 'put them in a bad light'. These processes of self-protection are used both consciously and unconsciously by people in organizations.

THE RESEARCH APPROACH

The study explores mistakes made by professionals at work, including their definitions of mistakes, their views on what learning has resulted from them and their perceptions of management or organizational responses and reactions. The study provided data on the experiences of individuals in an important, sensitive and under-researched area. My emphasis was not on the nature and prevention of error through observations of practice or laboratory experiments and simulations. Narrative approaches to research, which aim to learn about mistakes from the stories people tell about their experiences, were more appropriate for this study. The 'critical incident technique' was used given that the study aimed to investigate a potentially major event from the perspective of the actor (Chell 1998). Making a mistake can be a critical incident in the working life of professionals, leading individuals to make pivotal decisions, change priorities or direction or even to bring new aspects of the 'self' into being (Becker 1966, cited in Measor 1985). Certain aspects of the 'self' which can work to hinder learning and development may be reinforced. Analysing critical incidents can help us to gain insights into the way identities are built because 'we place the actor's definition of what is important at the forefront' (Strauss 1959).

The first stage of the study involved a questionnaire, completed by 90 respondents (45 men and 45 women), to determine whether individuals would be able to recall and be prepared to discuss details of mistakes they had made at work. Most respondents were 30 to 50 years old and experienced rather than new entrants to their professions. Participants were asked for their definition of a mistake, to describe a particular mistake they had made at work, their feelings about it (both at the time and in retrospect), what they were tempted to do and what they actually did about their mistake. They noted the consequences of the mistake, the managerial or organizational response to it (if any) and what and how they learned from the mistake, including whether they have avoided repeating their mistake and if it has affected how they deal with other people making mistakes.

The second stage of the research used narrative approaches to capture deeper qualitative data to enrich the findings. Twelve interviews which used elements of critical incident approaches were carried out. Participants told the detailed stories of their mistakes in the context of their career, their organization and working lives. The participants (six men and six women) all belonged to the people service sector. The nature of the research was exploratory and caution should be observed when making general inferences given the sample size, the age and experience level of participants, and the differences in organizational environments.

FINDINGS

Our Mistakes – Participants' Definitions and Descriptions

The questionnaires and the interviews started with the participants' definitions of a mistake. Women seemed to personalize their answers, thinking subjectively about the issue, whereas men tended to make more objective statements, more like dictionary definitions. Over half the men surveyed and four of six male interviewees defined mistakes primarily in terms of their undesirable or unacceptable consequences, for example 'An act or an omission which is outside accepted norms or established guidelines and may have an adverse resultant effect on individuals or the organization.'

Women mainly defined mistakes in terms of doing wrong. Wrong-doing emphasizes the actor's behaviour and actions, not just the outcome. According to a female interviewee a mistake is 'Something you do that is wrong but you didn't mean to'.

Pearn *et al.* (1998) found that 57 per cent of the mistakes they analysed fell into the category of information mistakes. While the result is not so strong here, almost half the women did report these types of error and it was also the most common error among men. These mistakes were classified as minor but still viewed as very important by the participants. For example, a teacher described confusing two chemical processes in her own mind and proceeding to teach them 'the wrong way round'.

Some mistakes were very serious and participants revealed, male and female, that they had never disclosed their mistake. A health professional described an error he had made in administering medication to a patient: 'I knew that medication errors were treated very seriously – I had recently seen a nurse sacked for it.' A female doctor similarly described a mistake of a medication error: 'I was dealing with a woman who was in a diabetic coma. I put in a drip and carefully checked the drugs. But I cocked up. I ended up keeping her in a coma for 24 hours longer than she should have been.'

A female senior police officer also described a mistake when she mistook an ill member of the public for a drunk. The person later died.

The major action taken by both men (15) and women (26) was to sort out or put right their mistakes. More men than women were tempted to cover up or deny their mistakes and in the end three men did so. Several men (but no women) quoted the exact cost of their mistake to their organizations. In discussing the consequences of their mistakes, the most common response from men concerned the damage to their own personal reputation:

> My credibility was reduced, which was rather over-reacting, as I actually discovered the mistake and corrected it. (Man)

> My personal record was tarnished. (Man)

The importance of honesty and owning up was again mentioned by several women. In the survey women made 33 mentions of the importance of owning up to their mistakes and apologizing. Only four men mentioned owning up and only two mentioned that they apologized. Twenty men chose their reported mistake because it was the only mistake they could think of or because it had happened recently or because something had happened recently to remind them of it. However, 22 women (but only four men) say they are still affected by their mistake or that it is always in their minds.

> I chose this mistake because after 12 years it's still vivid in my mind. I don't forget things easily, especially when they have such a profound effect on me. (Woman)

However, five men commented that the mistake was their biggest mistake and nine other men chose to report on it because of its seriousness or potential seriousness.

> Biggest mistake I made in my working life and I guess it has been hidden and not discussed by anybody. This gives an opportunity to release this. (Man)

Feelings about the Mistake

Women reported feeling strong emotions at the time of the mistake. Fifteen women (but only four men) said they felt 'silly, stupid or foolish'. Thirteen women (but only two men) said they felt 'embarrassed'. Eleven women (but only four men) described being 'angry with themselves'. Men were more likely to feel 'angry with others' although five men did describe themselves as feeling 'mortified, devastated, gutted or terrible' (as did ten women). Seven women described themselves as feeling a combination of 'sorry, remorse and regret' but no men mentioned that they were sorry.

It is interesting to note the large numbers of women who expressed feelings of embarrassment, stupidity and annoyance with themselves. These feelings are all directed at themselves and equate definition of mistakes as 'doing wrong'. Here, again, the emphasis is on the actor, rather than a depersonalized objective view of the situation. In contrast, twice as many men were angry at others as were annoyed or angry with themselves. A few respondents (men) described feelings which Marsick and Watkins (1990) might conclude showed 'inappropriate' learning. These included 'not bothered', 'smug' or 'sure I'd got away with it', 'lazy', 'cynical' and 'on an adrenalin high'.

Respondents were asked how they felt about their mistake now. The most popular response for men (15) was one which suggested that they view their mistake as over and as something with which they have come to terms. In contrast, 27 women (but only seven men) expressed strong feelings and emotions of embarrassment, that thinking of the mistake still makes them cringe, of still feeling very upset, being annoyed with themselves, of sickness, fear or panic, that they still feel hurt, resentful that the mistake was dealt with badly. The intensity of the some women's feelings after the event suggests an inability to put it behind them. For example:

> Although the experience is over six years old I have only just come to terms with my indecision and my own belief that I made an unforgivable personal mistake which had such a large impact on my life. (Woman)

Management/Organizational Reactions

Respondents were asked for the reactions to their mistake from within their organizations and a wide variety of responses resulted. Sometimes there was little response to relatively minor mistakes, but nonetheless this was sometimes a concern to the mistake-makers, who expected something more. Several women commented on the positive effect on their learning when their mistake had been well handled in their organizations. For example:

> The reactions of my manager had a positive effect on my learning. I admitted I'd made a mistake and knew it would be unlikely to happen again as I'd always double check in the future .... They were understanding .... I don't think they made a 'big thing' of it as the rest of my work was of a high quality and this was a one off. (Woman)

Another female respondent reported:

> I learned 'admit it and don't ever try to hide it'. He did a sort of a training session with me to check out that I did know what to do, could do it right ... I think it was an appropriate organizational response. There was no confession to the patient – she wasn't harmed. I had told my immediate manager, the SHO [senior house officer]

but I didn't want it sorted for me. I coughed up to the big boss myself. He was OK compared to most consultants and the kind of reaction you might expect.

A male health professional was asked whether his organization had found out about his mistake. He was emphatic in his answer:

> No. I didn't tell them. If they had found out I would probably have been sacked – certainly severely disciplined. I would have had a warning on my record for five years.

Eight men and six women said that their organization did not find out about their mistakes, while five women and three men said the organization accepted that it was a mistake and was 'one of those things' that happened. Six women but no men described the organization's reaction as 'supportive'.

> I got such a supportive response from my supervisors. Had they taken a more punitive attitude, I might have been tempted not to tell anyone if I made a mistake again. (Woman)

Four women but no men were allowed to, or helped to, sort out the mistake as illustrated by the following quote:

> I accepted that I had been at fault and then worked with my manager to try to find a damage limitation solution. This was only made possible by the positive attitude of my line manager. The initial reaction was anger from my line manager then the need to work out a suitable solution. (Woman)

Around one-third of respondents reported negative and unhelpful organizational responses including anger, being laughed at, being blamed, being unsupported and having their mistake covered up. The following statements illustrate the range of responses:

> My boss didn't help me work through this situation – did not inform me or brief me … I should have been given guidance. (Man)

> I never have, or ever would treat people the way I was treated. I received no support whatsoever. (Woman)

> They should have recognized it as a mistake and asked can we change the system to prevent future repetition? You can't legislate for human culpability. (Woman)

Respondents were asked their desired organizational reaction. The most popular response from women (12) was that the organization should have supported them; a very personal reaction compared to the most popular response from men (11) that the organization should have investigated the mistake and/or reviewed its procedures. The sample indicates a more objective and detached view from the men in the survey compared to personalized subjective responses of the women.

When Other People Make Mistakes

In considering how they respond to mistakes made by other people nine women (but no men) recognized the possible emotional impact of making mistakes, saying they helped others realize 'it's not the end of the world'. Women interviewees echoed these views:

> I'm tolerant of mistakes. It's usually not the end of the world. I'm a supportive colleague. (Woman)

> I'm more tolerant of other people's mistakes. I insist on honesty and if I get it then I won't blame. (Woman)

Helping others to sort out their mistakes and discussing other people's mistakes with them was important to men and women. Turning others' mistakes into a learning experience and checking out that the mistake-maker had learned from the experience were also important, as illustrated by this quote:

> I felt that I did not receive support to explain this issue, fully to learn from the mistake. I would do this for others. (Man)

However, nine men (but only one woman) claimed that mistakes will happen and saw little role for themselves, again de-centring the person from the mistake. For example, male a human resources manager stated:

> I always look for the cause of the error not who's to blame ... I don't blame. I follow total quality management which looks at systems not individuals to blame. I'm annoyed by the 'blame mode'. We should look at what went wrong, not who is to blame.

While a female health professional, throughout her interview, stressed the importance of honesty, owning up to mistakes, the importance of being allowed to sort out your own mistakes for yourself and the need for appropriate reactions from the organization to ensure learning and no repetition.

DISCUSSION AND DEVELOPMENT

The findings explore some interesting aspects of organizational life. It is clear that professional people do make mistakes at work and that they are sometimes serious mistakes with repercussions for individuals and organizations.

The women in this research felt and still feel powerful emotions connected to their mistakes and they tend to internalize and personalize that experience. Often the women's feelings of self-blame could be attributed to the fact that they felt that the clients had received a raw deal, even when the problem had been appropriately solved from the point of view of the organization or company policy. The women in this study emphasized work relationships, providing the best service to clients and colleagues and a sense of self-worth. Space, time and support are needed to come to terms with the mistake, rationalize it and re-build themselves. There are interesting resonances with Gilligan's (1982) argument that women find their own identity through their relationships with others. Belenky *et al.*'s (1986) typology of how women learn emphasizes that relationships, communication and intimacy are more important to women than to men. Women, in particular, need to forgive themselves and be reassured by their managers that they have been forgiven for their mistakes and are still viewed as valuable members of staff. Handy (1990: 198) claims forgiveness is crucial to learning; we must forgive ourselves and others must forgive us.

> Too many organizations neither forgive nor forget, unaware that by doing so they are putting brakes on the wheel, because learning needs space, the room to test and the freedom to get it wrong.

Many more men sampled in this study were able to rationalize their mistakes and appear to recover from them quickly, realizing that a whole range of circumstances (such as over-work) led to their error. The emotions of shame and embarrassment were hardly mentioned by the men in this study. Feelings appeared more likely to be directed outwards through anger at others or by blaming the pressure they were under or by emphasizing the particularities of the context in which they were operating. Men it seemed were more concerned than women to restore and re-build their personal reputations after making a mistake perhaps because in general, men are more likely to attribute success – or expected to attribute success – to their own actions and failure to external events, while women are the opposite, attributing failure – or expected to attribute failure – to their own actions and success to external events (McMahan 1971, cited in Wilson 1995).

Both men and women reported that they personally wanted to deal with the implications of their mistakes. For men this tied in with the notion of putting the record straight and restoring their public image. For women, this was reported as a strong desire to make things right, to apologize and reassure others. Many women remarked on the importance of personally apologizing to clients when they were affected by mistakes, but organizations can discourage apologizing to clients, perhaps because of fears of litigation. Moore (2000: 32) quotes the daughter of a woman killed through a mistake:

> If they had said at the start that they were really sorry that a mistake had been made, that would have been the end of it.

Moore's five suggestions (explanation, admission, prevention, redress and apology) for satisfying aggrieved patients are applicable more widely than to the medical profession and may, indeed, provide a template for how organizations should deal with mistakes. Moore (2000) suggests we should learn from high risk industries, which have pioneered the development of safer systems which limit the risk and minimize the effects of mistakes. These rely on mandatory and confidential reporting systems which log and investigate without having to find someone to blame. Minor incidents and near-misses are also recorded to provide 'free lessons' in prevention. The no-blame reporting systems are often anonymous and focus on learning lessons and putting them into practice. However, this study raised the possibility that such solutions alone are stereotypically masculine and rational, and may not deal with the important emotional effects that can be so damaging to mistake-makers. Models of successful managers emphasize the rational manager, working calmly and logically towards the right answers to organizational problems and are essentially stereotypically masculine (Patching 1999). He claims that the intellectual mode tends to be favoured by men rather than women, therefore men seem more willing to work to the rational model of manager, effectively denigrating the potential value, significance and contributions of all other aspects of the human mind. West (2005: 39) confirms the importance of paying attention to emotions:

> The idea that we can create effective organizations by focusing on performance and ignoring the role of our emotions is based on the false premise that emotions can be ignored at work.

Inappropriate organizational responses caused pain and distress, especially the actions and reactions of managers. None of the participants thought that their organization should have done nothing or very little. They wanted the organization to react and they were often frustrated when they were brushed aside when they wanted to discuss it. Even those who described their mistakes as minor felt that their organizations should react. When the organization's response was supportive and when they felt that their mistake had been supportively dealt with, participants commented very favourably. Women in particular felt 'they should have supported me' (only four men gave this answer). This is a further example of how women tend to personalize the experience of making a mistake. In contrast, the most popular answer among men was a more rational and objective suggestion that the organization should have investigated the mistake and reviewed its procedures if necessary. Men in this study neither expected nor received support from their organizations when they made mistakes. Overall, both men and women wanted their organizations to treat them fairly and take them seriously, let them sort out their mistakes for themselves (perhaps with help) and not have their mistakes taken from them and sorted out for them. It was important to women if their managers took the time to re-affirm to them their worth as a professional and to the organization, despite the mistake. The importance of support was carried forward into how sympathetically they dealt with mistakes made by others.

Sometimes organizational reactions to mistakes were so inappropriate that the mistake-makers were left feeling not just unsupported, but actively treated unjustly. Some organizational practice discourages openness and leaves mistake-makers with lasting feelings of unjust treatment. The disciplinary process should protect clients and enhance the learning and performance of the mistake-maker. If disciplinary policies are used to blame and let off steam, to punish rather than to ensure the correction of inappropriate practice, organizations may end up with resentful or risk-averse staff or with staff who do not know what is appropriate practice and who cover up mistakes.

Professionals did learn from making their mistakes at work and the learning took place mainly as a result of the impact of the experience itself and through self-reflection, often ongoing for many years after the event (particularly for women). Some learned new knowledge as a result of help from a lead professional, manager or professional colleague from another discipline, but most stated that they had learned to be more careful. These results were unsurprising, especially when many mistakes are careless slips or minor errors. It was clear that these professionals had learned something about themselves and about others. Several women, in particular, described their learning in terms of a re-affirmation of the importance of honesty, principles and moral values. Often the mistake had a long-term impact on their practice.

CONCLUSION

Helping staff to learn and to recover from mistakes is a key role for managers and senior professionals. This requires that managers (who are still largely male) recognize the different learning styles and requirements of their staff. Pearn *et al.* (1998: 15) are convinced that 'most managers simply lack the skills to manage mistake making in a constructive way'. This research suggests that managers and organizations have to be gender aware to ensure best practice. We need managers and organizations which can accept the emotions which accompany mistakes and help mistake-makers to deal with the emotions as well as the mistake. When people (mainly women in this study) continue to live with their mistakes it can undermine their professional practice and their willingness to take risks. If people (mainly men in this study) move on from their mistakes and are inappropriately managed, challenged and supported, there is a danger that their learning may be shallow or unsuitable.

Kotter's (1995) expressed concerns about the potentially catastrophic effects of even simple mistakes coupled with the need to make them in order to learn. Doherty and Horne (2002) asked how can managers manage the tension between the need to learn from mistakes and the need for employees to accept that they are accountable for the mistakes they make. The empirical data presented offers no easy solutions to these tensions, but show that rational, objective solutions which ignore emotional, subjective experiences may only cause further problems. Good management of mistakes will accept our human imperfections and will focus openly on learning and the improvement of practice. It will pay attention to the emotional and the rational and to the needs of all those affected (including the mistake-maker) in gender-inclusive ways.

REFERENCES

Argyris, C. (1990), *Overcoming Organizational Defences*, Needham Heights, MA: Allyn and Bacon.

Argyris, C. (1992), *On Organizational Learning*, Oxford: Blackwell.

Belenky, M.F., Clinchy, B.M., Goldberger, N.R. and Tarule, J.M. (1986), *Women's Ways of Knowing*, New York: Basic Books.

Billett, S. (1999), 'Guided Learning at Work', in D. Boud and J. Garrick (eds), *Understanding Learning at Work*, London: Routledge.

Boud, D. and Garrick, J. (eds) (1999), *Understanding Learning at Work*, London: Routledge.

Chell, E. (1998), 'Critical Incident Technique', in G. Symon and C. Cassell (eds), *Qualitative Methods and Analysis in Organizational Research*, London: Sage.

Clutterbuck, D. and Kernaghan, S. (1990), *The Phoenix Factor*, London: Weidenfeld & Nicholson.

Doherty, T.L. and Horne, T. (2002), *Managing Public Services*, London: Routledge.

Equal Opportunities Commission (2000), *A Checklist for Gender Proofing Research*, Manchester: Equal Opportunities Commission.

Fineman, S. and Gabriel, Y. (1996), *Experiencing Organizations*, London: Sage.

Fox, M. (2005), 'Survey Finds 80% of US Doctors Witness Mistakes', www.alertnet.org/printable.htm?URL=thenews/newsdesk/N26527689.htm January 2005.

Garrick, J. (1999), 'The Dominant Discourses of Learning at Work', in D. Boud and J. Garrick (eds), *Understanding Learning at Work*, London: Routledge.

Gilligan, C. (1982), *In a Different Voice*, Cambridge: Harvard University Press.

Handy, C. (1990), *Inside Organizations*, London: BBC Publications.

Hartley, R. (1994), *Management Mistakes and Successes*, New York: John Wiley & Sons.

Hine, J.A.H.S. (2004), 'Success and Failure in Bureaucratic Organizations: The Role of Emotion in Managerial Morality', *Business Ethics: A European Review*, **13**(4), 229–42.

Kotter, J.P. (1995), 'Leading Change: Why Transformation Efforts Fail', *Harvard Business Review*, **73**(2), 59–67.

Marsick, V. and Watkins, K. (1990), *Informal and Incidental Learning in the Workplace*, London: Routledge.

Matthews, J.H. and Candy, P.C. (1999), 'New Dimensions in Learning and Knowledge', in D. Boud and J. Garrick (eds), *Understanding Learning at Work*, London: Routledge.

Measor, L. (1985), 'Critical Incidents in the Classroom', in S.J. Ball and I.F. Goodson (eds), *Teachers' Lives and Careers*, Lewes: Falmer Press.

Moore, W. (2000), *Why Doctors Make Mistakes*, London: Channel Four Television.

Morgan, G. (1997), *Images of Organization* (New edition), Newbury Park, CA: Sage.

Patching, K. (1999), *Management and Organization Development: Beyond Arrows, Boxes and Circles*, London: Macmillan.

Pearn, M. (1995), 'Learning from Mistakes', Paper presented to the IPD National Conference, Harrogate: Institute of Personnel and Development.

Pearn, M. (1996), 'Managers Making Mistakes: Moving from a Blame Culture to a Gain Culture', Paper presented to the IPD National Conference, Harrogate: Institute of Personnel and Development.

Pearn, M. and Honey, P. (1997), 'From Error Terror to Wonder Blunder', *People Management*, 6 March, 42–5.

Pearn, M., Mulrooney, C. and Payne, T. (1998), *Ending the Blame Culture*, Aldershot: Gower Publishing Limited.

People Management (2005), 'An Informal Approach Gets Better Results,' *People Management*, 30 June, 14.

Personneltoday.com, 'UK Staff Top the Cover-up League Table for Mistakes at Work', www.personneltoday.com/Articles/Article.aspx?1iArticleID=27684 January 2005.

Popper, K. (1963), *Conjectures and Refutation: the Growth of Scientific Knowledge*, London: Routledge & Kegan Paul.

Reason, J. (1990), *Human Error*, Cambridge: Cambridge University Press.

Schon, D.A. (1995), *The Reflective Practitioner: How Professionals Think in Action*, Aldershot: Arena Ashgate Publishing.

Senge, P. (1991), *The Fifth Discipline*, London: Century.

Strauss, A.L. (1959), *Mirrors and Masks: The Search for Identity*, Glencoe: Free Press.

West, M. (2005), 'Hope Springs', *People Management*, 13 October, 38–9.

Wilson, F.M. (1995), *Organizational Behaviour and Gender*, Maidenhead: McGraw-Hill.

PART II

Business and public sector dimensions

7. Opening the boardroom doors to women directors

Val Singh and Susan Vinnicombe

INTRODUCTION

This chapter is about the appointment of women into the decision-making positions of corporations. In the UK, the FTSE 100 company boardrooms represent the pinnacle of private sector careers. But these boardrooms are dominated by men. Research has shown that women seeking directorships face challenges in their careers additional to those faced by their male peers.

Concern with the slow progress of women to top boards has led to a number of research initiatives in the last decade. In the USA since 1996, Catalyst has undertaken a census of Fortune 500 (later extended to Fortune 1000) companies with women directors, now reporting biennially. Following Catalyst's example, the Cranfield Centre for Developing Women Business Leaders has monitored progress in FTSE 100 companies since 1999, reporting annually.

This chapter will first examine the progress of women on to top corporate boards, the career barriers they face en route, and the position of women directors in the UK from 1989. An overview of theoretical perspectives will cast more light on the persistence of the barriers to the boardroom for women. The business case for gender diversity in the boardroom will identify the added value that diversity can bring. The 2005 statistics from the Female FTSE Index will be presented, featuring the characteristics of companies with women directors. The backgrounds of the women directors will be examined for patterns that help to explain their career success. The current situation in the top UK boardrooms will be compared with that in other European countries. Some initiatives for change will be reported, and the chapter concludes with consideration of the value of diversity and independence for building better functioning boards. Most of the UK's top boardroom doors are now opening to women, but generally still only a token proportion of those who are selected to enter are female.

REACHING THE BOARDROOM

Women face the same challenges as their male peers to get to the boardroom, but in addition, they have to overcome the consequences of sex discrimination in selection, development, pay and promotion. The Sex Discrimination Act came into force in the UK in 1975, but there is still enormous disparity in terms of career progression, and the gender pay gap was 17 per cent in 2005, improving but still significant (EOC 2006). The extremely low representation of women in senior ranks of organizations means that there are few female role models to emulate and few female mentors to learn from, as well as little same-sex social interaction. The visibility of the few women directors is both advantageous in that the few women are quickly noticed, but disadvantageous if the women are not successful.

A study of men and women directors' careers revealed that they had very similar career paths (Vinnicombe and Singh 2003). In the early stages, they consistently performed extremely well, gaining reputation for their technical prowess. They drew the attention of mentors, who were sources of support and information about opportunities in other areas, often with line and budget responsibility. As they undertook the challenging new jobs, they gained valuable experience in dealing with change, taking risk, and experiencing and learning from failure. Gradually accumulating a wide-ranging portfolio of developmental experiences, the men and women attracted attention from ever more senior sponsors, and so the cycle continued until they reached board level. There were some differences in that the men reported actively approaching their mentors and seeking out opportunities for development, whilst the women indicated that they were spotted by senior people, and made it clear to them that they would welcome some informal mentoring support. Some of the women reflected their reluctance to take some of the promotions offered to them, but recognized afterwards that these were an essential part of preparation for directorships.

Women face the challenge of stereotyping as they approach senior positions. 'Think director, think male' attitudes still prevail in the UK, particularly for executive directorships (see Chapter 1). Promotion at senior level depends not just on performance delivered but also on personal reputation and influence. This means having gathered the right kinds of career experiences (for example line and budget responsibility) and developing good relationships with the necessary sponsors. International experience is said to be valuable for those seeking directorships (Daily *et al*. 2000), but women's family responsibilities may impede their access to such experience (see Chapter 5).

Women tend to be excluded from the powerful corporate networks which are still almost all male (Ibarra 1992). Women often eschew the need for managing visibility and upwards influence, opting out of the 'promotion game' (Singh *et al.* 2002). Yet unless they are known to those responsible for board level appointments and to the executive search consultants, they are unlikely to be invited to apply or be shortlisted for the top positions. The Higgs Review (2003) found that only 4 per cent of new directors were interviewed for their positions; the rest were so well known to the appointers that interviews were not seen to be necessary.

THEORIES INFORMING WOMEN'S SLOW PROGRESS ON TO BOARDS

Social Identity Theory

There are many theories about women's slower and more limited career progression compared to that of men, and Singh and Vinniscombe (2004a) provides an overview of some theories with particular relevance to women's access to the boardroom.

A social identity theoretical perspective (Tajfel 1982) gives insight into the difficulties that women have in gaining access to the boardroom. Individuals are categorized and categorize others by their social identification with particular personal characteristics such as sex, race and age, and group characteristics such as job level and social class. The phenomenon of homophily is evident, as people in privileged groups such as high status males tend to prefer to associate with those similar to themselves (Ibarra 1992). They behave in ways congruent with their collective privileged identity, and tend to see in-group member performance as higher than that of dissimilar individuals. As corporate boards are comprised mainly of males from similar backgrounds, including exclusive schools, colleges and clubs, it is not surprising that females find it difficult to gain access to the boardroom. Social identity theory would predict that successful female directors would be likely to have similar backgrounds to male directors, but would need to have additional qualities such as higher performance or higher social capital to overcome the in-group similarity advantage held by male candidates. Women at the top often comment that they had to work harder and be better than their male peers at every stage en route.

Tokenism Theory

When women are in a minority at the top of large companies, they are said to be 'tokens' (Kanter, 1997). Token theory suggests that when percentages of representation in the community fall below around 15 per cent, those who are different are seen as representing their category rather than being seen as individual, because they are so unusual. With a minority of between 15 per cent and 30 per cent, the population is seen as skewed, whilst that between 30 per cent and 40 per cent is seen as tilted. In the skewed population, the minority individuals are less isolated and often provide social support for others. Splits of 60:40 are seen as more or less balanced, true balance being reached at 50:50. Token individuals in senior positions have to give attention and make decisions about how to behave in order to fit in the group, using energy that those in the dominant category (males) do not have to expend. Very often, the tokens will seek to be assimilated by having a public face at work, keeping a private face hidden, which for women can lead to feelings of inauthenticity at work. Kanter's view is that when there are two women in a senior team, the isolation is much less, and several women directors have confirmed to this chapter's authors that this is indeed the case in their experience on FTSE 100 boards.

Resource Dependency Theory

Coming from the strategy field, resource dependency theory holds that board members are recruited to provide the firm with access to valuable resources necessary for survival in the longer term (Pfeffer and Salancik 1978). Each new director brings resources in the form of human capital (education, knowledge, skills, experience) as well as access to others through their social capital (networks, contacts, links to critical resources).

Human Capital Theory

Human capital theory (Becker 1964) would predict that only those individuals with substantial human capital would be considered for a seat on the board of directors. Women may need to develop more extensive human capital than their male counterparts in order to overcome 'glass ceiling' barriers and to attract the attention of director selectors. Women are investing in education, with better results than their male peers even at university level. However, the interrupted nature of women's careers disadvantages women's human capital acquisition, in terms of fewer chances to gain new job skills and experiences (Ohlott *et al.* 1994). Inappropriate career decisions may prevent women from accessing the relevant work experience necessary for eventual leadership positions. Furthermore, investments in human capital are said to provide higher returns for men. As a result, women may be less well prepared for board appointments. Certainly there are many reports that chairmen and chief executives indicate that in their view, women do not have the necessary experience (Mattis 2000). In the Catalyst/Opportunity Now (2000) survey, 40 per cent of British chief executives believed that women had not been in the director pipeline long enough, indicating perceptions that women had not yet had the opportunity or taken the chance to obtain the necessary experience. Whilst 72 per cent of senior women disagreed with them, the chief executives held the view that it was the lesser human capital of aspiring women directors that formed a hurdle for their appointment to boards.

Social Capital Theory

Human capital acquisition is necessary for career success, but it needs to be used in conjunction with social capital. Whilst human capital is a quality of the individual, social capital is a quality of the interpersonal relationships of the individual that provides access to wider resources such as information, connection, power and influence (Burt 1997). Social capital provides opportunities to the individual and, by extension, to the organizations in which they work. Social networks are a manifestation of social capital, and social capital theory would predict that managers higher up in organizational hierarchies (in most institutions, that would mean mostly males) would have more powerful connections through their networks to others at senior levels (also mostly male), that would make them attractive to boards seeking new directors. Examination of the backgrounds of the pioneer women directors reveals that they were usually very well connected to powerful 'old families' or those with political influence.

Social capital theory also explains why directors with interlocking directorships are sought after by board appointing committees. The network of connected directors and companies provides resources far beyond those of the individual at the node in the network. New board members are appointed with the expectation that they will contribute their particular expertise to the hiring board, but they also bring advantages based on connections to multiple parties within the network, providing indirect benefits such as information about opportunities for business, problems across the sector and government or community plans. These benefits are accessible also to other members of the wider network.

SLOW PROGRESS TO DIRECTORSHIPS IN THE UK

Despite optimism that barriers to women's careers would soon be removed by the UK's equal opportunities legislation of the mid-1970s, the Hansard Society raised concern in the late 1980s that women were still not visible on large corporate boards. Their Commission on Women at the Top (Howe and McRae 1991) found that 80 per cent of the 190 largest companies in 1989 had no women on the board. The four female executive directors represented only 0.5 per cent of all main board executive directors in the top 190 companies, whilst the 26 female non-executive directors formed only 4 per cent of the non-executive directors. Women were slightly more evident as executive directors on subsidiary boards (almost 2 per cent). A third of them were finance directors, a quarter held managing director positions, but surprisingly, less than one in ten of the women executives held the position of personnel director. Most of the appointments of women directors had been made in the last three years prior to the survey. Following the issue of the Hansard Report, the Opportunity 2000 organization was formed by a group of employers to benchmark progress of women into management in the participating companies. However, recognizing that there was still a long way to go to achieve the goals set in 1991, Opportunity 2000 renamed itself in 2000 as Opportunity Now.

The barriers for women directors in 1991 were stated to be the need to follow a typical male full-time and uninterrupted career path with total commitment to the company or profession and the continued sex-role stereotyping of men and women, particularly in terms of leadership which was seen as masculine. The 'old boys' club was seen to play a major hurdle to the appointment of women, as chairmen sought directors known to their networks. Similarly, executive search consultants drew on a limited pool of talent already known to the chairmen. The view was that a new generation of chairmen would lead to more open attitudes to change in the boardroom. The scarcity of women in executive positions was seen to be the precursor to the few women in the talent pool for non-executive directorships. The report concluded: 'We are confident that in ten years, the absence of women from the board will seem [...] unthinkable and that women will have become an accepted and much valued part of company life' (Howe and McRae, 1991: 14).

A follow-up study by McRae (1995) showed some improvements. Forty-six per cent of the 120 top companies had a woman in the boardroom by 1995. Women held 10.4 per cent of non-executive positions, up from only 4 per cent in 1989, but although the proportion of women executive directors doubled over the five-year period, this was still abysmally low at 1 per cent. Women were described as restricted by glass walls as well as the 'glass ceiling'. A further five years saw little progress. By 2000, Singh *et al.* (2001) found that 58 per cent of FTSE 100 companies had at least one woman on the board, whilst women made up 9 per cent of non-executive directors and 2 per cent of executive directors.

THE BUSINESS CASE FOR GENDER DIVERSITY AT BOARD LEVEL

There are a number of business reasons why having women represented on the board should be beneficial. In the UK and across Europe, there are concerns about changing demographic profiles, and by 2010, the UK government predicts that just 20 per cent of the UK workforce will be male and under age 45. Four-fifths of workforce growth will be among women (Department of Trade & Industry 2003).

It obviously makes good business sense to draw directors from the widest possible qualified talent pool – but the scarcity of women at senior management levels means that there are even fewer women with equivalent experience to men in that talent pool at present. This also means that the talents of half the working population are not being fully developed, which is a serious waste of resources. Yet companies talk of the 'war for talent' as they scour the world for the best brains to develop into future business leaders. Why have they for so long ignored the talents of ambitious young women, who then do not get the opportunities to develop into potential directors?

Diversity in teams should lead to better decision-making, as individuals with diverse experiences, qualifications and backgrounds contribute a variety of perspectives to the issue at hand. Such variety should have a better chance of generating innovative solutions. This process helps to avoid the dangers of 'group think' where those who have similar backgrounds are more likely to think in similar ways, achieving consensus prematurely, before all angles have been explored (Maznevski 1994).

Understanding the female consumer, purchaser, stakeholder, client and employee perspective may be difficult for an all-male board. Yet in retail companies even in the early 2000s, males held positions such as director of childrenswear and womenswear, where there would presumably be a talent pool of women in those particular departments.

Fondas and Sassalos (2000) reported that where boards included female directors, there was better governance. Women achieving such positions were highly prepared and keen to be responsible members of boards that governed well and that considered diverse voices. Studies had noted earlier that women directors tended to prepare extremely well for board meetings (Izraeli 2000), so that challenging of governance issues should be more effective. Fondas and Sassalos also suggest that given women's preference for transformational and collaborative leadership styles, the female director's presence is likely to lead to more civilized boardroom behaviours.

Other more recent studies indicate a positive relationship between corporate governance and the presence of women directors. A Canadian study (Conference Board 2002) highlighted that companies with multiple women directors showed significantly higher performance than those with all-male boards on measures related to strong and independent boards of directors, where particular consideration was given to non-financial measures of performance. In addition, the presence of multiple women was associated with more board attention given to ethics, codes of conduct, and conflict of interest guidelines.

In the UK, the Female FTSE studies revealed that top companies with women on board had higher overall scores than those with all-male boards on a number of indicators of good corporate governance and compliance in line with the recommendations of the Higgs Review and new reporting codes (Singh and Vinnicombe 2005). The indicators of board independence were the balance of non-executive and executive directors on the board, a separate chairman and chief executive, a nominated senior independent director, and less than one third of the non-executive directors having more than seven years' tenure. Companies with women directors had significantly higher scores than those with all-male boards in terms of board independence ($p = 0.022$). They were significantly more likely to have transparency in reporting compliance with codes of practice, and other board processes such as succession planning, reporting of board appointments, the use of search consultants and an annual review of board skills, knowledge and experience ($p = 0.002$). Significantly more companies with women directors also had induction and on-going development programmes for board members ($p = 0.018$). So companies with good governance processes in place are those that are more likely to have appointed women to their boards.

The presence of women directors has been associated with significantly higher levels of market capitalization in several international studies, including the USA and Canada (Catalyst 2004) and the UK (Singh and Vinnicombe 2004b). However, whilst some would credit this to the presence of women on board, it is likely that larger companies are more open to the appointment of women directors. Having a diverse board may attract funds from certain groups of investors, such as trade union or ethical pension fund managers (Bilimoria 2000). In 2005, women owned 48 per cent of the personal wealth of Britain, and this is expected to rise to 60 per cent by 2025 (Department of Trade & Industry 2003). So women will be increasingly important as investors in the future, and may prefer to invest in companies demonstrating confidence in women directors.

Investors may also prefer to avoid investment in companies where repeated sex-discrimination claims by senior women employees are upheld by courts, wasting financial resources in terms of huge pay-outs and fines, destroying corporate reputation and deterring the best female talent from entering the company. Newspaper reports show that in New York and also in the City of London, a number of firms have been exposed for discrimination in pay and promotion of their senior women, leading to successful prosecutions. Such firms have corporate cultures that are hostile to women.

An interesting study by Ryan and Haslam (2005) building on the Cranfield Female FTSE Report 2003 (Singh and Vinnicombe 2003) indicates that new women directors are often appointed when companies are at the beginning of a period of decline, and hence their positions are more precarious than those of men directors, who are more likely to be appointed when the business is stable. Ryan and Haslam suggest that women directors appointed at such a time are standing on a 'glass cliff', highly visible and potential scapegoats for declining performance.

The presence of women directors has symbolic value for women lower down the organization. The females in the boardroom symbolize the possibility that women can get right to the top of the particular company. The presence of executive women is even more important in terms of career aspirations. Studies show that women feel more satisfied with their careers and are more ambitious in such companies, and hence would be likely to develop their potential (Bilimoria 2000; Institute of Management 2001). Some women directors are proactive in leading change in their companies, by engaging in women's networks and mentoring junior women (Singh *et al*. in press). This again makes the junior women feel less isolated and keen to further their careers.

FTSE 100 COMPANIES WITH WOMEN DIRECTORS

The Female FTSE Report 2005 (see Table 7.1) shows an increasing pace of progress of women into the boardroom as almost four in every five of the top 100 companies now have at least one woman on the board. Almost half of the companies with no women directors in 2000 had appointed women by 2005. The number of companies with female executive directors has hardly changed since 2000, rising from ten to eleven. This indicates that women are not breaking through the 'glass ceiling' in executive roles despite the progress of non-executive women into the boardroom.

The leading companies in the Female FTSE 100 Index 2005 had 30 per cent female boards, and in 13 companies, women made up at least 20 per cent of the board. Twenty-five companies had at least 15 per cent female boards. It is noteworthy that companies with more than one woman on board have increased from 12 in 2000 to 30 in 2005. As Kanter (1977) indicated, where there is a sole woman on a board, she is likely to be marginalized on grounds of her sex, whereas where there are at least two women, this is much less likely. In 2004, a few companies which previously had women directors on their board, then returned to all-male boards, due to the inevitable turnover of directors. However, by 2005 most of those companies had again appointed women directors, which together with the increase in companies with multiple female directors indicates a promising trend towards a more equitable distribution of men and women on top boards.

Table 7.1 FTSE 100 companies with women directors

FTSE 100 (October 2005)	2005	2004	2003	2002	2001	2000
Companies with women executive directors	11	13	13	12	8	10
Companies with women directors	78	69	68	61	57	58
Companies with multiple women directors	30	29	22	17	15	12
Companies with 1 woman director	48	39	46	44	42	46
Companies with 2 women directors	19	19	13	11	12	12
Companies with 3 women directors	9	7	7	6	3	0
Companies with 4 women directors	2	2	2	0	0	0
Companies with no women directors	22	31	32	39	43	42
Female FTSE Indices (2000–2005)	2005	2004	2003	2002	2001	2000
Female-held directorships	121	110	101	84	75	69
	10.5%	9.7%	8.6%	7.2%	6.4%	5.8%
Female executive directorships	14	17	17	15	10	11
	3.4%	4.1%	3.7%	3.0%	2.0%	2.0%
Female NEDs	107	93	84	69	65	60
	14.5%	13.06%	11.8%	10.0%	9.6%	9.1%
Women holding FTSE directorships	99	96	88	75	68	60
Women chief executives	1	1	1	1	1	1
Women chairmen	1	1	1	1	0	0
Female % of new appointments	17%	17%	13%	11%	12%	11%

COMPANIES WHERE WOMEN SUCCEED

Companies with Women Executive Directors

First, the 11 FTSE 100 companies with female executive directors are considered. Their boards have between eight and 15 directors, and ten are in the top 30 companies of the Female FTSE Index, indicating not only openness to appointing women executives but also having a higher than average proportion of women on the board. Five companies have three women executive directors, and a further five companies have two women executives on their boards. The companies were in various sectors: two utilities, one oil and gas company, two retailers, two from banking and financial services, and one each from media, leisure and hotels, transport and real estate, so there was no strong pattern of better progress in companies with female dominated workforces and/or customers such as retail. Only five of the companies were in the top half of the FTSE 100 by market capitalization (a proxy for size) so there was no strong indicator that size of company was a factor related to the appointment of women executive directors, in contrast to the position for women non-executive directors.

Companies with Women on Board Compared with All-male Boards

Although in 2005, only 11 companies had women executive directors, 78 of the top 100 companies had women directors. Most had only non-executive women. So how did the 78 companies compare with the 22 where only men sat at the boardroom table? Overall there were a number of ways in which they differed. In particular, the higher market capitalization of the company, the more likely it was to have appointed women directors. This is a finding that has been consistent since the Female FTSE Index was started in 1999, and has been found in the USA and Canada by Catalyst. As well as significantly higher market capitalization, such companies had an average of 12 board members, compared with only ten in all-male boards. Companies with women on the board also had more non-executive directors than the all-male board companies.

Women were more likely to be on boards where the non-executive directors were younger and had shorter than average board tenure. Not only did these boards have gender diversity, but they were also significantly more likely to have ethnic minority directors, although only 23 companies out of the 100 actually had directors from ethnic minorities. From the start of the Female FTSE Index in 1999 until 2003, the long tenure of the chairman was a significant factor, although age was not significant. Where the chairman had been in place for more than seven years, there was a significant likelihood that there would be no women on the board. Age and tenure of the chief executive were also investigated but there was no relationship with the presence of women on the board.

Sector Differences in Companies with Women Directors

Women directors are most likely to be found in banks, telecoms and tobacco companies, followed by retailers, the utilities and pharmaceuticals. All eight banks had women on board, as did the four telecoms and three tobacco companies in the FTSE 100. It could be expected that women would be on boards in banks and retailers because of the high proportion of female staff and female customers. It could also be expected that the utilities and privatized telecoms companies would have at least one woman on the board as their boards were set up initially by the government. Most such companies did have gender diversity on their boards, despite the male-dominated workforces in those sectors.

A more specific way to consider the impact of sector on women's advancement is to examine the directorate of each sector, for the proportion of the total directorships held by women. Women make up 17 per cent of directors in the transport sector, and over 14 per cent of directors in banking, closely followed by the finance, insurance, assurance and investment sector group at 13 per cent. These figures reveal that women are making good progress in these sectors. Given the high proportion of female staff and customers, the retail directorate was disappointing with only 11.5 per cent female representation, despite eight of the nine retailers having at least one woman on the board.

The lowest proportion of women directors is in the real estate sector, where only 4 per cent of directors are women. The real estate companies are large developers of office and retail properties for investment purposes, with only a small business in residential housing. Interestingly the cover page of the annual report of one such land company shows six businesswomen entering and having meetings in a futuristic office foyer – is gender diversity only symbolic?

WOMEN DIRECTORS IN THE FTSE 100

Although the pace is slow there are some significant and steady improvements. The number of women directors has increased from 60 to 99 women, and the overall percentage of female held directorships has almost doubled since 2000 (see Table 7.1). But only one woman holds a chief executive position, and there is one female chairman, with three female deputy chairmen too. Importantly, women are maintaining their proportion of new appointments (17 per cent), at a time when boards are tending to reduce the number of executive directors.

It is clear from the difference between the number of women holding directorships and the number of female-held directorships that some women hold more than one such position. Whilst 82 per cent of females and 86 per cent of males hold only one seat, one female director holds four seats, and two hold three seats, but a slightly higher proportion of women compared with men hold multiple directorships. This means that the pool of talent is not being extended as far as the improvements would indicate, as some women in the existing pool are getting second or even more directorships in FTSE 100 companies.

Earlier US research indicated that women non-executive directors often did not get to sit on the powerful board committees, particularly the audit, remuneration and nomination committees (Bilimoria and Piderit 1994). There was no evidence that this was the case in the FTSE 100 companies in 2005 in terms of membership, but women were more likely than men to sit on the audit committee, half of the women but only a third of the men doing so. However, men were significantly more likely to chair the audit and nomination committees, whilst women were just as likely as men to chair the remuneration committee.

Characteristics of FTSE 100 Women Directors

With an average age of 53 years, the FTSE 100 cohort of women directors are younger than their male peers, whose average age is almost 56. When age is examined by director role, women executive directors are younger (average age 48 compared with 50.5) than the men executives, and whilst male non-executives have an average age of almost 59, the average age of their female peers is under 54.

Tenure in the boardroom also differs by sex, with women having 3.2 years and men having five years' tenure on average. Most directorships are for a period of three years. The gender differences reflect the fact that many of the women directors have been appointed in the last five years, whilst there are many males who have had several renewals of their directorships.

In the past, it was noted that many of the women gaining FTSE 100 directorships had titles (Howe and McRae 1991). Commenting on the bias for 'brand name directors' in the US Fortune 500 companies, Daily *et al.* (2000) said that this might constrain the supply of new directors. It could be argued that women had to prove themselves before appointment whereas men were appointed on a promise based on their fit with the existing model of directors. In the FTSE 100 2001 study, 32 per cent of women and 27 per cent of men directors had titles, but by 2005, this had reduced to 25 per cent and 21 per cent respectively, indicating that women may no longer be seen as such a risk by appointing committees. In 2005, lords held 35 directorships, compared with 11 held by baronesses, and three seats were held by dames, compared with 87 by knights. These titles were a mix of hereditary and life peerages and knighthoods given as civic honours. Around 10 per cent of the directors held titles indicating doctorates or professorships.

Only five of the 121 women directors (4 per cent) came from ethnic minority backgrounds, including one Asian baroness, a baroness from Hong Kong, two African-Americans, and the first woman director from Saudi Arabia to be appointed in a FTSE 100 firm. Overall, 2.4 per cent of FTSE 100 directors came from an ethnic minority in 2005.

However, there is considerably more interest in the recruitment of directors from other countries. Whilst overall, 29 per cent of males and 35 per cent of females appear to have non-UK nationality, around 10 per cent of both males and females hold European citizenship. Interestingly, North American women hold one fifth of the female directorships, compared with 13 per cent for their male counterparts. The UK does have diversity on its boards, as recommended by the Higgs Review (Higgs 2003) and Tyson Report (Tyson 2003), but nationality and international experience would appear to be valued more highly than gender and ethnic diversity. Women from outside the UK offer a variety of perspectives, drawing on their differences from the traditional white middle-aged male director, not just in terms of adding gender diversity but also their international experience and connections.

An examination of the biographies of 144 recently appointed directors of whom half were female revealed some interesting differences by gender. Whilst 72 per cent of the male directors had UK backgrounds, only 61 per cent of the females came from the UK. New female directors were more likely to be from the USA (32 per cent compared with 7 per cent for the males), whilst 17 per cent of males were from other European countries compared with only 6 per cent of females. Men and women had equivalent profiles in terms of titles, civic honours and Google references. Whilst 42 per cent of the males compared to 22 per cent of the females had prior FTSE 100 board experience, women did have slightly more experience on FTSE 250 boards and 63 per cent of them had sat on other boards, compared with 39 per cent of the men. A greater proportion of the women had work experience spanning several sectors, presenting themselves as more rounded directors, with career histories including work in financial institutions, management consultancy, law, politics, academia, public sector, voluntary and charity sectors and other government boards. Differences were significant in terms of women having more management consultancy and more public sector experience than their male peers. Indeed a third of the women had been in senior positions in the public sector. This variety of profiles suggests that boards are extending the talent pool for board appointments beyond the set of directors with prior FTSE 100 experience.

COMPANIES WITH WOMEN DIRECTORS: EUROPEAN AND NORDIC COMPARISONS

Women are making inroads into European boardrooms. The European Commission reported statistics for the top 50 companies for the first time in 2004, and again in 2005 (see Table 7.2). The first Nordic index of companies with women directors started in 2004 (Hoel 2004). It is important to note that governance structures differ by country, so that direct comparisons are difficult. The UK company has a single tier board comprising executive and non-executive directors, a chief executive and a chairman, all with legal liability as directors. In contrast, many European countries have a two-tier system with a chairman heading the supervisory board, whilst the chief executive sits on a separate management board. In many countries, the supervisory board includes employee representatives, and sometimes community representatives as well. In some countries, boards may include directors who represent major shareholders. In Europe, family-owned companies may have several family members on the board, although this is not common in the top companies of the UK. Employee representation presents an opportunity for women to gain board experience without having to progress through the ranks to top management.

The average percentage of female representation on top boards rose in just one year from 8 to 10 per cent in 2005. Indeed, following pressures from the Norwegian government in 2002, where legislation was threatened to impose a 40 per cent female representation on all corporate boards within three years, women now make up 21 per cent of top boards, closely followed by Sweden with 20 per cent. The newest group of countries into the EU (the Balkans, Central European and smaller Baltic countries) also have a higher than average proportion of women directors. Poland leads in terms of female chief executives with one in five of the top 50 companies headed by a woman, in contrast to the UK with none.

In January 2006 the new coalition government of Norway decided to enforce the previous government requirement that company boards should have 40 per cent female representation within three years (that is by 2005), given that only a fifth of the 590 listed companies achieved that target. The proposal is that companies will be forcibly closed if they do not comply within a further two years, although there are strong views against this from the employers' association. Family owned company boards are also likely to be

Table 7.2   Women directors in the top 50 companies in EU countries 2005

Country	Top companies on Stock Exchange	Companies for whom data are available	Companies with female chief executives (%)	Female heads and directors on main board (%)	Female heads and executive directors (%)
Austria	49	48	2	5	0
Belgium	50	50	0	7	2
Bulgaria	50	38	3	18	11
Cyprus	50	50	0	7	6
Czech Republic	50	49	6	10	0
Germany	50	50	0	12	0
Denmark	50	48	0	11	2
Estonia	16	16	0	19	6
Greece	50	50	4	9	4
Spain	50	50	2	5	0
Finland	50	50	2	15	0
France	50	49	4	6	0
Hungary	48	48	2	11	7
Ireland	49	47	1	5	0
Iceland	47	46	0	5	0
Italy	50	50	2	2	2
Lithuania	43	28	0	11	7
Luxembourg	28	23	0	3	5
Latvia	50	32	7	12	17
Malta	12	12	8	2	0
The Netherlands	50	50	0	5	0
Norway	50	50	4	21	2
Poland	50	49	10	8	6
Portugal	50	48	4	5	7
Romania	50	39	0	15	6
Sweden	49	49	0	20	0
Slovenia	50	40	8	18	5
Slovakia	30	24	9	10	0
United Kingdom	50	50	0	14	2
Average (%)			3	10	3

Source: European Commission (2005).

included in this affirmative action measure. Norway is already ahead of the rest of Europe, Australia and New Zealand and North America, in terms of numbers of women directors, but political pressures are continuing to drive change at a faster pace. The UK's Equal Opportunities Commission (EOC 2006) says it will take 40 years for women to achieve equality on FTSE 100 boards at the present pace, so no doubt, the Norwegian case study is being watched with great interest in other countries.

CONCLUSIONS: BEST PRACTICE IN MANAGING THE FEMALE DIRECTOR PIPELINE

For the 2005 Female FTSE report, a number of leading companies were asked to comment on their strategies for increasing the talent pool of women in their companies. Companies included Anglo-American, British Airways, Centrica, HBOS, HSBC, Lloyds-TSB, National Grid, O2, Pearson, Reuters, Scottish Power and Shell. Understanding the current position of women at management levels in the company is a key first step to action, but for global companies with differing human resource management systems, this can still be a challenge. In the sample of companies investigated, the women in the tier below the main board formed between 10 and 20 per cent of that level. Three of the companies set targets expressed as overall percentage of women at particular senior grades or in terms of continuous improvement year on year, to avoid a backlash reaction. Others preferred not to set public targets.

It is important not only to establish at what level the lack of senior women becomes visible, but also to ascertain what the perceived barriers are. This can be done by including relevant questions in employee surveys, for instance about inclusion and diversity, perceptions of the company's commitment to progression of women to the highest echelons of management, concerns about taking advantage of work-life balance and flexibility policies, and perceptions of women's roles and abilities as future leaders.

For successful and sustainable results, the visible and active support of the chief executive and chairmen is essential, so that understanding and acceptance of the need for change can happen. This is particularly important in companies where there may be lack of interest or even resistance in the middle tiers of management and lower line management levels.

The companies reported a range of initiatives to address the issue of developing women for future senior positions, including recruitment, talent identification and development, assessment of potential, succession planning, leadership development, mentoring and networking. Companies involved their senior women in recruitment drives, especially in the technology sector where it was difficult to gender-balance the intake of new graduates. Several of the companies used executive search firms to identify more senior external talent, and Shell built in 'diversity and inclusion' capability as part of their tender process when using executive search firms for senior appointments. Talent reviews was a mechanism used by most of the companies to plan director and senior position succession. Assessment systems were examined for evidence of gender bias, so that any sex role stereotyping of women as less suitable for leadership could be explored and addressed if necessary. Job rotation was used by both Scottish Power and National Grid to develop their senior most women, as well as putting them through leadership programmes, coaching and mentoring. Whilst all of these 'best practice' companies were now proactive in developing the talent of their senior women, initiatives specifically for the development of women lower down the hierarchy were less evident. This appears to be due to the companies' expectation that the talent management process at lower levels, and in some cases, the additional corporate support for women's network activities, would allow women to come through to the middle management talent pool.

Diversity awareness initiatives help managers to understand gender differences and to see that women's ways of management and leadership may be different but just as effective as the traditional approaches generally used by men. Courses for senior managers and those responsible for talent identification can be used to challenge sex role stereotyping and identify unintended biases about the suitability of women for leadership. Reverse mentoring is an example of an intervention whereby women can directly engage senior managers in discussion of the negative impact of stereotyping and masculine culture on women's careers, helping them to see that the apparently gender-neutral organization is actually gendered in its informal structures and processes.

Not all the companies involved had formal accountability for diversity management in place, but leaders in National Grid and Lloyds TSB already had personal diversity objectives, and HBOS was introducing diversity accountability linked to the rewards system. In Pearson, diversity was an integral part of the quarterly business review meetings with the chief executive. In a few companies, the action planning and reporting processes have become fully integrated, so that diversity of talent has become a key consideration for measuring the health of the talent pool.

The most critical factors to be addressed for sustained change are listed below:

- Continuous communication from individual top leaders of the strategic need to build the female talent pipeline, and of performance expectations.

- Robust management disciplines, including goal setting and accountability for improvement, being applied to the problem, as in the case of any other critical business priority.
- Diversity being fully integrated into the talent agenda and processes.
- Creation of an inclusive culture (starting with education and awareness of business leaders, HR business partners and line managers), so that the talents and differences that women bring to business are recognized and valued in the talent process.

This chapter has highlighted the history of women directors' progress into the top boardrooms of UK companies, identifying some progress in terms of women non-executive directors but stagnation in terms of women executive directors over a period of 15 years. The Rt Hon. Patricia Hewitt, Secretary of State for Trade and Industry and also Minister for Women in 2004, commented: 'If we are serious about creating a modern economy, recognising diversity and utilising the skills of everyone, there is still much more to do' (Singh and Vinnicombe 2004b).

REFERENCES

Becker, G.S. (1964), *Human Capital*, Chicago: University of Chicago Press.

Bilimoria, D. (2000), 'Building the Business Case for Women Corporate Directors', in R.J. Burke and M. Mattis (eds), *Women on Corporate Boards of Directors: International Challenges and Opportunities*, Dordrecht: Kluwer, 25–40.

Bilimoria, D. and Piderit, S. (1994), 'Board Committee Membership: Effects of Sex-based Bias', *Academy of Management Journal*, **37**(6), 1453–77.

Burt, R.S. (1997), 'The Contingent Value of Social Capital', *Administrative Science Quarterly*, **42**(2), 339–65.

Catalyst (2004), *The Bottom Line: Connecting Corporate Performance and Gender Diversity*, New York: Catalyst.

Catalyst/Opportunity Now (2000), *Breaking the Barriers: Women in Senior Management in the UK*, London: Catalyst and Opportunity Now, Business in the Community.

Conference Board of Canada (2002), *Women on Boards: Not Just the Right Thing … But the 'Bright' Thing*, Ottawa: Conference Board of Canada.

Daily, C.M., Certo, S.T. and Dalton, D.R. (2000), 'The Future of Corporate Women', in R.J. Burke and M. Mattis (eds), *Women on Corporate Boards of Directors: International Challenges and Opportunities*, Dordrecht: Kluwer, 11–23.

Department of Trade & Industry (2003), *Brighter Boards for a Brighter Future*, London: Women & Equality Unit, Department of Trade & Industry.

Dulewicz, V. and Herbert, P. (2004), 'Does the Composition and Practice of Boards Make any Difference to the Performance of their Companies?' *Corporate Governance: An International Review*, **12**(3), 263–80.

Equal Opportunities Commission (2006), *Sex and Power: Who runs Britain 2006?* Manchester: Equal Opportunities Commission.

European Commission (2005), *Database on Women and Men in Decision-making*, Luxembourg: Directorate General for Employment and Social Affairs.

Fondas, N. and Sassalos, S. (2000), 'A Different Voice in the Boardroom: How the Presence of Women Directors affects Board Influence over Management', *Global Focus*, **12**(2), 13–22.

Higgs, D. (2003), *The Higgs Review of the Role and Effectiveness of Non-Executive Directors*, London: Department of Trade & Industry.

Hoel, M. (2004), *The Nordic 500*, Oslo: Center for Corporate Diversity.

Howe, E. and McRae, S. (1991), *Women on the Board*, London: Hansard Society.

Ibarra, H. (1992), 'Homophily and Differential Returns: Sex Differences in Network Structure and Access in an Advertising Firm', *Administrative Science Quarterly*, **37**, 422–47.

Institute of Management (2001), *A Woman's Place*, London: Institute of Management.

Izraeli, D. (2000), 'Women Directors in Israel', in R.J. Burke and M. Mattis (eds), *Women on Corporate Boards of Directors: International Challenges and Opportunities*, Dordrecht: Kluwer, 75–96.

Kanter, R.M. (1977), *Men and Women of the Corporation*, New York: Basic Books.

Mattis, M. (2000), 'Women Corporate Directors in the United States', in R.J. Burke and M. Mattis (eds), *Women on Corporate Boards of Directors: International Challenges and Opportunities*, Dordrecht: Kluwer, 43–56.

Maznevski, M.L. (1994), 'Understanding Our Differences: Performance in Decision-Making Groups with Diverse Members', *Human Relations*, **47**(5), 531–52.

McRae, S. (1995), *Women at the Top: Progress after Five Years*, King-Hall Paper No 2, London: The Hansard Society.

Ohlott, P.J., Ruderman, M.N. and McCauley, C.D. (1994), 'Gender Differences in Managers' Developmental Job Experiences', *Academy of Management Journal*, **37**(1), 46–67.

Pfeffer, J. and Salancik, G. (1978), *The External Control of Organizations: A Resource Dependence Perspective*, New York: Harper & Row.

Rosener, J.B. (1990), 'Ways Women Lead', *Harvard Business Review*, Nov/Dec, 119–25.

Ryan, M. and Haslam, A. (2005), 'The Glass Cliff: Evidence that Women are Over-represented in Precarious Leadership Positions', *British Journal of Management*, **16**, 81–90.

Singh, V. and Vinnicombe, S. (2003), *The Female FTSE Report 2003*, Cranfield: Cranfield School of Management.

Singh, V. and Vinnicombe, S. (2004a), 'Why so Few Women Directors in the Top UK Boardrooms? Evidence and Theoretical Explanations', *Corporate Governance: An International Review*, **12**(4) 479–88.

Singh, V. and Vinnicombe, S. (2004b), *The Female FTSE Report 2004*, Cranfield: Cranfield School of Management.

Singh, V. and Vinnicombe, S. (2005), *The Female FTSE Report 2005*, Cranfield: Cranfield UK.

Singh, V., Kumra, S. and Vinnicombe, S. (2002), 'Gender and Impression Management: Playing the Promotion Game', *Journal of Business Ethics*, **37**(1) 77–89.

Singh, V., Vinnicombe, S. and Johnson, P. (2001), 'Women Directors on top UK Boards', *Corporate Governance: An International Review*, **9**(3) 206–16.

Singh, V., Vinnicombe, S. and Kumra, S. (forthcoming), 'Women in Formal Corporate Networks – An Organizational Citizenship Perspective', *Women in Management Review*.

Suroweicki, J. (2004), *The Wisdom of Crowds*, London: Abacus.

Tajfel, H. (1982), *Social Identity and Intergroup Relations*, Cambridge: Cambridge University Press.

Tyson, L. (2003), *The Tyson Report on the Recruitment and Development of Non-Executive Directors*, London: London Business School.

Vinnicombe, S. and Singh, V. (2003), 'Locks and Keys to the Boardroom: A Comparison of UK Male and Female Directors' Careers', *Women in Management Review*, **18**(6) 325–33.

8. The smaller business context: a conducive environment for women in management?

Susan M. Ogden and Gillian A. Maxwell

INTRODUCTION

The small and medium sized enterprises (SMEs) that together make up much of the smaller business sector can be differentiated from larger organizations in terms of their human resource management approaches and practices. For example, as Kinnie *et al*. (1999: 218) note, a 'lack of resources of time, money and people is thought to inhibit the use of sophisticated management strategies [and] the appointment of human resource specialists'. Further, the 2004 Workplace Employee Relations Survey undertaken in the UK confirms that the practice of employee relations varies significantly between smaller and larger workplaces, as well as between different sectors of industry and between public and private sectors (Kersley *et al*. 2004). The survey provides a rich source of evidence about the SME sector given that 46 per cent of the 3000 workplaces surveyed were SMEs (between 10–249 employees), with over half (56 per cent) of all private sector employers surveyed falling into this category. At the same time, it has been asserted that strategic human resource management (HRM) issues in smaller businesses in industrialised high growth countries are becoming more important (Brand and Bax 2002).

The strategic HRM issue under examination in this chapter is the progress of women into management. Much of the research on this topic is set within larger organizations, such as Singh and Vinnicombe's (2004) work (see Chapter 7). In contrast this chapter aims to investigate how the smaller business context may impact on the prospects for females' progression in management. It seeks to address the question of whether the smaller business environment constitutes a conducive environment for women in management. The increasing proportion of women in the general labour market is well documented, with females now comprising 51 per cent of the UK workforce (Equal Opportunities Commission 2001). However, behind these headline figures there are other significant patterns and trends in relation to female participation in management, with female participation uneven across sectors and levels. For instance, in the private sector while females make up 40 per cent of the workforce, they occupy only 28 per cent of management positions, while in the public sector, where 60 per cent of the workforce is female, 40 per cent of its managers are female (Equal Opportunities Commission 2002). As research into women in management in SMEs is relatively lacking, this chapter address a significant knowledge deficit.

The chapter begins with an outline of the general characteristics of the SME sector, before examining human resource management and development issues arising in the smaller business context. It then discusses organizational culture and work-life balance in SMEs, followed by case studies of females in management in a range of smaller businesses. Finally, conclusions are drawn on the significance of the smaller business context for the progression of female managers.

CHARACTERISTICS OF THE SMALLER BUSINESS SECTOR

By 2004 SMEs (defined by DTI as organizations with less than 250 employees) account for 'more than half of employment (58.5 per cent) and turnover (51.3 per cent) in the UK' (DTI 2005: 1). Analysis of DTI figures show that the total number of small businesses in the UK rose 50 per cent between 1980 and 2000, from 2.4 million in 1980 to 3.7 million in 2000 (Keynote 2000: 28), and it was predicted to grow to 4 million by 2006 (Keynote, 2000: 130).

Although there is steady growth in the SME sector, a key feature is the survival, or failure, and start-up rates of smaller businesses. Several studies have been undertaken to examine the extent to which the gender of the owner/manager influences organizational success (see Carter *et al.* 2001). Watson (2003: 262) found that 'while female-owned businesses do have higher failure rates compared with male-owned businesses, the difference is not significant after controlling for the effects of industry'. In other words, there is a suggestion that many female-controlled businesses operate in 'riskier' sectors of the economy. A study of the role of gender in financial performance of small accountancy practices, although finding no significant relationships between gender and financial performance, did find that female-owned small businesses had enhanced financial performance where the female proprietors had expressed a strong commitment to work-life balance policies (Collins-Dodd *et al.* 2004). A fuller review of issues relating to women's business ownership, including performance and growth statistics, as well as management characteristics of female-owned firms is provided by Carter *et al.* (2001).

HUMAN RESOURCE MANAGEMENT PRACTICES IN SMALLER BUSINESSES

Given the predicted growth in the SME sector, it is vital that organizations take steps to ensure they retain and develop their human resources. In 2001, a lack of skilled or trained staff was reported by SMEs as the third most important business problem faced, after 'low turnover/lack of business' and 'government regulations and paperwork' in a survey of 720 businesses by Natwest Small Business Research Trust (SBRT 2000 reported in Keynote, 2000: 100). Further the staffing problem was reported more often by the larger SMEs, with 25 per cent citing this as their main business problem (ibid: 101). In the 2001 SBRT survey, employment regulations were considered to have occupied the most time in compliance activity by 21 per cent of all SMEs with over 50 employees. As one of the critical advantages offered by the SME sector is their ability to respond quickly and appropriately to changes in the marketplace, employment regulation is a concern to many businesses (Bridge 2004). From the perspective of women employees though, one such regulatory compliance challenge – the potential for flexible working framed in recent employment law – supports their progression in management, as highlighted by Mattis (1995).

There remains significant variation in HRM practices in smaller businesses. Gray and Mabey (2005) report that firms with fewer than 100 employees are likely to have very informal approaches to HRM. The degree of formality in relation to HRM practices can be expected to vary according to the SME size and may also be shaped by the personal influence of one or a few individuals (Brand and Bax 2002). Kotey and Slade's (2005) Australian data of 1330 SMEs generally supports the view that in 'micro firms the close relationship between employer and employee replaces formal controls and reduces the need for detailed documentation' (Kotey and Slade 2005: 21). This reflects the view of Carroll *et al.* (1999) that many smaller firms find it cheaper and quicker to rely on informal channels and networks in recruiting staff rather than resorting to a formal and lengthy advertising and application process. Furthermore, informal recruitment processes such as job try-outs have been found to be used extensively in manufacturing SMEs as they are inexpensive and an effective way of assessing the suitability of a person with the job demands (Duberley and Walley 1995; Brand and Bax 2002). However, unsurprisingly Kotey and Slade (2005) find that as firms grow in size they do rely more and more on formal application and reference checks of candidates.

On the one hand, too much informality may result in a business failure to implement the new employment rights on flexible working; on the other hand it can be argued that too much formality may act to restrict smaller businesses' response to individual requests for flexible work. A recent study of flexible working arrangements in smaller businesses in Scotland found that much employment practice operated informally yet permitted supportive responses to employee driven requests for flexible working (MacVicar *et al.* 2005). Therefore it seems the combination of employment rights, and formal and informal HRM practices, is critical in constructing a conducive environment for women in management in smaller businesses. In this, the smaller business sector can be seen to have a distinct advantage over the need of larger businesses to formalize HRM practice in order to ensure consistency and fairness across large numbers of employees.

HUMAN RESOURCE DEVELOPMENT IN SMALLER BUSINESSES

In the UK, public policy has supported the development of best practice human resource development though the promotion of Investors in People (IIP). IIP accreditation is seen as a way of improving an organization's performance through better employee retention, and enhancements in productivity and quality. Brand and Bax (2002) suggest that programmes such as pushing uptake of IIP among SMEs are measures to improve the sector's image and to interest more and better qualified employees. In 2002, 38 per cent of IIP uptake was by smaller firms, with general uptake said to cover 27 per cent of the UK workforce (IIP 2003) The IIP programme has been specifically targeted at the smaller business sector in recent years with a total of £30 million to support the smaller business sector in England to develop the skills of their workforce using the IIP accreditation process (ibid). IIP has set a target to ensure that 65 000 small firms have achieved or are working towards IIP status by December 2007, and report that by the end of 2004, 20 000 new smaller businesses in this category had been signed up (IIP 2005). This measure has already more than doubled the number of smaller companies working towards the standard, given that the starting figure was around 14 500 small employers (IIP 2003). With the focus on training that is at the centre of IIP, women have the potential opportunity to undertake training that supports their wider career development. This opportunity is enhanced further when organizational training includes training for managers to assume responsibility for developing women in particular (Mattis 1995).

Nevertheless some concerns have been expressed about the lack of investment in management development, given the importance of smaller businesses to economic development. Gray and Mabey (2005: 469) recognize that smaller organizations may find it harder to release 'precious' employees for development activities due to difficulties in covering staff absence from the work place due to the 'time and skill pressures related to their small size'.

Analysis of their survey findings from 191 small firms across Europe suggests that 'only a minority of small firms have formal, written management development policies but most of them do discuss and appraise their managers' development needs and support a wide array of formal management development activities' (Gray and Mabey 2005: 480). This informality is associated with the flexibility and adaptability of smaller firms which give them much of their competitive advantage, as outlined earlier. However, half of the small firms surveyed have a dedicated training budget, despite concerns that employees may be approached by larger firms offering better remunerations and career prospects. This fear is said to account for the finding that smaller firms spend more on firm-specific competences than on generic management skills. Storey (2004: 113) argues that the less frequent use of formal management training within smaller businesses is attributable more to the 'market protection' than the 'ignorance' explanation. For females seeking management progression, lack of management development is a career inhibitor, though it may be offset by job competency specific training. The authors have found that difficulty in accessing training provision can be a source of discontent for female and male employees alike, while, conversely, opportunities to participate in management training is considered positively by female and male employees (Maxwell and Ogden 2006), if not by smaller business employers.

The loss of staff whose development has been invested is partly attributable to the shorter career paths and absence of internal labour markets in smaller businesses (Storey, 2004). Moreover, less than transparent and informal career processes can be detrimental to women's progression in management (Tomlinson *et al.* 1997). As a consequence, there is a need for a degree of formality in the career structures offered by smaller businesses to help women in management. Overall, career advancement in the smaller business sector is likely to depend on the acceptance of multi-directional rather than linear – or uninterrupted, vertical – career paths described by Baruch (2004). The importance of moving between companies for career development can also depend on the sector. For example, it has been reported as a critical career success factor in studies of the retail sector. Maxwell *et al.* (2006) stated that in the retail sector employees report that career progression requires vocational mobility. However, a mobility policy is only a requirement for promotion in the larger organization studied and this appears to be curtailing career aspirations of some employees, particularly women with family responsibilities. In these circumstances, networking skills can be helpful in building profile and reputation needed to take full opportunity of any career openings in the local vicinity. Profiling activities like attending external professional association activities (for example seminars or social gatherings) can be important in building the social capital to enable career progression. On the other hand, it can be argued that internal visibility within smaller organizations is more effortless. Thus impression management behaviour, which is deemed to be an important variable in career success, but one which many women avoid (Singh and Vinnicombe 2001), may be less important in smaller organizations. Instead advancement may be based on performance merit and, for example, 'ambition, ability and commitment' (Maxwell and Ogden 2006: 117).

ORGANIZATIONAL CULTURE AND WORK-LIFE BALANCE IN SMALLER BUSINESSES

It has been noted that smaller organizations may have more homogeneous cultures than larger organizations and their cultures are likely to be more influenced by the dominance of owner-managers or the chief executives. Mukhtar's (2002: 289) wide-scale survey of the management of established smaller businesses in the USA, for instance, examines 'whether gender has an impact on management characteristics of male and female business owner-managers'. A key finding is that female owner-managed businesses 'differ markedly in their managerial styles compared to male businesses ... [in being] more informal, and thus more flexible owner-managers with little or no documented procedures' (Mukhtar 2002: 300–301). According to this study then, the degree of formality and informality in HRM and HRD practices may well have a gendered element. Beyond this, the study indicates the influence of management style on organizational culture. Other studies indicate that flexible informal cultures and 'people-centred management styles' (Maxwell and Ogden 2006: 117) are conducive to females' progression in management.

More broadly, research on organizational culture in small organizations highlight the need for tight financial control, while at the same time employees are likely to experience 'values of procedural informality, practicality, and cooperation' (Haugh and McKee 2004: 391). Haugh and McKee's case study research indicates five frequently occurring values representing the cultural paradigm of the small firm: survival, independence, control (internal and external), pragmatism and financial prudence. Of particular interest is the value of 'pragmatism' which addresses the need for action and behaviour to be designed by practical bearing upon individual and organizational interests rather than strict adherence to formal and legal requirements (ibid: 390). This brings benefits and possibilities in terms of work-life balance for many employees.

Quality of working life, work-life balance and conditions of employment may be an important part of the psychological contract in smaller businesses, particularly for female employees. It has been suggested that in a tight labour market, the 'underdog position' of SMEs on the external labour market should be addressed by using a 'softer contract' drawing upon commitment to the vision and values of the organization, and the benefits of an organic culture and an enhanced quality of working life (Brand and Bax 2002: 459). Thus, 'SMEs could use their known strengths such as internal flexibility, direct communications and integrated tasks to design jobs which fit available personnel' (ibid). In this way 'serendipitous' job design (Lado and Wilson 1994 in ibid) perhaps incorporating work-life balance dimensions can be used to attract new employees or to present existing employees with interesting job opportunities in order to reduce employee turnover.

There is some empirical evidence that career success can be linked to work-life balance rewards rather than linear or remunerative career progression. Though evidently not often formalized, work-life balance opportunities are presented in the smaller business sector (MacVicar *et al.* 2005). Arguably this is facilitated by the direct relationships between managers and employees as a function of business size. This is supported by evidence from a survey of 13 000 SME employees from 203 companies which reports that smaller businesses 'excel in the leadership stakes' where the top 100 small business employers score 4.9 per cent higher than the matching survey of the best 100 large business employers, with a 76.8 per cent average positive score (Rodrigues and Whyatt 2005: 2). This is explained with reference to the 'greater intimacy of smaller companies [that] means that senior managers and directors are more visible and influential' (ibid.). Maxwell's (2005a) study of the role of managers in work-life balance, which includes small business cases, also highlights both the centrality of managers and significance of organizational culture in work-life balance.

Further, business benefits associated with flexible working in smaller business have been identified, notably in staff retention and recruitment, employee relations and employee motivation (Maxwell *et al.* forthcoming 2007). In a similar vein, case study evidence presented by Harris and Foster (2005) points to the evidence that many small employers in the service sector are offering flexible working practices in order to retain employees. In addition, it is reported that smaller employers recognize that larger firms are able to offer better remuneration packages and career prospects to employees, but feel they can compensate by being 'more responsive to individual circumstances' and are more likely to be aware of these circumstances due to better communications channels (Harris and Foster 2005: 11). Their findings are based on 12 case studies (constructed from 50 telephone interviews with management) of firms with less than 100 employees from across five service sectors: entertainment, hotel and catering; retail; financial services; voluntary services; and business services. Given that female employees are present in significant numbers in these sectors, this provides an interesting base from which to explore further female progression into management within SMEs in the service sector.

CASE STUDIES OF FEMALES IN MANAGEMENT OF SMALLER BUSINESSES

It is notable in the above discussion that a largely 'gender blind' stance is adopted in studies of training, management and career development, particularly pertaining to the SME sector. Studies of female career progression into management generally do not differentiate between organizational size nor focus on the smaller business sector. It has been identified that females find it easier to progress in female-dominated contexts (Dreher 2003), and literature is now beginning to examine sectoral differences in female managerial career progression. In the voluntary sector, where 73 per cent of the workforce is female, 47 per cent of chief executives are also female (SCVO 1999). The proportions of female managers in finance and retailing is less, at 29 per cent and 41 per cent respectively (Equal Opportunities Commission (EOC) 2002). Generally in these two sectors, female representation at management levels remains disproportionate to their overall representation in the workforce, with a gap of 23 per cent in finance and 19 per cent in retail between the percentage of females in the workforce and the percentage occupying management positions, as shown in Table 8.1 (see also Broadbridge 1999; EOC 2002; Schmidt and Parker 2003). These data are drawn from case study research conducted between 2003–2005 on organizations in these sectors. In the cases represented here, most senior managers committing their organization to participation in the research study believed their organization performs well in gender balance terms and, indeed, the employment statistics provided show that in all organizations women are moving into managerial positions in greater proportions than the average for their sector. Further as shown in Table 8.1, in six of the seven smaller businesses, the difference between the proportion of female managers in relation to the proportion of females in the workforce is less than shown by the EOC sector average statistics.

Qualitative evidence to explore the factors underpinning the statistics described in the case studies was gathered from interviews with male and female managers at various levels in organizational hierarchies. Focus group meetings were also held in the larger SMEs with non-management employees, usually on a gender-defined basis as same gender peer support may foster deep levels of discovery (Morgan 1997). The lines of inquiry centred on different aspects of gender in management including HRM and HRD practices,

Table 8.1   Managerial gender balance, by sector and organizational size

Case descriptor	1. No. of employees (approx.)	2. Female employees (%)	3. Female managers – middle and senior (%)	4. Gap between (2) and (3)
Finance sector statistics*	–	52	29	–23
Finance case 1	144	65	49	–16
Finance case 2	34	65	54	–9
Finance case 3	23	83	60	–23
Retail sector statistics*	–	60	41	–19
Retail case 1	230	33	85	+52
Retail case 2	35	37	57	+20
Voluntary sector statistics* (health and social work)	–	–80	–52	–28
Voluntary case 1 (health and social work)	30	70	60	–10
Voluntary case 2 (health and social work)	17	83	75	–8

*Source: EOC (2002)

organizational culture and career progression. A sample of 79 people provided some prima facie evidence of factors that are conducive to females' career progression in smaller organizations and businesses.

The finance sector cases point to three significant enablers of women achieving management levels, as reported by Ogden (2005). First, 'an open door, relational and supportive management style where employees are given appropriate feedback about their performance and encouragement to make the time to attend appropriate training and development activities' (Ogden 2005: 19). Second, an organizational culture that allows for flexible working hours and work-life balance policies is important. Third, access to and funding of training and development emerges as an important enabler. Conversely, practices of networking and long working hours come out as career inhibitors for the development of female managers as the following quotations illustrate:

> Networking is very important. Men are more willing to be out in the evening with clients. (Ogden 2005: 16)

There's an attitude that beyond admin grades, time off in lieu doesn't happen anymore ... you have to start putting in extra hours. (Ogden 2005: 15).

The networking pressures are strongly associated with working in many parts of the finance industry, regardless of organizational size, due to the importance of developing business contacts (Ogden *et al*. 2006), although this issue was not raised by informants in Finance Case 3, a not-for-profit credit union which had the highest female representation at management levels.

The retail cases too reveal that management style, organizational culture and training and development practices are all important to females in management (Maxwell 2005b). In particular, 'individually orientated and people-centred management styles that allow employees to exercise initiative and thus gain the experience and confidence necessary for working at managerial level' (Maxwell 2005b: 21) are enabling. In Retail Case 1, the (male) Managing Director encapsulated the pervasive management style as stemming from the business' chairman thus:

We've tried to focus on investing in individuals. Our very charismatic chairman provides leadership and motivates through training and development and succession planning. The management style is fairly informal ... listening managers ... the business growing requires a balance between leadership and valuing people as individuals. (Maxwell 2005b: 12)

Approachability and sensitivity to family responsibilities are highlighted as supportive aspects of management as well. Like in the finance cases, manageable working hours and some commitment to flexible working are helpful aspects of organizational culture, alongside a generally open and supportive culture in which employees are valued and receive feedback. A range of HRM and HRD practices are highlighted: support and encouragement for training and development; structured management development; promotion based on performance merit; female role models in management; and employee appraisal and coaching activities. Principal among the barriers to women in management in the retail sector were long working hours, the absence of development opportunities and promotion based on length of service.

Again, in the voluntary sector, management style, organizational culture and HRM and HRD features are perceived to support women in management (Beattie 2005). People-centred, supportive and approachable managers, valuing employee diversity, HRD opportunities – often informal – role models, flexible working and formal HRM practices such as performance appraisal all emerge as important enablers, reflecting the findings in the small finance and retail cases. Conspicuous in the voluntary sector cases alone though is the organizational ethos and values element of organizational culture. In Voluntary Case 1 for instance, one employee expresses this succinctly as 'We're committed to values and to our colleagues' (Beattie 2005: 18). In Voluntary Case 2 the organizational ethos is evidently the main factor of women's career development. Here, 'there is a high level of collegiality and commitment to the cause, aims and objectives of the organization' (Beattie 2005: 19). Whilst the voluntary sector cases offer a number of factors that are conducive to females in management, at the same time a number of barriers are recognized. These barriers include limitations for progression as a direct function of small size and flat organizational structures, long working hours, together with limited formal HRD opportunities, and informal and inconsistent HRM practices.

Therefore it can be seen that the finance, retail and voluntary sector cases have in common key factors that are conducive to females in management. These are approachable, people-centred management; organizational cultures that allow for flexible working; and training and development opportunities. Because of the sheer size of smaller businesses, it can be argued that these factors may be readily applied where there is the all-important senior management commitment (Maxwell and Ogden 2006). Thus the hub of effecting a conducive working environment for females in management is the pivotal role played by owner-managers (Brand and Bax 2002; Mukhtar 2002) – or equivalent – in smaller businesses that can operate without the constraints of scale in larger organizations. However, the tendency for the cases to rely on informal practice in these areas may undermine the benefits achieved, which echoes Gray and Mabey's (2005) report. The balance between informal and formal practices in SMEs is then critical: structured, but flexible practices seem to be more enabling to women in management than wholly informal practices. As a consequence there is a need for SMEs to bring more formality to their HRM practices, not just as a result of business growth (Kotey and Slade 2005), and to their HRD practices, particularly as regards management development (Storey 2004).

CONCLUSIONS

In its investigation of how the smaller business context may impact on the prospects for females' progression into management, this chapter identifies and discusses several factors that, in concert, may make up a conducive environment for women in management. In the economically significant SME sector, where senior managers are both visible and influential, elements of HRM and HRD practices, organizational culture and work-life balance contribute to the creation of an environment that actively supports women in management.

In terms of HRM practices, recent legislation on flexible working increased the prospects of women being better able to manage work and non-work commitments (Mattis 1995). However, while SMEs may be characterized by business flexibility as a function of their size, it is apparent that there is a challenge for businesses operating in this sector to strike a balance between the advantages of informality and structuring work-life balance environments, which require a degree of formality. This has the potential to be mutually advantageous to SME businesses and employees alike, not least because the absence of consistent HRM practices have been found to be detrimental to women in management. Further, appropriate feedback, appraisal and performance based promotion are elemental to women in management – all requiring formalism.

As regards HRD practices, the uptake of the Investors in People standard in SMEs (IIP 2003) has arguably brought with it attention to training and development which has been identified as underpinning the progression of females into management. Where training centres on encouraging managers to shoulder responsibility for developing women, the prospects for women in management are further enhanced (Mattis 1995). Access to and manager support of training may be especially important facets of development for women in SMEs too, as indicated in the finance, retail and voluntary sector cases covered in this chapter. Again though, this research raises the need for applying greater formality to SME business practice in this area.

Turning to organizational culture wherein management style is important, there is evidence that flexible cultures and 'people-centred management styles' (Maxwell and Ogden 2006: 117) are conducive to females' progression in management. This is a recurrent finding across the finance, retail and – especially – voluntary sector smaller business cases profiled earlier in the chapter. Lastly, work-life balance, facilitated by flexible working arrangements, is a notable aspect of organizational culture. Although SMEs have the potential to support this, case study evidence presented here strongly suggests, once more, that there is a need to structure work-life policies more to contribute to consistent and supportive organizational cultures. As managers are the linchpin in this the proximity between managers and non-managers in SMEs presents a real opportunity to support women in management in the smaller business context.

To conclude, the smaller business context evidently offers at least a potentially conducive environment for women in management. In large measure this lies in the proximity between managers and their employees but relies upon the degree of formality and informality in HRM and HRD practices which themselves have been found to have a gendered element (Mukhtar 2002). In general, it appears that there is a need for greater formality in smaller businesses in the enabling HRM and HRD practices that buttress women in management. This, above all, may be the key to making the smaller business context a conducive environment for women in management.

REFERENCES

Baruch, Y. (2004), 'Transforming Careers: From Linear to Multidirectional Career Paths: Organizational and Individual Perspectives', *Career Development International*, **9**(1), 58–73.

Beattie, R.S. (2005), *Gender Balance in Management: the Voluntary Sector in Scotland*, Glasgow: Glasgow Caledonian University.

Brand M.F. and Bax E.H. (2002), 'Strategic HRM for SMEs: Implications for Firms and Policy', *Education and Training*, **44**(8/9), 451–63.

Bridge R. (2004), 'Small Firms Drowning Under a Tide of Employment Legislation', *Sunday Times*, 15 September.

Broadbridge, A. (1999), 'A Profile of Female Retail Managers: Some Insights', *The Service Industries Journal*, **19**(3), 135–61.

Carroll, M.M., Marchington, J., Earnshaw, J. and Taylor, S. (1999), 'Recruitment in Small Firms: Processes, Methods and Problems', *Employee Relations*, **21**(3), 236–50.

Carter, S., Anderson, S. and Shaw, E. (2001), 'Women's Business Ownership: A Review of the Academic, Popular and Internet Literature', Report to the Small Business Services, www.business.kingston.ac.uk (accessed January 2006).

Cassell, C., Nadin, S., Gray, M. and Clegg, C. (2002), 'Exploring Human Resource Management Practices in Small and Medium Sized Enterprises', *Personnel Review*, **31**(6), 671–95.

Collins-Dodd, C., Gordon, I.M. and Smart, C. (2004), 'Further Evidence on the Role of Gender in Financial Performance', *Journal of Small Business Management*, **42**(4), 395–417.

Department of Trade and Industry (DTI) (2005), 'Statistical Press Release', Small Business Service (SBS), 25 August, www.sbs.gov.uk (accessed January 2006).

Dreher, G.F. (2003), 'Breaking the Glass Ceiling: The Effects of Sex Ratios and Work-life Programs on Female Leadership at the Top', *Human Relations*, **56**(5), 541–62.

Duberley, J.P. and Walley, P. (1995), 'Assessing the Adoption of HRM by Small and Medium-sized Manufacturing Organizations', *International Journal of Human Resource Management*, **6**(4), 891–909.

Equal Opportunities Commission (2001), *Analysis of Labour Force Survey*, ONS: EOC, Manchester, Spring.

Equal Opportunities Commission (2002), *Women and Men in Britain: Management*, EOC: Manchester.

Gray, C. and Mabey, C. (2005), 'Management Development: Key Differences Between Small and Large Businesses in Europe', *International Small Business Journal*, **23**(5), 467–85.

Harris, L. and Foster, C. (2005), 'Small, Flexible and Family Friendly: Work Practices in Service Sector Businesses', *Employment Relations Research Series No. 47*, www.dti.gov.uk/er/inform.htm (accessed January 2006).

Haugh, H. and McKee, L. (2004), 'The Cultural Paradigm of the Smaller Firm', *Journal of Small Business Management*, **42**(4), 377–95.

Investors in People (2005), 'Company Report, 2004–5', www.iip.co.uk (accessed December 2005).

Investors in People (2003), 'Small Firms to Benefit from £30 Million Injection to Invest in Training and Development', Press Release, 27 February, www.iip.co.uk (accessed December 2005).

Keynote (2002), 'Small Businesses and Banks: 2002 Market Assessment', www.keynote.co.uk (accessed December 2005).

Kersley, B., Forth, J., Alpin, C., Bewley, H., Dix, G. and Oxenbridge, S. (2004), 'Inside the Workplace: First Findings from the 2004 Workplace Employment Relations Survey', Department of Trade and Industry, Ref No: Y8095, London, www.dti.gov.uk (accessed December 2005).

Kickul, J. (2001), 'Promises Made, Promises Broken: An Exploration of Employee Attraction and Retention Practices in Small Businesses', *Journal of Small Business Management*, **39**(4), 320–35.

Kinnie, N., Purcell, J., Hutcheson, S., Terry, M., Collinson, M. and Scarborough, H. (1999), 'Employment Relations in SMEs: Market-driven or Customer Shaped?' *Employee Relations*, **21**(3), 218–35.

Kotey, B. and Slade, P. (2005), 'Formal Human Resource Management Practices in Small Growing Firms', *Journal of Small Business Management*, **43**(1), 16–40.

Lado, A.A. and Wilson, M.C. (1994), 'Human Resource Systems and Sustained Competitive Advantage: A Competency Based Perspective', *Academy of Management Review*, **19** (October), 699–727.

Marlow, S. and Patton, D. (2002), 'Minding the Gap between Employers and Employees: the Challenges for Owner-managers of Smaller Manufacturing Firms', *Employee Relations*, **24**(5), 523–40.

Mattis, M.C. (1995), 'Corporate Initiatives for Advancing Women', *Women in Management Review*, **10**(7), 5–14.

Maxwell, G. (2005a), 'Checks and Balances: the Role of Managers in Work-life Balance Policies and Practices', *Journal of Retailing and Consumer Services*, **12**(3), 179–89.

Maxwell, G. (2005b), *Gender Balance in Management: The Retail Sector in Scotland*, Glasgow: Glasgow Caledonian University.

Maxwell, G. and Ogden, S. (2006), 'Career Development of Female Managers in Retailing: Inhibitors and Enablers', *Journal of Retailing and Consumer Services*, **13**(2), 111–20.

Maxwell, G., Rankine, L., Bell, S. and MacVicar, A. (2007), 'The Incidence and Impact of Flexible Working Arrangements in Smaller Businesses', *Employee Relations*, **29**(2).

MacVicar, A., McDougall, M., Bell, S., Maxwell, G. and Rankine, L. (2005), *Work-life Balance in Scotland: Encouraging the Expansion of Flexible Working Policies and Practice*, Glasgow: Glasgow Caledonian University.

Morgan, D. (1997), *Focus Groups as Qualitative Research* (2nd edn), California: Sage.

Mukhtar, S.M. (2002), 'Differences in Male and Female Management Characteristics: A Study of Owner-manager Businesses', *Small Business Economics*, **18**(4), 289–305.

Ogden, S. (2005), *Gender Balance in Management: the Finance Sector in Scotland*, Glasgow: Glasgow Caledonian University.

Ogden, S.M., McTavish, D. with McKean, L. (2006), 'Clearing the Way for Gender Balance in the Management of the UK Financial Services Industry: Enablers and Barriers', *Women in Management Review*, **21**(1), 40–53.

Rodrigues, N. and Whyatt, C. (2005), 'Small Firms Prove a Knock Out to Work For', *The Sunday Times*, 6 March, www.business.timesonline.co.uk (accessed December 2005).

Schmidt, R.A. and Parker, C. (2003), 'Diversity in Independent Retailing: Barriers and Benefits and the Impact of Gender', *International Journal of Retail Distribution Management*, **31**(8), 428–39.

Singh, V. and Vinnicombe, S. (2001), 'Impression Management, Commitment and Gender: Managing Others' Good Opinions', *European Management Journal*, **19**(2), 183–94.

Singh, V. and Vinnicombe, S. (2004), *Women Pass a Milestone: 101 Directorships on the FTSE 100 Boards: The Female FTSE Report 2003*, Bedford: Cranfield University School of Management.

SCVO (1999), *Gender and Job Role*, Edinburgh: SCVO.

Small Business Service (SBS) (2005), 'SME Definitions', www.sbs.gov.uk (accessed January 2006).

Storey, D.J. (2004), 'Exploring the Link, Among Small Firms, Between Management Training and Firm Performance: a Comparison Between the UK and other OECD Countries', *International Journal of Human Resource Management*, **15**(1), 112–30.

Tomlinson, F., Brockbank, A. and Traves, J. (1997), 'The "Feminization" of Management? Issues of "Sameness" and "Difference" in the Roles and Experiences of Female and Male Retail Managers', *Gender, Work and Organization*, **4**(4), 218–29.

Wagner, J. (1997), 'Firm Size and Job Quality: A Survey of the Evidence from Germany', *Small Business Economics*, **9**, 411–25.

Watson, J. (2003), 'Failure Rates for Female-controlled Businesses: Are they Different?', *Journal of Small Business Management*, **41**(3), 262–77.

9. Female entrepreneurship: challenges and opportunities – the case for online coaching

Sandra Fielden and Carrianne Hunt

INTRODUCTION

The creation of new businesses plays a pivotal role in the creation of new jobs. In the UK, new businesses, specifically small businesses, have been found to be the greatest single source of new jobs, providing employment at all stages of the economic cycle (Dale and Morgan 2001). Despite the increase in female entrepreneurship, women are only half as likely to be involved in entrepreneurial activity as their male counterparts (Harding 2004). Relevant business skill and knowledge is a key barrier for female entrepreneurs, with service providers acknowledging that the number of women who approach them for support remains low (Fielden *et al.* 2003). There are a variety of reasons why women do not access the support that is currently available, including: social background, lack of confidence, childcare responsibilities, and ethnicity (Fielden *et al.* 2003). Coaching has the potential to overcome these barriers to entrepreneurial activity. E-coaching could provide the ideal form of support for women entering business ownership. This chapter will report on a qualitative study, co-funded by the European Social Fund (ESF) and Manchester Business School. This study is an important step forward for research examining the experiences of women business owners in accessing business support and their views towards e-coaching as an alternative targeted form of business support. The project covered four North West regional areas: Greater Manchester, Liverpool and Merseyside, Lancashire, and Cheshire. Sixty women business owners were interviewed, which included a variety of businesses, from marketing and public relations, to landscape gardening.

DEFINING ENTREPRENEURSHIP

Some would argue that the characteristics of entrepreneurs and small business owners are inherently different. Entrepreneurs focus on inventive tactics that help them achieve their long-term growth and profitability. In contrast, small business owners tend to be motivated towards their own individual goals rather than that of expansion and profitability (Carland *et al.* 1984; Glueck 1980; Vesper 1990). Despite this distinction it can be difficult to identify any differences at the pre start-up stages of business, as the behaviour patterns are not easily distinguishable. Therefore, for this study, no differentiation will be made between entrepreneurs and small business owners.

FEMALE ENTREPRENEURSHIP

A Barclays Bank survey (2003) found that the number of females setting up in business increased from 117 000 in 2000 to 150 000 in 2003. This increase in female entrepreneurship has reduced the gap between male and female entrepreneurship in the UK, however women continue to encounter many barriers to entrepreneurship as a direct result of gender discrimination and social exclusion (Fielden *et al.* 2003). The GEM UK (Harding 2004) report found that women are less likely than men to be expecting to start a business, know an entrepreneur, see good business opportunities, and think that they have the necessary skills to start a business (Harding 2004). Barriers to female entrepreneurship cover the whole spectrum of business development, from pre-start-up to maturity. A main barrier reported by women is a lack of relevant business skill and knowledge. Furthermore, women do not access the support that is currently available to them. This is because of a variety of reasons, including: social background, lack of confidence, childcare responsibilities, and ethnicity (Schmidt and Parker 2003).

Over the past two decades, research has identified several central areas where female and male entrepreneurship are similar and, while female and male entrepreneurship share similarities, female entrepreneurship continues to display unique characteristics (Greene *et al.* 2003). A deeper understanding of the issues adversely impacting on women's entrepreneurial activity is a fundamental starting point in providing the business support for female entrepreneurs (Gatewood *et al.* 2003). Hurley (1999: 59) asserts that, 'the professionalization of entrepreneurship is creating a profession with the same male-dominated standards as traditional organizational theory'. To ensure that researchers examine the real experiences of women entrepreneurs it is essential to explore how male dominated standards are transferred to an entrepreneurial setting. By exploring these issues, researchers will have a deeper understanding of women's experiences of business ownership (Mirchandandi 1999). Many authors, particularly those from a liberal feminist perspective, have argued that self-employed women remain disadvantaged when compared with self-employed men. Women can face barriers relating to education, families and workplace (Kalleberg and Leicht 1991). Liberal feminist theorists would argue that men and women need access to equal opportunities for true equality to be achieved (Lowe and Bentson 1984). Social feminists, however, suggest that men and women are subjected to different socialization processes. These different socialization processes can result in women and men having different characteristics, experiences, and motivations (Fischer *et al.* 1993) and these differences in socialization can leave women at a disadvantage to their male counterparts, specifically when starting their own business (Jones and Tullous 2002).

Studies have identified an array of factors which can create barriers for women deciding to set up their own business, for example: greater responsibility for domestic and or caring arrangements, lack of confidence, credibility, lack of role models, and limitations on mobility (Chell 2002). Women also face conflict between work and family roles (Parasuraman *et al.* 1996) and women who have families are more inclined to face primary domestic responsibilities (Aldrich 1989). When establishing a business it is often necessary to work long hours. In the UK, domestic responsibilities and the impact of domestic work and family issues is significantly greater on the working lives of women than men (Barclays Bank 2000; Mitchell and Weller 2001).

In addition to domestic barriers, women's entrepreneurial networking activity is significantly lower than that of men (Katz and Williams 1997), with women frequently excluded from traditional networks or lacking information about relevant networks (Buttner and Rosen 1988; Kramer 1992), and having fewer role models (Mattis 2004). Women too are more likely to set up a business from home (Loscocco and Smith-Hunter 2004), which may consider-ably reduce their networking opportunities. This is of particular concern, since networks are undeniably effective for sharing and exchanging information, which can have a positive impact on business success (Doe 1998; Schor 1997; Rosenfeld 1996). Women have different requirements from networks, tending to use them as sounding boards (Moore and Buttner 1997).

COACHING

The potential of coaching as a professional and organizational development approach (now well documented in the literature) has only been recognized in the last two decades, with Tim Galleway (1986) being amongst the first to document movement of coaching from the sporting arena to business, presenting a method of coaching which could be applied to almost any situation (Whitmore 2002).

The literature produced on coaching is primarily discursive (Gorby 1937; Parkes 1955; Carroll 1975; Barratt 1985; Popper and Lipshitz 1992; Peterson 1993; Katz and Miller 1996; Day 2000; Wilkins 2000; Frisch 2001; Greenburg 2002; Storey 2003; Kilburg 2004), with few empirical studies examining this developmental intervention (Gershman 1967; Gant 1985; Sergio 1987; Thompson 1987; Miller 1990; Deviney 1994; Peterson 1993; McGibben 1995; Conway 2000; Wenzel 2001; Charbonneau 2003; Smither *et al.* 2003; Liljenstrand 2004).

To date there is no clearly agreed definition of coaching (Grant and Cavanagh 2004). Coaching is generally viewed as a form of mentoring, or as a certain aspect of mentoring, but simply having a more narrowed focus, usually relating to an individual's specific responsibilities or skills (Hopkins-Thompson 2000). Megginson and Boydell (1979) refer to coaching as on-the-job activity whereby one individual will give guidance to another to help them to improve their performance. Popper and Lipshitz (1992) believe that coaching involves psychosocial aspects, is not merely a focus on skills and tasks and has two components: first, improving performance at a skill level and second, establishing relations that allow a coach to develop the coachees psychological development (Popper and Lipshitz 1992).

It is evident that coaching relationships are a highly personalized development intervention and therefore require an examination of the coaching relationship in an entrepreneurial setting (Edwards 2003). Utilization of the internet and its link with business support development is an emergent area of interest, where there has been limited research (Evans and Volery 2001).

Despite the number of toolkits and models developed for coaching, there is a paucity of empirical research examining this development intervention. Furthermore, there is an absence of literature and empirical studies focusing on coaching in an entrepreneurial setting, with the available literature tending to focus on mentoring schemes (Stokes 2001; Sullivan 2000). The majority of coaching literature typically focuses on large organizations (Zeus and Skiffington 2004; Whitmore 2002). It is imperative to understand the learning processes of entrepreneurs, specifically when designing and delivering effective support (Sullivan 2000). Evans and Volery (2001: 340) state that 'generation, rather than cumulation of knowledge is needed' in this area of business support development. This chapter contributes to entrepreneurship theory, by combining women business owners' needs and requirements, with regard to business support, and the potential of an e-coaching programme provided by women for women: providing an evidence-based model of e-coaching, which can be used to facilitate business support provision. Bierema and Merriam (2002: 214) state, 'all sorts of barriers such as time, work responsibilities, geographical distance and lack of trust often reduce if not halt interaction'. Information technology can provide a method of communicating to overcome many of the problems and barriers experienced with traditional forms of business support.

AIM OF THE STUDY

The aim of this study was to ascertain the barriers to business support provision for female entrepreneurs, in order to develop an evidence-based approach to the design of a targeted e-coaching programme for women entrepreneurs. An inductive, qualitative approach was adopted. The study focused on ascertaining the needs, requirements and experiences of new and existing women business owners in the North West of England. Women business owners were interviewed across the four regional areas of the North West of England: Greater Manchester, Lancashire, Liverpool and Merseyside, and Cheshire.

DATA COLLECTION

Semi-structured interviews were conducted with 60 women business owners, with businesses ranging from pre-start-ups to those at the development and maturity stages. Businesses were in a range of sectors, including: retail, service and manufacturing. A purposive and snowballing sampling technique was used throughout the study. Participants were grouped as potential coaches ($n = 30$) and potential coachees ($n = 30$): women who were established and experienced business owners were identified as potential coaches, whereas women business owners, who were at the pre-start-up or start-up stages, were identified as potential coachees (see Table 9.1).

The ages of the women business owners ranged from 22 to 55 years of age, with an average age of 40 years. The majority of coaches (17) were married, whilst the majority of coachees were single (13). Over half (39) of the women in the study had children. The majority of women (50) in the study had attained qualifications post-GCSE, including degree, masters and diplomas and a high proportion (52) had been running their own business for five years or less. There was a fairly equal split across business sectors between the coaches and coachees.

Semi-structured telephone and face to face interviews were conducted, lasting between 20 and 60 minutes. Interviews were used to probe fully into the business experiences of women and, more specifically, to ascertain women's level of understanding of coaching and coaching relationships and their preferences with regard to this form of development. The interviews explored: current business support needs, current business support provision available, current formal and informal business support accessed, problems and barriers accessing formal business support, business support provision gaps, and understanding of coaching and e-coaching relationships.

Table 9.1   Personal demographics of North West's 60 women business owners

	Coaches ($n = 30$)	Coachees ($n = 30$)
Age:		
21–30	6.6%	6.6%
31–40	40%	60%
41 and over	53.3%	33.3%
Education:		
GCSEs/O-Levels	26.6%	6.6%
A-Levels	6.6%	6.6%
Degree	26.6%	50%
Postgrad diploma/Masters	40%	36.6%
Marital status:		
Married	56.6 (17)	13.3 (4)
Single	13.3 (4)	43.3 (13)
Divorced/widowed	16.6 (5)	23.3 (7)
Cohabiting	13.3 (4)	20 (6)
Number of children:		
None	20%	50%
One	0%	33.3%
Two	56.6%	13.3%
Three	23.3%	3.3%
Business age (years):		
Pre-start-up	0%	16.6%
1–5	73.3%	83.3%
6–10	6.6%	0%
11–15	6.6%	0%
16 and above	13.3%	0%
Business sector:		
Services	73.3%	73.3%
Retailing	6.6%	6.6%
Manufacturing	16.6%	10%
Other	3.3%	10%

KEY CONCEPTS

Business Support Availability

Despite an understanding that women can make a huge contribution to the growth of the UK economy (Shaw *et al.* 2001) and the variety of programmes developed to assist women in business (including start-up) there has been only limited success increasing the number of women-owned businesses (MaCaulay 2003). A study conducted by Fielden and Dawe (2004) concluded that many women are unaware of the initiatives that are supposedly available to them.

It is perhaps unsurprising that the availability of business support was an important issue raised by the majority of women interviewed and it was clear from initial investigations that many women were unaware of the support and advice available. The research showed that many women had found out about business support services by accident. Whilst this may also be an issue for men as well, women entrepreneurs tend not to access networks to the same degree as their male counterparts (Aldrich 1989), so are more reliant on the business support provided by organizations and agencies. As the following quotes illustrate:

> First of all, the hardest thing is where to find support. I only got involved with the Chamber of Commerce by chance and even then this was six months into my business set up. When you work for yourself you are isolated and so you don't know what is out there and don't know where to turn to. Once you have tapped into the support it's easier to get what you need, however, most women in business for the first time don't even know what they need in the first place. (46-year-old female entrepreneur, two-year-old business, service sector)

The Small Business Service (2003) annual survey, based on a sample of 8693 small businesses in the UK, found that just over one-third of respondents surveyed had not sought advice before starting up their business (Hurstfield and Atkinson 2004). A causal factor for this relatively low number of entrepreneurs accessing business support may have been that entrepreneurs are simply unaware of the support which is currently available to them.

Locality and Access of Business Support

An additional barrier facing women in business was the locality of business support organizations. First impressions would suggest that this is not a gender issue. However, women typically have primary responsibility for childcare and domestic responsibilities (Parasuraman *et al.* 1996), and they are more likely than their male counterparts to set up a business from home (Loscocco and Smith-Hunter 2004). Thus, basing service provision in central locations, for example city centres and town centres, can be an effective barrier, particularly for women business owners who have young children (Fielden *et al.* 2003).

> Normal business hours can be a real problem for women with children. (37-year-old female entrepreneur, one-year-old business, service sector)

A number of women ($n = 13$) in the study had not accessed any form of formal business support, the main reasons being a lack of knowledge and time pressures, particularly when considering the location of support agencies.

Networking

Research on female entrepreneurship has often highlighted the importance of networks and networking and the impact such activities can have on the success and indeed survival of businesses (Aldrich and Baker 1997; Rosa and Hamilton 1994; Aldrich 1989). Networking is seen as an invaluable method of gaining business support and advice. It is also seen as a way in which women can gain necessary contacts and combat feelings of loneliness and isolation that many women in business face. In an under-researched area, Carter *et al.* (2001) state that there are distinct gender differences apparent at the establishment stage of networks, in network management and in the use made of networks. They indicate that women are more likely to establish and become part of women only networks as are male entrepreneurs.

Networks are undeniably useful and effective, particularly in sharing and exchanging information (Doe 1998; Schor 1997; Rosenfeld 1996). Entrepreneurs are constantly being encouraged to establish and become part of networks as this can have a positive impact on business development (Birley *et al.* 1991). It was evident from this study that women understood the importance of networking, particularly with other women, as the following quote illustrates:

> Women need to learn how to network. Networking can help women in so many ways. (28-year-old female entrepreneur, 18-month-old business, service sector)

Despite this awareness, only half of the women in this study were part of an ongoing networking group, in keeping with previous research by Aldrich (1989), and Katz and Williams (1997), who conclude that women's networking activity is less developed than their male counterparts (see also

Kramer 1992 and Buttner and Rosen 1988). This was an experience common to the majority of women in this study who, while understanding that networking is fundamental to business success, highlight obstacles that remain, such as: knowledge, time and confidence, as the following quote illustrates:

> Networking support would be useful but it's very difficult for women just to walk into a room and network. (41-year-old female entrepreneur, five-year-old business, service sector)

> It can sometimes be difficult to access some of the organizations, especially if you live outside of towns. The travelling time eats into your day and when you are setting up every minute is very precious to you. (51-year-old female entrepreneur, four-year-old business, service sector)

Women prefer to work in clusters, not only to establish their business but also to maintain and, if decided, expand their business (Harding 2003). These clusters represent a number of women working together and accessing support from one another, similar to a network group. This once again highlights the need for women to work collectively to share their ideas, solutions, experiences, aspirations and inspirations.

> Mutual support from other women would be very helpful. (38-year-old female entrepreneur, seven-year-old business, service sector)

> Networking is important and learning from other female entrepreneurs' experiences, listening to their experiences can be a huge help. (41-year-old female entrepreneur, five-year-old business, service sector)

Many respondents believed that mutual support received from other women in business would be invaluable. The reasons for joining a network and the importance of networking tended to be focused on sharing experiences rather than networking in order to increase their customer base and profits. Rather than using a male model of networking, women prefer smaller, more intimate groups, where they feel less threatened and tended to want smaller and more personal networks (Aldrich 1989). This was supported by women in this study, as the following quote illustrates:

> It's more 'real' if it's a smaller and intimate group. (Focus group, Chamber of Commerce, Manchester, February 2005)

Tailored Support

Tailored support and advice was seen as imperative for women in this study. As Evans and Volery (2001: 337) state, 'in some cases, general information is ill suited to the entrepreneurs' needs'. Women required advice and support which was specific to their business, rather than the general information which was often provided by the business support organizations. When starting a business it is often difficult for the entrepreneur to know exactly what their needs are. Whilst this is not a gender issue, one must consider that female entrepreneurs often have reduced access to networks, particularly those with a home-based business and therefore rely heavily on gaining information and resources from conventional business support sources.

In such cases tailored advice and support targeted at a particular problem and a particular entrepreneur is required. A 'just in time' approach to assistance and learning may be more effective than a prescribed approach. This of course can be resource-intensive from both business support service and entrepreneurial perspectives. It is therefore essential that the learning process of entrepreneurs is fully researched and understood before programmes and initiatives are designed, developed and delivered. As Deakins (1996: 22) asserts, 'there is now a need for re-focusing research away from the emphasis on picking winners, to identify key issues in the learning and developmental processes of entrepreneurship'.

Participants, particularly potential coaches, believed that women needed 'intangible' business support, whereby at certain stages in the creation of a business, women may just need to talk through ideas, rather than receiving practical training. A general consensus among women was that talking about problems would help to clarify issues and would enable women business owners to gain a different viewpoint and perspective. This type of support may also bring to light problems or issues which women had not previously considered.

> I personally think women need a sounding board to think things through ... they need extra support that you can't get from practical support, so I suppose it's more intangible support. (32-year-old female entrepreneur, one-year-old business, service sector)

This finding is consistent with the work of Moore and Buttner (1997) who stated that women primarily use networks for sounding boards rather than for gaining actual resources. Women felt that a coaching relationship, unlike other business support provision, would allow them to share their ideas and discuss problems.

> A problem shared is a problem halved. (32-year-old female entrepreneur, one-year-old business, service sector)

Numerous studies have identified factors which affect women's propensity to set up in business, for example: greater responsibility for domestic and or caring arrangements, lack of confidence, credibility, lack of role models and limitations on mobility (Chell 2002). In addition, women-owned businesses tend to be perceived as 'lifestyle' businesses and not necessarily growth businesses (Lerner and Almor 2002). Thus, women need to be considered as individuals and their businesses should also be viewed in this way: each business is unique and therefore it is imperative that women receive support and advice that is unique to their experience.

> Coaching would provide you with one on one support, it will focus solely on your specific problem, issues, wants and needs, it will be tailored not generalist. (28-year-old female entrepreneur, 18-month-old business, service sector)

The lack of follow-up provided by business support agencies results in women business owners feeling isolated. Over half of the women in this study focused on the desirability of regular one-to-one support over an extended time period. By keeping in regular contact women believed that this would help them feel that they had someone to turn to who would provide them with some continuity of advice and support. The GEM UK (Harding 2003) report stated that women can have a lower perception of their skills and are less likely to know other entrepreneurs. Having one-to-one support would provide women with the advice that is pertinent to them and provides them with an insight into the type of issues that they need to address. This could reduce the fear that many women face when starting out in business and can help to establish and sustain confidence.

> Continued support that is the important thing. (37-year-old female entrepreneur, pre-start-up, service sector)

Coaching Versus Business Support

There was a consensus among respondents that coaching, by women for women, could provide the necessary support and personal service that is not currently available from business support agencies. Women believed that coaching could be tailored to the needs of the individual and would provide one-to-one support.

> I think it would provide a personal service and a service which is dedicated to the needs of women. It would be a personalized relationship, helping individual women achieve their individual needs. (38-year-old female entrepreneur, seven-year-old business, service sector)

The importance of individual support was believed to be important for providing motivation and guidance, as the coach would have an understanding of the coachee's business and future direction:

> Someone to work alongside you, to think about things in a different way, not a lecture style as training can be ... I don't know what I don't know. Business support organizations can't help you with this. (34-year-old female entrepreneur, 18-month-old business, service sector)

Coaching was also seen as an important development tool. Women believed that a coaching relationship would be more focused on specifics and that this form of support would be appropriate for women business owners. A number of women also stated the need for support in terms of personal skills and development, for example, confidence building and motivation. Coaching was seen as being more focused on individual requirements, specifically when compared with training courses that are aimed at a wide spectrum of individuals, as one woman stated:

> Each support process is different for each client/coachee when coaching, a woman in business could just have a problem with self-esteem, and you wouldn't be able to get support for this from a business support organization. Sometimes women do not know exactly what they need before they start and in that case a coach can provide this intangible support as and when it's required. (32-year-old female entrepreneur, one-year-old business, service sector)

E-coaching

Women viewed online coaching as a way in which they could access support at a time that was most convenient to them, overcoming many of the obstacles which women face when attempting to access traditional forms of business support, as indicated in the following interview:

> Women who are setting up their own business probably have a family and other commitments, this is good as it means they can access support when the kids are in bed. (32-year-old female entrepreneur, one-year-old business, service sector)

> Anytime, anywhere, anyplace advantage of online. (46-year-old female entrepreneur, twenty-three-year-old business, manufacturing sector)

Three-quarters of women in the study who had young children faced problems with childcare, and the problems of juggling family and work roles impacted both on the development of their business and also on their ability to access business support provision outside the home. Women tended to highlight these issues when discussing the advantages of online support:

> Online coaching can be accessed out of business hours, not like the nine to five which it is normally. (37-year-old female entrepreneur, pre-start-up, service sector)

CONCLUSION

An online coaching programme would provide a 'one-stop shop', whereby women business owners would be able to: receive support and guidance from their individual coach, network with other women business owners, and access information on pertinent issues relating to small business ownership. Women have very different experiences with regards to balancing their home and work life, often having primary responsibility for childcare and domestic responsibilities (Parasuraman *et al.* 1996; Aldrich 1989). Thus, whilst they are working hard to set up their business, they are also trying to perform a 'balancing act' between their work and family roles. Only by raising awareness of this and ensuring that business support provision goes someway to reconciling these opposing forces can there be a true levelling of the playing field for women and men in business start-up. Providing a programme online will enable women to access support at a time and place which is convenient for them, therefore fitting more appropriately with their lifestyle and daily responsibilities. An online coaching programme would also provide women with a discussion forum and a place to network with other women business owners. This would help to combat feelings of isolation and provide role models, by providing a forum whereby women can tap into networks that can provide them with support and guidance (Kramer 1992; Buttner and Rosen 1988).

The findings from this study tend to suggest that, in contrast to liberal feminist theory, women do not want identical opportunities to men. It is apparent that women require tailored support, which appreciates that women and men have different motivations and experiences of business ownership. If it is accepted that women have different experiences to men (Carter *et al.* 2001; Feldman and Bolino 2000; Hisrich *et al.* 1997), then it is imperative for women to be provided with support by someone who understands their experiences. An online coaching programme providing support, for women and by women, would provide an opportunity for women business owners to share similar experiences. Online coaching, for women business owners, provided by women business owners, provides both the method and the medium by which women can access appropriate support which truly satisfies their needs. As Evans and Volery's (2001: 334) Delphi study suggests; 'the internet is a powerful medium to provide the business development services much needed by entrepreneurs'.

It is acknowledged that small businesses are not simply large businesses scaled down, but that they have distinct and unique characteristics (Hill 2001). Thus, it is essential that developmental interventions, such as coaching, are not only examined in the context of large organizations, but are also studied within the small business sector, particularly as small businesses now contribute so greatly to the UK economy.

ACKNOWLEDGEMENTS

This study was funded by the European Social fund in collaboration with Manchester Business School. The authors would also like to thank the respondents who gave their time freely and participated in the study.

REFERENCES

Aldrich, H. (1989), 'Networking among Women Entrepreneurs' in O. Hagen, C. Rivchum and D. Sexton (eds), *Women-Owned Businesses*, New York: Praeger.

Aldrich, H. and Baker, T. (1997), 'Blinded by the Cites? Has There Been Progress in Entrepreneurship Research?', in D.L. Sexton and R. Smilor (eds), *Entrepreneurship 2000*, Chicago: Upstart Publishing, 377–401.

Barclays (2000), *Women in Business – the Barriers Start to Fall*, Barclays Bank plc, London, September.

Barclays (2003), *Women in Business Report*, www.business.barclays.co.uk/BBB/A/Content/Files/women_in_business.pdf

Barratt, A. (1985), 'Management Development: The Next Decade', *Journal of Management Development*, **4**(2), 3–9.

Bierema, L.L. and Meriam, S.B. (2002), 'E-mentoring: Using Computer Mediated Communication to Enhance the Mentoring Process', *Innovative Higher Education*, **26**(3), 211–27.

Birley, S., Cromie, S. and Myers, A. (1991), 'Entrepreneurial Networks: Their Emergence in Ireland and Overseas', *International Small Business Journal*, **9**(4), 56–74.

Butner, E.H. and Rosen, B. (1988), 'Bank Loan Officers' Perceptions of the Characteristics of Men, Women and Successful Entrepreneurs', *Journal of Business Venturing*, **3**, 249–58.

Carland, J.W., Hoy, F., Boulton, W.R. and Carland, J.A.C. (1984), 'Differentiating Entrepreneurs from Small Business Owners', *Academy of Management Review*, **9**, 354–9.

Carroll, A.B. (1975), 'The Joining-up Process: Issues in Effective Human Resource Development', *Training & Development Journal*, **29**(8), 3–7.

Carter, S., Anderson, S. and Shaw, E. (2001), *Women Business Ownership: A Review of the Academic, Popular and Internet Literature*, London: Small Business Service. Census 2001, www.statistics.gov.uk/census2001/default.asp

Charbonneau, M.A. (2003), 'Media Selection in Executive Coaching: A Qualitative Study', *Dissertation Abstracts International*, **64**(1), 450.

Chell, E. (2002), 'Women in Science Enterprise: an Exploration of the Issues, Some Policy Implications and Research Agenda', Paper presented at the Gender Research Forum, 8 November, Women & Equality Unit, London.

Clutterbuck, D. (1992), *Mentoring*, Henley: Henley Distance Learning.

Conway, R.L. (2000), 'The Impact of Coaching Mid-level Managers Utilizing Multi-rater Feedback (Managers)', *Dissertation Abstracts International*, **60** (7-A) 2672, US: University Microfilms International.

Dale, I. and Morgan, A. (2001), *Job Creation – The Role of New and Small Firms*, Small Business Service.

Day, D.V. (2000), 'Leadership Development: A Review in Context', *Leadership Quarterly*, **11**(4), 581–613.

Deakins, D. (1996), *Entrepreneurship and Small Firms*, Maidenhead: McGraw-Hill.

Deviney, D.E. (1994), 'The Effect of Coaching Using Multiple Rater Feedback to Change Supervisor Behavior', DAI-A 55/01, 114, Jul 1994.

Doe, H. (1998), 'An Exploratory Study of Networking Among Small Independent Midwest Specialty Store Retailers', unpublished Master's thesis, Ames, IA: Iowa State University.

ECOTEC Research and Consulting Ltd. (1997), 'Encouraging Sustainable Development Through Objective 2 Programmes: Guidance for Programme Managers', Final Report Manuscript, Birmingham.

Edwards, L. (2003), 'Coaching – the Latest Buzzword or a Truly Effective Management Tool?', *Industrial and Commercial Training*, **35**(7), 298–300.

Evans, D. and Volery, T. (2001), 'Online Business Development Services for Entrepreneurs: an Exploratory Study', *Entrepreneurship and Regional Development*, **13**, 333–50.

Feldman, D.C. and Bolino, M.C. (2000), 'Career Patterns of Self-employed: Career Motivations and Career Outcomes', *Journal of Small Business Management*, **38**(3), 53–67.

Fielden, S.L. and Dawe, A. (2004), 'Entrepreneurship and Social Inclusion', *Women in Management Review*, **19**(3), 139–42.

Fielden, S.L., Davidson, M.J., Dawe, A.J. and Makin, P.J. (2003), 'Factors Inhibiting the Economic Growth of Female Owned Small Businesses in North West England', *Journal of Small Business and Enterprise Development*, **10**(2), 151–66.

Fischer, E.M., Reuber, R.A. and Dyke, L.S. (1993), 'A Theoretical Overview and Extension of Research on Sex, Gender, and Entrepreneurship', *Journal of Business Venturing*, **8**(2), 151–68.

Frisch, M.H. (2001), 'The Emerging Role of the Internal Coach', *Consulting Psychology Journal: Practice & Research*, **53**(4), 240–50.

Gallway, T. (1986), 'The Inner Game of Tennis', in Whitmore, J. (2002), *Coaching for Performance: Growing People, Performance and Purpose* (3rd edition), London: Nicholas Brealey.

Gant, A.V. (1985), 'Coaching for Application of Inservice Training: Impact on Stages of Concern and Levels of use of Mainstreaming Concepts', *Dissertation Abstracts International*, **46**(4-A), 855.

Gatewood, E.J., Carter, N.M., Brush, C.G., Greene, P.G. and Hart, M.M. (2003), *Women Entrepreneurs, Their Ventures, and the Venture Capital Industry: An Annotated Bibliography*, Stockholm: ESBRI.

Gershman, L. (1967), 'The Effects of Specific Factors of the Supervisor–subordinate Coaching Climate upon Improvement of Attitude and Performance of the Subordinate', *Dissertation Abstracts International*, **28**(5-B), 2122.

Glueck, W.F. (1980), *Business Policy and Strategic Management*, New York: McGraw-Hill.

Gorby, C.B. (1937), 'Everyone Gets a Share of the Profits', *Factory Management & Maintenance*, **95**, 82–3.

Grant, A.M. and Cavanagh, M.J. (2004), 'Toward a Profession of Coaching: Sixty-five Years of Progress and Challenges for the Future', *International Journal of Evidence Based Coaching and Mentoring*, **2**(1) 1–16.

Greenberg, L.S. (2002), 'Coaching for Emotional Wisdom in Couples', in L.S. Greenberg (2002), *Emotion-focused Therapy: Coaching Clients to Work Through their Feelings*, Washington, DC: American Psychological Association.

Greene, P.G., Hart, M.M., Gatewood, E.J., Brush, C.G. and Carter, N.M. (2003), *Women Entrepreneurs: Moving Front and Center: An Overview of Research and Theory*, Commissioned by the Coleman Foundation, www.usasbe.org/knowledge/whitepapers/greene2003.pdf

Harding, R. (2003), *Global Entrepreneurship Monitor (GEM) Report*, London: London Business School.

Harding, R. (2004), *Global Entrepreneurship Monitor (GEM) Report*, London: London Business School.

Hill, J. (2001), 'A Multidimensional Study of the Key Determinants of Effective SME Marketing Activity: Part 1', *International Journal of Entrepreneurial Behaviour and Research*, **7**(5), 171–204.

Hisrich, R.D., Brush, C.G., Good, D. and DeSouza, G. (1997), 'Performance in Entrepreneurial Ventures: Does Gender Matter?', *Frontiers of Entrepreneurship Research*, Wellesley, MA: Babson Center for Entrepreneurship.

Holmquist, C. and Sundin, E. (1989), 'The Growth of Women's Entrepreneurship: Push or Pull Factors?', Paper presented to EIASM Conference on Small Business, University of Durham Business School.

Holmquist, C. and Sundin, E. (1988), 'Women as Entrepreneurs in Sweden – Conclusions from a Survey', *Frontiers of Entrepreneurship Research*, Wellesley, MA: Babson College.

Hopkins-Thompson, P.A. (2000), 'Colleagues Helping Colleagues: Mentoring and Coaching', *NASSP Bulletin*, **84**(617), 29–36.

Hurley, A.E. (1999), 'Incorporating Feminist Theories into Sociological Theories of Entrepreneurship', *Women in Management Review*, **14**(2), 54–62.

Hurstfield, J. and Atkinson, J. (2004), *The Annual Small Business Survey 2003: UK*, UK: Small Business Service.

Jones, K. and Tullous, R. (2002), 'Behaviours of Pre-Venture Entrepreneurs and Perceptions of Their Financial Needs', *Journal of Small Business Management*, **40**(3), 233–49.

Kalleberg, A.L. and Leicht, K.T. (1991), 'Gender and Organizational Performance: Determinants of Small Business Survival and Success', *Academy of Management Journal*, **34**(1), 136–61.

Katz, J.H. and Miller, F.A. (1996), 'Coaching Leaders through Culture Change', *Consulting Psychology Journal: Practice & Research*, **48**(2), 104–14.

Katz, J.A. and Williams, P.M. (1997), 'Gender, Self-employment and Weak-tie Networking through Formal Organizations', *Entrepreneurship and Regional Development*, **9**(3), 183–97.

Kenton, B. and Moody, D. (2001), *What Makes Coaching a Success?*, UK: Roffey Park Institute.

Kilburg, R.R. (1996), 'Towards a Conceptual Understanding and Definition of Executive Coaching', *Consulting Psychology Journal: Practice and Research*, **48**(2), 134–44.

Kilburg, R.R. (2004), 'Trudging Toward Dodoville: Conceptual Approaches and Case Studies in Executive Coaching', *Consulting Psychology Journal: Practice & Research*, **56**(4), 203–13.

Kramer, K.L. (1992), 'A Qualitative Study of an Educational Entrepreneurship

Program (Doctoral Dissertation, The Ohio State University, 1992)', *Dissertation Abstracts International*, **53**.

Lerner, M. and Almor, T. (2002), 'Relationships among Strategic Capabilities and the Performance of Women-owned Small Ventures', *Journal of Small Business Management*, **40**(2), 109–25.

Liljenstrand, A.M. (2004), *A Comparison of Practices and Approaches to Coaching Based on Academic Background*, San Diego: Alliant International University.

Loscocco, K. and Smith-Hunter, A. (2004), 'Women Home-based Business Owners: Insights from Comparative Analyses', *Women in Management*, **19**(3), 164–73.

Lowe, M. and Bentson, M.L. (1984), 'The Uneasy Alliance of Feminism and Academia', *WSIF*, **7**(3), 177–83.

Macaulay, C. (2003), 'Changes to Self-employment in the UK: 2002 to 2003', *Labour Market Trends*, London: Office for National Statistics.

Matthews, C.H. and Moser, S.B. (1996), 'A Longitudinal Investigation of the Impact of Family Background and Gender on Interest in Small Firm Ownership', *Journal of Small Business Management*, **34**(2), 29–43.

Mattis, M.C. (2004), 'Women Entrepreneurs: Out from Under the Glass Ceiling', *Women in Management Review*, **19**(3), 154–63.

McGibben, L.W. (1995), 'Evaluating Coaching Skills Training Through Subordinate's View of Organizational Climate and Managerial Skills', *MAI*, **33**(01), 261, February.

Megginson, D. and Boydell, T. (1979), *A Manager's Guide to Coaching*, London: Bacie, in M. Wallace (1991), *School-Centred Management Training*, London: Paul Chapman.

Miller, D.J. (1990), 'The Effect of Managerial Coaching on Transfer of Training', *Dissertation Abstracts International*, **50**(8-A), 24–35.

Mirchandani, K. (1999), 'Feminist Insight on Gendered Work: New Directions in Research on Women and Entrepreneurship', *Gender, Work, and Organization*, **6**(4), 224–35.

Mitchell, J. and Weller P. (2001), *The Small Business Service's Research Agenda on Female Entrepreneurship*, London: SBS Research & Evaluation Unit.

Moore, D.P. and Buttner, E.H. (1997), *Women Entrepreneurs: Moving Beyond the 'Glass Ceiling'*, Thousand Oaks, CA: Sage.

O'Connor, J. and Lages, A. (2004), *Coaching with NLP*, London: Element.

Orhan, M. and Scott, D. (2001), 'Why Women Enter into Entrepreneurship: an Explanatory Model', *Women in Management Review*, **16**(5), 232–43.

Parkes, R.C. (1955), 'We Use Seven Guides to Help Executives Develop', *Personnel Journal*, **33**, 326–8.

Parasuraman, S., Purohit, Y. and Godshalk, V.M. (1996), 'Work and Family Variables, Entrepreneurial Career Success and Psychological Well-being', *Journal of Vocational Behavior*, **48**(3), 275–300.

Parsloe, E. (1999), *The Manager as Coach and Mentor*, UK: CIPD.

Peel, D. (2004), 'Coaching and Mentoring in Small to Medium Sized Enterprises in the UK – Factors that Affect Success and a Possible Solution', *International Journal of Evidence Based Coaching and Mentoring*, **2**(1), 46–56.

Peterson, D.B. (1993), 'Skill Learning and Behavior Change in an Individually Tailored Management Coaching and Training Program', *DAI-B*, **54**(03), 1707, September.

Popper, M. and Lipshitz, R. (1992), 'Coaching on Leadership', *Leadership & Organization Development Journal*, **13**(7), 15–18.

Rosa, P. and Hamilton, D. (1994), 'Gender and Ownership in UK Small Firms', *Entrepreneurship Theory and Practice*, **18**(3), 11–28.

Rosenfeld, S.A. (1996), 'Does Cooperation Enhance Competitiveness? Assessing the Impacts of Inter-firm Collaboration', *Research Policy*, **25**(2), 247–63.

Sarason, Y. and Morrison, Y. (2005), 'Hispanic Women Entrepreneurs and Small Business Owners in the USA', in S.L. Fielden and M.J. Davidson (eds), *International Handbook of Women and Small Business Entrepreneurship*, Cheltenham, UK and Northampton, MA: Edward Elgar.

Schmidt, R.A. and Parker, C. (2003), 'Diversity in Independent Retailing: Barriers and Benefits – the Impact of Gender', *International Journal of Retail and Distribution Management*, **31**(8), 428–39.

Schor, S. (1997), 'Separate and Unequal: The Nature of Women's and Men's Career-building Relationships', *Business Horizons*, **40**(5), 51–8.

Sergio, J.P. (1987), 'Behavioral Coaching as an Intervention to Reduce Production Costs through a Decrease in Output', *DAI-B*, **47**(08), 3566, February.

Shaw, E., Carter, S. and Brierton, J. (2001), 'Unequal Entrepreneurs: Why Female Enterprise is an Uphill Business', *Policy Paper*, London: The Industrial Society.

Smither, J.W., London, M., Flautt, R., Vargas, Y. and Kucine, I. (2003), 'Can Working with an Executive Coach Improve Multisource Feedback Ratings over Time? A Quasi-experimental Field Study', *Personnel Psychology*, **56**(1), 23–44.

Stokes, A. (2001), 'Using Telementoring to Deliver Training to SMEs: a Pilot Study', *Education and Training*, **43**(6), 317–24.

Storey, M.A. (2003), 'Bringing Head and Heart to Coaching', *Organization Development Journal*, **21**(2), 77–81.

Sullivan, R. (2000), 'Entrepreneurial Learning and Mentoring', *International Journal of Entrepreneurial Behaviour and Research*, **6**(3), 160–75.

Thompson, A.D., Jr (1987), 'A Formative Evaluation of an Individualized Coaching Program for Business Managers and Professionals', *DAI-A*, **47**(12), 4339, June.

Vesper, K.H. (1990), *New Venture Strategy. Englewood Cliffs*, NJ: Prentice-Hall.

Wenzel, L.H. (2001), 'Understanding Managerial Coaching: The Role of Manager Attributes and Skills in Effective Coaching', *Dissertation Abstracts International: Section B: the Sciences & Engineering*, **61**(8-B), 4462, US: University Microfilms International.

Whitmore, J. (2002), *Coaching for Performance: Growing People, Performance and Purpose* (3rd edition), London: Nicholas Brealey.

Wilkins, B.M. (2000), 'A Grounded Theory Study of Personal Coaching', *Dissertation Abstracts International, A (Humanities and Social Sciences)*, **61**(5), 1713.

Zeus, P. and Skiffington, S. (2003), *The Complete Guide to Coaching at Work*, McGraw-Hill: Australia.

10. Gender and public management: education and health sectors

Duncan McTavish, Karen Miller and Robert Pyper

INTRODUCTION

The main focus of this chapter is a study of the emergence and development of gender as a key issue in two specific areas of public management: higher education and the National Health Service (NHS). The case studies are based upon ongoing programmes of empirical research. Health and higher education are particularly important loci for gender management research as they employ high proportions of women, face typical but significant challenges associated with the need to increase female representation in senior managerial roles.

The gender management issues and challenges in these key areas of public service can best be understood if they are located within a broader context which establishes the significance of gender as a feature of the Blair government's modernization strategy. Before turning our attention to the detailed cases of higher education and health, therefore, we can contextualize the discussion in the light of these broader parameters.

CONTEXT: GENDER AND MODERNIZATION IN UK PUBLIC MANAGEMENT

Traditional textbook descriptions of the UK unitary state tended to be misleading, even during the 'golden era' of British constitutional orthodoxy, in the sense that they minimized the complexities of the system in favour of apparent simplicities. Such descriptions no longer pass muster, even at the most basic level, in the era of the differentiated polity, the move from 'government' to the more complex modes of 'governance' and beyond all of this to the realms of multi-level governance (Kooiman 1993; Rhodes 1997; Pierre 2000; Newman 2001). Nonetheless, it would be wrong to dismiss the potential for even a modern UK central administration, albeit hedged-in by the complex interactions of an increasingly tangled set of governing systems, to send out clear signals of intent and set the tone for the prevailing managerial ethos in the public services.

> The significance of the politics of modernization, its form, pace and combination of ideological imperatives, means that the state must be understood not only in terms of its new, 'steering' form, shaping the actions of the plurality of agencies involved in dispersed governance, but also in its traditional role as legislator, regulator and policymaker. (Newman, 2005: 85)

The Blair administration, from 1997 onwards, attempted to deploy its power, in part at least, towards the end of establishing an agenda for the modernization of public service management and delivery. This was encapsulated in the *Modernising Government* White Paper, which, *inter alia*, enshrined the commitment to 'achieve greater diversity within public service' (Prime Minister 1999).

As a key sub-set of the modernization programme, the diversity agenda aimed to build upon the generally slow and patchy progress being made towards more proportional representation in public services employment (especially at senior levels) of women, people with disabilities, and people from ethnic minority communities. The gender dimension of the diversity agenda was encapsulated in a series of initiatives stemming from the very heart of Whitehall, some of which were largely symbolic. A Women and Equality Unit was established within the Cabinet Office, with a watching brief over these elements of the modernization agenda. A raft of social welfare policy developments, including child tax credits, the minimum wage, the New Deal for single parents, and measures designed to produce more 'family-friendly' workplaces, were promoted as part of the government's commitment to improve the social and economic position of women. In 2006, the government's Equality Act proposed the appointment of a Commissioner for Equality and Human Rights, and contained some key clauses on the issue of sex equality. The legislation places a gender duty on public sector organizations to ensure gender equality at policy and implementation levels. As one critical observer has noted, however, New Labour's primary commitment was to the fluid and imprecise concept of 'modernization' rather than to gender equality for its own sake. This critic argued that the strategy was

> based not on overcoming inequality or celebrating diversity but on the attempted installation of a homogeneous, consensual representation of the people ... Labour operated in an imaginary 'post-feminist' world in which conflict around gender issues was viewed as yesterday's agenda. (Newman, 2001: 155)

Notwithstanding this perspective, and whatever its precise motivation might have been, at a practical level the Blair government perceived the importance of leading by example, and saw that its calls for greater diversity in general, and gender balance in particular, across the public services would only have meaning if the organs of central government were seen to be embracing the new challenges. This led to the establishment of continuous monitoring of the gender balance within the civil service, agreement on key performance targets and regular reporting of outcomes.

Under the auspices of the Civil Service Management Board, a 'Diversity Champion' (Bill Jeffrey) and 'Chief Diversity Adviser' (Waqar Azmi), identify emerging policy issues for the civil service as a whole, share best practice across departments via a benchmarking exercise, support departments as they develop and implement their own diversity policies, promote a 'senior women's network' and a 'partnership scheme' designed to pair junior and senior female civil servants, and liaise with the Equality Coordination Unit in the DTI (which coordinates legislation, policy and public sector targets) and the Women and Equality Unit in the Cabinet Office. This work is taken forward in the context of a '10-point plan' for delivering a more diverse civil service (Cabinet Office 2005). The plan contains specific targets, which are to be achieved by 2008:

- 37 per cent of the Senior Civil Service to be women
- 30 per cent of top management posts in the civil service to be occupied by women.

While progress is being made towards the achievement of these targets, there remains a long way to go. The most recent, fully collated, published figures (from autumn 2004) show that women occupied 52.3 per cent of the 554 110 civil service posts in the UK. Women were disproportionately represented in the ranks of part-time staff (89.7 per cent). At Senior Civil Service level, women occupied 25.7 per cent of the 4510 posts (all figures from www.civilservice.gov.uk/management_of_the_civil_service/statistics). This leaves the government with a challenging target – to increase women's representation in the ranks of the Senior Civil Service by 11.3 per cent by the time the 2008 statistics are collated.

The government's modernization agenda focuses on valuing public sector employees, improving diversity and the human resource capacity of the public sector in order to improve upon the performance of public service delivery. The government has introduced a number of legislative and policy initiatives such as the Equality Act (2006), pay modernization schemes, continuous professional development programmes, family-friendly working directives, and so on. In order to ensure value for money and accountability for performance, the government has also introduced increasing number of performance and other new public management measures to ensure the effective use of financial and human resources. These and other managerialist interventions in addition to masculine, agentic organizational cultures converge to affect the career progression of women within the public sector despite policies which seek to create parity within the workplace.

The next section of the chapter explores the issue of managerialism, equal opportunities and female career progression within the education and health sectors in the UK. These sectors were specifically chosen as case studies given their socio-public objectives; high levels of relative public expenditure; the political and media attention each receives; and moreover the high levels of female employment in these sectors but the low representation of females at senior levels.

HIGHER EDUCATION: A TRADITIONALLY MALE ENVIRONMENT UNDERMINED?

It is not difficult to depict higher education traditionally as a male dominated space. It was only in the latter half of the nineteenth century that women were admitted (and then in a limited sense) as students at Cambridge, Oxford and London and only in the mid-1890s were women first appointed as university lecturers and professors (Brooks 1997; Rendell 1980). The male dominated 'club', collegiate academic culture – gender exclusive – has been well documented (for example Hearn 1999; Lewis and Copeland 1998).

This historically rooted traditional gendering has of course been severely undermined. First, there has been a longer term decay taking place from the Robbins Report (Robbins 1963) increasing social access from the 1960s, the continual increase in the numbers of female students (now the majority) and the creation of new cadres of institutions in the 1960s and again in the early 1990s.

Second, more recent legislative and other initiatives have dealt a blow (indeed targeted to do so) to the traditional gendering of the sector, attempting to force the pace of modernization. The equal opportunities environment has shifted from a position in the 1980s where the existence of such policies in higher education institutions was extremely patchy (Heward and Taylor 1994; Davies and Holloway 1995) to an environment from the late 1990s when almost all institutions have equal opportunities policies, with a shifting focus from individual discrimination to the current position where institutional discrimination and institutional responsibility is key (Deem *et al.* 2005). This responsibility will be intensified with the introduction of the Equality Act (2006) (see discussion above). From the mid–late 1990s increasing evidence of gender (and other) inequalities has helped drive these matters on to the public policy landscape, highlighting the requirement for action on unbalanced and inequitable gender outcomes. The Bett Report (1999) found that gender and ethnic discrimination in higher education pay and conditions was widespread. The pressure brought to bear from women within the sector must not be overlooked: 'Through the "glass ceiling"' (a network of women in senior positions, at or above the level of Dean or equivalent) claims to have played an important role in bringing such issues to the top of the agenda. Higher education institutions have collectively responded to this equality deficit. Universities UK (the body representing higher education principals) established the Commission on University Career Opportunity. In the late 1990s this became the Equalities Challenge Unit, a full-time staffed unit concerned with equality issues related to academic staff in higher education: universities are unusual in having such a sector-wide body to address staff equality issues; evidence perhaps of its necessity.

Finally there are the impacts of new public management on higher education, the rising prominence of accountability for the achievement of specified outputs, the availability of more women in the talent pool filling and flowing through the pipeline (for example in a number of institutions, research now shows initial recruitment and female promotion to senior/principal lecturer level moving towards proportionality (Docherty and Manfredi 2005)) and the apparent openness of meritocratic performance and output-based management regimes. Managerialism is distinctive for universities in that previously largely autonomous institutions which allocated resources as they saw fit are now subjected to an externally driven environment of controls, internally organized by forms of corporate and managerial hierarchy (Docherty and Manfredi 2005; Saunderson 2002; Thomas and Davies 2002; Goode and Bagilhole 1998; Davies and Holloway 1995; Morley and Walsh 1995). This meritocratic and managerial environment accentuating outputs and outcomes, while recognized as breaking down traditional gendered segregation patterns and providing openings for some women (for example Thomas and Davies 2002), may not however be gender neutral.

Clearly the traditional gendering of the sector has been undermined in many respects. Universities are no longer male dominated; there is not the same male collegiate gender-exclusive institutionally autonomous paradigm. Universities, neither from staff nor student perspectives, are not exclusively male-dominated spaces. Greater external controls and accountability, increased diversity of representation amongst staff and students, greater policy and public awareness of institutions' responsibilities for equal opportunities, increased internal accountability with its narrative of performance-based meritocracy have all challenged the traditional paradigm. What is now found is a different type of institution. The key issues are whether this post-traditional university is, in gender balance terms, a modernized institution with patterns of gender imbalance severely compromised, making male dominance difficult to detect; or indeed whether what exist now are re-gendered organizations. These issues can be viewed through first, the parameters of the equal opportunities environment in the sector; second, the senior management profile of the sector; and third, the prevailing academic career dynamic. The extent to which managerial regimes with accountability and meritocracy at their core have an impact will be explored.

HIGHER EDUCATION IN THE 2000S: MODERNIZED AND APPROACHING GENDER BALANCE, OR RE-GENDERED?

The Equal Opportunities Environment

Studies in the 1990s have outlined that the 'gap between rhetoric and reality [of equal opportunities] is relatively universal' (Bagilhole and Robinson 1997; Heward and Taylor 1993; Burton and Weiner 1993; Morley and Walsh 1996) and that equal opportunities policies have little effect on women academics (Heward and Taylor 1993).

The complexity of equal opportunities policies is captured in a range of literature. Although a recent detailed study of a representative group of UK universities found that 'compared with work done on equal opportunities issues for staff in higher education in the 1980s and 1990s, considerable progress has been achieved, in at least some fields and forms of equality' (Deem *et al*. 2005: 108). The same study noted a considerable variety of response from the higher education community on how equal opportunities policies impact on different groups. Other research has shown that equal opportunities policies are perceived as benefiting different groups unequally – with mothers seen to be benefiting most, followed by childless women and fathers, with childless men seen to benefit least (Bagilhole 2003). This has raised the possibility of equal opportunities policies actually being divisive. The multi-faceted nature of equality is just one indicator of complexity in this area. There are other indicators requiring explanation. Despite sector-wide recognized patterns of occupational and career segregation as well as disproportionality (in favour of men) in senior academic and managerial positions, a recent study assessing staff perception of the impact of equal opportunities policy on career development in a UK university found that women had more positive perceptions than men. The authors of this research have indicated that equal opportunities may have different meanings for males and females arising from diverse and far from unitary expectations and perceptions; 'grateful girls and grumpy old men' as the research paper is titled (McColl and Isles 2005).

Perhaps most significant of all is that the concept of mainstreaming equal opportunities (to develop and embed at policy, managerial, and all other levels of institutional operation) is not at all well understood in UK universities (Deem *et al*. 2005) and this may leave gendered and unequal practices in place – this could be of significance in various aspects of university activity and may help explain some of the practices and patterns observed below.

Senior Management in Universities

Are women still outsiders in higher education senior management? Over the UK as a whole 8 per cent of vice chancellors are women, 6 per cent of deputy vice chancellors, 21 per cent of pro vice chancellors, 20 per cent of deans (Bagilhole 2004). A more recent survey of Scottish universities shows a similar pattern (see Table 10.1).

Research from Australia (which has a mixed though in general more balanced gender profile than the UK) highlights the importance of 'critical mass' in increasing the numbers of females in senior positions in universities

Table 10.1   Scottish universities: senior management profile (at December 2005)[a]

Grade	Male	Female	% Male	% Female
Principals/Vice Chancellors	11	2	84	16
Depute Principals	17	3	85	15
Vice Principals/Pro Vice Principals/Pro Vice Chancellors/ Assistant Principals	35	7	83	17
Senior Management Group/ Principals Group	102	23	81	19
Dean/Dean equivalent[b]	69	17	80	20
Total	234	52	82	18

Source: McTavish (2005)

Notes:
[a]   The survey includes all Scotland's universities – 13 institutions. Excluded from the sample are two higher education institutions without university status, two specialist art schools, one specialist music and drama school, one specialist agricultural college, the University of the Highlands and Islands, as yet without university status. The Open University was also excluded.
   Institutions surveyed ranged from one with no females in any of the above categories, to the most gender balanced with around one-third of the Senior Management Group female, another with around one third of Deans female. One institution had more female than male Deans.
[b]   A number of institutions have a devolved college structure with the designated post 'Head of College'. This post has been treated as a Dean equivalent.

(Chesterman 2005). Given the UK numbers it would appear there is little prospect soon of critical mass being reached for women in the more senior positions in the nation's universities.

An explanatory framework for imbalance is in the area of career trajectory. A survey of the career background of the most senior positions in the UK (Vice Chancellors) indicates a science, engineering and technology background as the most common route (almost 60 per cent have this background); women are more likely to come from an arts, social science and humanities background (Bagilhole 2004). The picture for Scotland is similar (61 per cent with a science and technology background, the remainder with an arts, social science or business/professional background (McTavish 2005)). Research has also shown senior women are less likely than men to have experienced international mobility in their career (Bagilhole and White 2005). This it should be noted is in contrast to some European countries, for example Denmark (Langberg 2004 cited in Bagilhole and White 2005).

In addition to these differing trajectories, there appears to be career progression blockages which have a gendered dimension. Recent figures from the Higher Education Statistics Agency as well as some institutional-based research show that women are now progressing proportionally to the initial promoted lecturer grade (Docherty and Manfredi 2005). However, in terms of reaching the most senior levels a gender proportioned progression is unlikely any time soon: the overwhelming majority of heads of institution (over 80 per cent) are Professors (Halvorson, 2002), yet only 13.1 per cent of Professors are female (Hill 2003); other research shows that 4 per cent of female academics progress to Professor, whereas 14 per cent of males do (NATFE, 2002). All this has led one writer to suggest that by projecting current practices it will be 68 years before 50 per cent of Professors are female (Halvorsen 2002). This is in contrast with some other parts of the public sector where there appears to be determined action to address this misrepresentation. Other efforts include targets for the next five years and under new rules, meeting these targets will be one of the criteria used in annual appraisal to determine performance bonus payments for Permanent Secretaries (Report in *The Guardian*, 12 November 2005).

Other strands of explanation have looked at women's conscious career behaviour in the context of achieving a 'critical mass' of female representation. Kanter (1977) recognized that small numbers of women in an organization could lead to skewed or tilted groups leading to various behaviours from both the dominant and minority groups. Martin (2004) writes of tipping points, indicating that small proportions of women (he suggests up to 20 per cent) can receive a backlash but with over 40 per cent performance and morale substantially increase. This perhaps helps explain the well documented reticence and apprehension many women have in applying for senior posts (Bagilhole and White 2005). '[Women] are still being defined as outsiders in the world of management' (Chesterman 2004). The deeply gendered assumptions of senior management and professional life may lead to instability and setback even when it seems gradual but steady progress is being made towards greater gender balance. There is indeed accumulating international evidence in a variety of sectors of an attrition rate amongst senior women unwilling or unable to operate in this unwelcoming environment: Chesterman's study of senior women executives in public, private and higher education organizations (Chesterman 2004); Daniel's study of women leaving corporations in record numbers to start their own businesses (Daniel 2004); Hewlett and Luce's study of senior female executives in a range of US blue chip companies (Hewlett and Luce 2005).

Academic Career Dynamic

If achieving significant female representation at senior levels, especially at professional grades, is the key to critical mass, then it is important to focus on activity immediately beneath the senior management promotional structure – in other words to get a broad picture of the academic dynamic as it occurs to people developing and enhancing their careers. There are three aspects of this dynamic addressed: the apparent success in greater gender equality in appointment to the initial promotional grades; the levels of human capital by gender; the gendered implications of the managerial model applied in universities and in particular the role of research activity.

The increasing number of females entering the senior lecturer/principal lecturer position has been indicated above. This may not herald the start of an uninterrupted journey to a more gender balanced promotional and management structure. Like other sectors, family and caring responsibilities do not fall equally on males and females in academia. Probert (2005) has argued that the flexibility of the academic job often enables academics to work from home and this gives even more domestic responsibilities to women 'making it difficult for women to exert the power of absence'. Probert's study has pointed to the higher rates of separation and divorce among female academics, far higher rates of partnering among men than women (these having impacts on family care responsibilities) as particular explanations for the plateau women academics reach at senior lecturer level in their 40s.

Some trans-national studies have shown men to have higher levels of human capital than women, with higher proportions of men with PhDs on commencement of employment or gained after employment; men having more work experience in higher education; men having higher research productivity than women (Stoddart and Probert 2005). Other studies also indicate higher research productivity for men, but this being more related to academic rank –

within the same category there being no significant gender difference (Bordons *et al*. 2003). However Stoddart and Probert's study found that while women were just as successful as men when they applied for promotion, men applied earlier and more often leading the authors to conclude: 'even though men and women indicated similar ambitions about their academic futures, men more intensively and aggressively pursue their academic careers than women' (Stoddart and Probert 2005).

Organizational practices in universities illustrate a strong focus on managerialism. Performance targets and output focused activity as part of the new public management regime are now integral parts of higher education management with a regime of external controls and internal institutional hierarchies (for example Barrie *et al*. 2001). On the one hand some new opportunities and career areas offered by these practices have been captured by women, for example in academic programme management and quality assurance and improvement, but much of this has been at the cost of research (Morley 2005; Thomas and Davies 2002). On the other hand there is a view that this focus on managerialism represents an essentially 'male model' (notwithstanding that many males may feel alienated from it), agentic based (Deem 2003; Brooks and McKinnon 2001; Ozga and Deem 2000) which may make women 'aliens' (Harley 2003; Acker 1992), operating in a foreign environment.

A particular factor in the academic dynamic is the role of research which is a vital aspect of academic career advancement. The gendered dimension of research activity is clear, for the 2001 RAE men were twice as likely to be entered than women (Knights and Richards 2003). Less than 25 per cent of panel members and one in seven of panel chairs were women; the panels chaired by women were responsible for allocating less than 10 per cent of RAE funding (Morley 2005; also see Chapter 2). The position was such that the Roberts Review of the 2001 RAE recommended that 'the funding councils should monitor and report upon the gender balance of sub-panel members, sub-panel chairs, panel chairs, moderators and senior moderators' (Roberts 2003 Recommendation 13f). The gender composition of panel chairs for the 2008 RAE is nine males and six females (all figures from Funding Councils RAE 2008, www.rae.ac.uk/). The gender composition for sub-panel chairs is 57 males and ten females (ibid). For all panel and sub-panel members the gender composition is 746 men (74 per cent) and 259 women (26 per cent) (ibid).

So although the proportion of women main panel chairs is approaching balance with males, the composition of sub-panel chairs and panel and sub-panel members is little changed from the 2001 RAE. Beyond the boundaries of the RAE, there is other evidence of the gendered nature of research. A National Centre for Social Research survey of UK research councils and other major grant awarding bodies indicated that women made smaller numbers of applications than men and were less likely to be principal applicant; they also sought lower amounts of funding than males (National Centre for Social Research 2000). In 2002–2003 only 22 per cent of ESRC grants were allocated to women (Morley 2005).

Underlying explanations for this deeply gendered pattern of research activity include the broad ranging and the more specific. Some of these explanations are linked to the prevailing culture of managerialism as outlined. Many of the components of a successful research profile which include mobility between organizations, networking, reputation and prestige via publication, conference presentation, etc. (Kaulisch and Enders 2005) can present barriers to women given their unequal burden of domestic and family responsibility in relation to men (Deem 2003; Aveling 2002), making it more difficult for them to perform in a research environment which (particularly with the RAE focus) has a strong managerial target and output-based regime. Other explanations, also based on empirical research, show that the types of research women often do and the reference groups they develop are more likely to be local than cosmopolitan (Inglis 1999) with an adverse impact on the perceived prestige of research. Other research based on institutional practice has reported that women may spend significantly more time teaching and much less in research than men (Glazer-Raymo 1999) and also spend more time preparing for their classes and in advising students than male colleagues (Brooks 1997).

HEALTH SECTOR: FEMALE DEPENDENCE AND MALE DOMINANCE

The health sector in the UK is dominated by the NHS, the largest employer in Western Europe with approximately 1.3 million personnel (Department of Health 2004a). The health sector in the UK consists of personnel from diverse occupational groups such as management, health care professions (for example doctors and nurses), technical fields and hospitality and cleaning services, with a high proportion of highly trained and qualified staff. There is a high proportion of women employed in the health sector. In each of the health services for England, Scotland and Wales women constitute approximately 78 per cent of the workforce (Department of Health 2002a; ISD Scotland 2005; Welsh Assembly 2005). Almost half of the workforce consists of nurses, most of which are female with many employed on a part-time basis (ibid). Currently and increasingly there is a shortage of nurses, doctors and other health care professionals. This shortage has implications for health care as well the capacity of the NHS to deliver quality health care services. It is suggested in the Wanless Report (2002) that in the next 20 years there needs to be a substantial increase in doctors and nurses in order to meet increasing public health care demands. The capacity of the NHS is very much dependent on the size, composition and skills mix of its workforce, especially with demographics changes of an increased life expectancy and ageing population (Wanless 2002).

The capacity of the NHS is dependent mostly on a female workforce, but which functions within a masculine organizational culture and management system. Despite the high proportion of female employment in the NHS throughout the UK, relatively few women have reached senior levels in the NHS. In Scotland for example women constitute 33 per cent of senior management at Health Board level (all figures from www.show.scot.nhs.uk/organizations/orgindex.htm), while in England the representation of women is slightly better with 43 per cent of executive directors of NHS Trusts being women (Department of Health 2004a). However, given that there is a high proportion of female employment in the NHS, it would be expected that the representation of women at senior levels would be higher, but there is approximately a 30 to 40 per cent gender gap in leadership positions. Moreover, given that there are 535 NHS Trusts in England, thereby presenting more career opportunities than Scotland's 15 regional Health Boards, it would also be expected that there would be a higher proportion of women at leadership levels in the NHS.

NHS AND THE MODERNIZATION AGENDA

The NHS is probably that part of the public sector that has experienced most reforms and restructuring. Each successive government has placed its ideological mark on the NHS with the aim of improving public health at the same time as delivering an efficient and effective health service, that is modernizing the NHS. The NHS, like most public sector services, has a difficult task of balancing the infinite demand placed on the service with the finite means with which to deliver the service (Klein 2001). During the Conservative government years from the 1980s to the mid-1990s the NHS has seen the adoption of New Right thinking with the introduction of efficiency savings, private sector management principles, contracting out of services, the internal market, and the split of services by purchaser and provider, that is new public management. Many of these reforms were concerned with financial efficiency and control, responsiveness to the consumers of the service, performance management and target-setting, and de-regulation. New Labour has continued this trend of cost containment at the same time demanding more value for money, responsiveness to patients and continuous performance improvement. The New Labour government has maintained the purchaser–provider split in the NHS in England and has recently introduced Foundation Trusts as an incentive to better performing NHS organizations. Thus, in England the NHS still maintains a quasi-market as an effort to improve the efficiency and effectiveness of the NHS within financial constraints. In Scotland however, the NHS has abandoned the quasi-market by abolishing Trusts in 2004 and establishing Health Boards.

The New Labour government has sought to mainstream performance management within the NHS by instutionalizing it through systems such as clinical governance and organizations such as the National Institute for Clinical Excellence. At the core of this is a dilemma, endemic to the NHS since its inception. Most health care professionals through years of training and commitment to professionally regulated norms are committed to providing the best care possible. There are increasing health care demands and costs and political and public accountability to meet demands and expectations and contain public expenditure. Resolution of this dilemma is often articulated into government modernization policies and managerialist strategies such as increased performance measures, more efficiency savings, and even reforming or restructuring the health care system. These managerialist and agentic strategies and reforms often have negative outcomes for a female workforce. As mentioned above, Scotland has gone further than most health care systems in the UK by completely reforming and restructuring its NHS. The following section, based on primary research, explores the NHS in Scotland as a case study of attempts at modernization and the implications for its workforce, in particular female employees' career progression.

AN NHS CASE STUDY: SCOTLAND

Scotland presents an interesting case study. It has a high incidence of ill-health, but spends much more per capita on health care than England and Wales (Ham 2005). Scotland is reforming and restructuring its NHS by abolishing the internal market and establishing a single system of health care structure and organization for its 15 regions. NHS Scotland has adopted many of the modernization and managerialist strategies of England and Wales such as performance management, cost-containment and clinical governance. Scotland has the same workforce profile and issues as England and Wales, that is, a high proportion of female employment, shortages in health care professionals, a high proportion of nurses on part-time employment and low levels of female representation at senior managerial positions.

The health sector in Scotland employs approximately 198 000 people which constitutes almost 10 per cent of all employee jobs in Scotland (Scottish

Executive 2003a). The employment profile of NHS Scotland is that it has the highest employment rates for women, almost 78 per cent, relative to other sectors in Scotland; nurses constitute the largest proportion its workforce, approximately 43 per cent; approximately 90 per cent of its nursing and midwifery staff are female; and 50 per cent of female nurses and midwives are employed on a part-time basis (ISD Scotland 2005).

Scotland has a high incidence of ill-health and its health indices remains poor in comparison with other European countries despite high public expenditure levels (approximately 8 per cent of GDP) (Ham 2005). Scotland's life expectancy for women is the lowest in the European Union and there are high mortality rates for adults of working age (above the European mean) (Scottish Executive 2004). The Scottish Executive introduced the White Paper, *Partnership for Care*, in 2003 in an effort to modernize the health care system and meet political priorities such as health improvement; the reduction of health inequalities; high standards of healthcare and improved access; focusing on youth, the workplace and communities; involving patients and partners in health care; and devolving decision making to frontline staff (Scottish Executive 2003b). Most of the NHS in Scotland is in a process of restructuring and reforming to a single system of working. A number of NHS Trusts have now merged to form single unified NHS Health Boards. Thus, previously separate organizational entities are amalgamating into larger organizations with a consequent alignment of systems, processes, personnel, financial and physical arrangements, and services, as well as the attempted integration of organizational cultures.

NHS Reform in Scotland

In Scotland the dissolution of Trusts and the amalgamation of NHS bodies have resulted in a steeper hierarchy with less career progression opportunities for managers. Previously there would have been a number of executive positions for every Trust, now there are only 15 regional executive positions which will limit senior managerial and leadership opportunities. Research with male and female managers revealed that in order to progress in their career they may have to seek promotable posts outwith NHS Scotland (Miller 2005). An outcome of the NHS reforms in Scotland has resulted in limiting senior career opportunities for managers and may lead to increased attrition of management. There appears to be a consensus among managers who were interviewed, that change is a constant feature of the NHS which creates uncertainty, increased job demands and sometimes stress, often resulting in many managers and health care professionals seeking employment and career opportunities elsewhere. The current round of restructuring in NHS Scotland has, according to an interviewee, limited career opportunities and removed incentives for career progression: 'The way the NHS is now structured in Scotland has removed obvious career pathways' (ibid). And according to another interviewee 'with the new single system there is obviously going to be less opportunity for promotion in the future' (ibid).

In addition to continual reforms and restructuring, managerialist work practices and a masculine organizational culture of the NHS, there are other factors which affect the career progression of female employees. The lack of flexible work practices within the NHS Scotland and throughout the UK makes it difficult to achieve a work-life balance. Women still carry the burden of domestic and child care responsibilities in society. The lack of work practices which allow for female employees to accommodate their reproductive and domestic roles in part explains the high level of female part-time employment in the NHS. The difficulty of achieving a work-life balance is compounded when there are increasing political and managerialist demands placed upon the workforce. Many managers and health care professionals perceive promotion as compromising their work-life balance as it requires increased associated responsibilities and pressure to meet managerialist demands with increased performance assessment targets. The compromise of a work-life balance discourages employees from seeking career progression. The managerialist demands, emanating from political expectations, have seen the NHS held accountable for meeting performance targets within a resource constrained environment. Many within the NHS view this increased managerialism as having negative outcomes on retention rates, career advancement and succession planning.

Research with managerial and health care professionals reveals high levels of job demands and work-related stress (Miller 2005). For example a survey of an NHS organization indicated high levels of stress (60 per cent) and further research with medical practitioners revealed that 64 per cent experience high levels of stress (ibid). Furthermore, participants in the research were specifically requested to respond to a statement; 'I believe that too much bureaucracy makes promotion unattractive in the health sector', which revealed a strong cumulative agreement, almost 61 per cent, with the statement (ibid). This finding indicates that increased bureaucracy is an inhibiting factor to career progression within the NHS. NHS employees balance the idea of promotion and the consequent increase in job demands, bureaucracy, long working hours, demands to meet performance targets and associated stress, with the little received rewards and compromised work-life balance. Most are therefore reluctant to seek career advancement. Moreover, given the high proportion of women employed in the NHS it partly explains the low levels of female representation at senior levels within the NHS as it is becoming more difficult to balance work and life with increased political and managerialist demands. The following are qualitative statements made by research participants and are indicative of many views regarding the outcome of managerialism on retention rates and career progression within the NHS.

> When jobs or promotion do come up people now consider do they really want it, do they really want to go there! Is it worth the extra hours, money or work? There are too many targets, we are not in control of workload, we are driven by national policy initiatives.

> The biggest pressure is public perceptions or expectations. The public wants promises delivered. Politicians promise but clinicians and management have to deliver. The thumb screws get turned that we cannot meet expectations. I am all for targets but as a health service these can be unrealistic. Decisions are made nationally that are out of our control. They are unrealistic and unachievable expectations.

> [there is a] new generation of clinical and professional staff who do not find career progression attractive because of little reward.

The Medical Profession

The organizational culture within the NHS tends towards masculinity with job demands, structures and practices inconsistent with the needs of a largely female workforce to balance work and life. This is no more evident than in the medical profession. Research with medical practitioners reveals that 75 per cent believe it is more difficult for women to achieve senior clinical grades (Miller 2005). The difficulty lies in balancing a family with training for specialties in acute services, which follows a traditional male career path with full-time employment and training. The gender composition of the medical profession throughout the UK is changing with increasing numbers of women entering and employed in the profession. In Scotland women constitute almost 42 per cent of medical and dental staff in hospital and community health services (ISD Scotland 2005). Over 50 per cent of students in medical schools are female (Federation of Royal Colleges of Physicians 2001), but many prefer a general practitioner career which offers more flexible work practices. This preference for part-time employment has implications not only for the career development and progression of female health professionals, but increased shortages in clinical specialties and therefore the capacity of the NHS to deliver acute services. Female medical practitioners, because of their reproductive and domestic roles, are regarded by some as a professional or organizational liability. It is more expensive for Health Boards to employ trainee doctors on a part-time basis and the training framework does not allow for more flexible professional development, despite the introduction of Modernizing Medical Careers (Department of Health 2004b). Furthermore, in Scotland there is no workforce and financial planning for the increasing number of female medical practitioners on maternity and/or career breaks.

Research with medical practitioners revealed that almost 72 per cent of female respondents believe that if they took time off for family responsibilities it would harm their career as opposed to 17 per cent of male respondents (Miller 2005). Many within the medical profession believe that in order to prevent a gender occupational segregation between acute consultants and general practitioners, and moreover to increase the number of doctors in the NHS, the Scottish Executive (and for that matter the UK government) will need to provide adequate financial resources for training of doctors, provide more flexible work and professional development practices, and provide support (for example child care facilities) that accommodates or is cognizant of female employees' reproductive and domestic roles.

The UK government has recognized the need for flexible work practices in an effort to attract and retain staff given the increasing shortages of health care professionals. It has also launched a number of initiatives and policies to encourage flexible work practices and family-friendly work environments such as Women in the NHS – Opportunity 2000 and in Scotland the Partnership Information Network. However, flexible work practices are somewhat counter-intuitive to the managerialist ethos of cost-containment and agentic demands to meet performance targets. Despite the policy rhetoric of flexible work policies, the financial resources are not available or limited to enable these policies to be implemented. Many managers interviewed for this research indicated that there are no financial resources available, and no financial and workforce planning for increased flexible work practices. According to one interviewee;

> More female doctors are being qualified but nothing is being done to plan for it.
> What happens when three out of five cardiologists are on maternity leave?

The Nursing Profession

The lack of flexible work practices is indicative of the level of part-time employment in the NHS with 60 757 NHS Scotland employees of a total of 149 896 employees (40.5 per cent) employed on a part-time basis (ISD Scotland 2005). Nurses constitute the highest proportion of the workforce with half of all employed nurses employed on a part-time basis (ibid). Research conducted by Whittock *et al*. (2002) revealed that almost 60 per cent of nurses worked part-time due to child care commitments and a further 45 per cent took career breaks for reasons related to child care. Part-time employment offers the many females employed in the health sector the flexibility to balance work and family/child care commitments. Interviewees and respondents to a questionnaire stated that the lack of flexible work practices necessitated part-time employment, which often limited their career development (Miller 2005). The following statements are indicative of responses:

> In nursing there are many women, part-time nurses. Most are part-time because of family commitments ... a ward nurse would have to be on the ward the busiest time when patients' need, in the morning when they need their food, medication, etc. and it is the same time that mother is needed to get her kids ready.

> There is more of a huge issue about size of the jobs. People often work 12 hours a day, it's hard to balance work life ... there is also an issue of salary for example there is not enough money between grades E to G.

> career breaks for family and unfortunately the need of the family are often seen as less important by employers or peers, etc.

The NHS and its managers often perceive employees, mostly female, who opt for part-time employment as an organizational liability. Managers perceive part-time employment less favourably, viewing part-time employees as less committed to their work and career. This perception, particularly in the case of nurses, affects their opportunities to be considered for promotion, training and professional development, and therefore creates difficulties in meeting the clinical and registration standards set by the Nursing and Midwifery Council (Edwards *et al*. 2001; Whittock *et al*. 2002). Research conducted by Lane (1999) indicated that almost a quarter of part-time nurses experienced a change in grade when they opted from full- to part-time employment. In the nursing profession career breaks often result in career stagnation or regression and if nurses do not maintain their clinical knowledge and practice they invariably regress to a lower grade or at worse lose their registration status. This is often de-motivating and a disincentive to return to nursing. Lane's (1999) research revealed a concentration of women, especially those working part-time, in the lower echelons of the profession. Similar research by Whittock *et al*. (2002) showed that men occupy a disproportionately high number of senior grades in the nursing profession with 56 per cent of male nurses employed in grade H compared with 31 per cent of female nurse managers. Research with nurses showed that female nurses are aware of the disproportionate representation of male nurses at higher, particularly managerial grades, with many reporting a subsequent traditional male culture and attitude at managerial level (Miller 2005).

The lack of flexible work practices, agentic managerial and organizational attitudes, and regulatory and managerialist demands contribute to the career stagnation or regression of female nurses and thereby the concentration of female nurses at lower echelons of the NHS; at worst it contributes to increased attrition of nurses. Moreover, this will have implications for attracting and retaining nurses and other female health professionals as well as filling vacancies in senior clinical and managerial grades. It is recognized that the UK government and the Scottish Executive is attempting to address the gender inequalities which exist in the NHS. However, the organizational culture, managerialist demands and financial arrangements are biased towards full-time traditional training, professional development and career paths. The lack of flexible work practices and the perception of women as an organizational liability create barriers to female employees' career development and perpetuate gender inequalities in the health sector.

CONCLUSION

The traditional model of a hegemonic male dominated culture, and at worse gender discrimination, is still prevalent within the public sector despite legislative and policy efforts to improve the representation and career progression of women (and other excluded groups) to senior management and leadership positions. Government's 'modernization' and legislative efforts such as equal opportunities, equal pay and other sectoral and institutional initiatives should be acknowledged. However legislative and policy efforts to increase women to leadership positions within the public sector have been in existence for 30 years. The implementation (in some cases the lack thereof) of these policies reveal the complex nature of the relative positions of men and women in the workplace. As the two sectors discussed above reveal, the introduction of these policies has had inconsistent outcomes for women in the workplace. Moreover, the introduction of other modernization initiatives such as managerialist measures have reinforced agentic, masculine organizational cultures with a focus on outputs, performance and external accountability to the sacrifice of a work-life balance and the career progression of women in the public sector.

REFERENCES

Acker, S. (1992), 'New Perspectives on an Old Problem: the Position of Women Academics in British Higher Education', *Higher Education*, **24**(1) 57–75.

Aveling, N. (2002), 'Having it All and the Discourse of Equal Opportunity: Reflections on Choice and Changing Perceptions', *Gender and Education*, **14**(3) 265–80.

Bagilhole, B. (2003), 'One Step Forward and Two Steps Back? A Case Study of a Strategy to Promote Gender Equality in a UK University and the Resistance Encountered', in V. Maione (ed.), *Gender Equality in Higher Education. Proceedings of the Third European Conference in Genoa*, Milano: Franco Angeli.

Bagilhole, B. (2004), *Website Survey of Senior Managers in UK Universities*, Loughborough University, UK.

Bagilhole, B. and Robinson, E. (1997), *A Report on Policies and Practices on Equal Opportunities in Employment in Universities and Colleges of Higher Education.* London: Commission on University Career Opportunity, Committee of Vice Chancellors and Principals of the Universities of the UK (CVCP).

Bagilhole, B. and White, K. (2005), 'Benign Burden: Gender and Senior Management in the UK and Australia', Paper presented at the Fourth European Conference on Gender Equality in Higher Education, Oxford.

Barrie, J., Chandler, J. and Clark, H. (2001), 'Between the Ivory Tower and the Academic Assembly Line', *Journal of Management Studies*, **38**(1) 87–102.

Bett, M. (1990), *Independent Review of Higher Education Employment and Conditions,* London: HMSO.

Bordons, M., Morillo, M., Fernandez, T. and Gomez, I. (2003), 'One Step Further in the Production of Bibliometrics Indicator at the Micro Level: Differences in Gender and Professional Category of Scientists', *Scientometrics,* **57**, 159–73.

Brooks, A. (1997), *Academic Women,* Buckingham: The Society for Research into Higher Education and Open University Press.

Brooks, A. and MacKinnon, A. (eds) (2001), *Gender and the Restructured University: Changing Management and Culture in Higher Education*, Buckingham: Open University Press.

Burton, C. and Weiner, G. (1993), 'From Rhetoric to Reality: Strategies for Developing a Social Justice Approach to Educational Decision Making', in I. Siraj-Blatchford (ed.), *Race Gender and the Education of Teachers*, Buckingham: Open University Press.

Cabinet Office (2005), *Delivering a Diverse Civil Service, A 10-Point Plan*, London: Cabinet Office.

Chesterman, C. (2004), 'Senior Women Executives and the Cultures of Management: a Brief Cross-examination of Public, Private and Higher Education Organizations', *Senior Women Executives and the Cultures of Management Conference, ATNWEXDEV*, www.uts.edu.au/oth/wexdev.

Chesterman, C. (2005), '"Not Just a Token Female": the Importance of "Critical Mass" of Women in Senior Management in Higher Education', Paper presented at the Fourth International Conference of Gender Equality in Higher Education, Oxford.

Daniel, T. (2004), 'What "Glass Ceiling?" How Women Owned Small Businesses are Re-defining True Female Empowerment', Paper presented at the Fourth International Conference on Diversity in Organizations, Communities and Nations, UCLA.

Davies, C. and Holloway, P. (1995), 'Troubling Transformations: Gender Regimes and Organizational Cultures in the Academy', in L. Morley and V. Walsh (eds), *Feminist Academics*, London: Taylor and Francis.

Dearing, R. (1997), *National Committee of Enquiry into Higher Education*, London: HMSO.

Deem, R. (2003), 'Gender, Organizational Cultures and the Practices of Manager – Academics in UK Universities', *Gender, Work and Organization*, **10**(2), 239–59.

Deem, R., Morley, L. and Tlili, A. (2005), *Negotiating Equity in Higher Education Institutions – Project 3 of Equal Opportunities and Diversity for Staff in Higher Education Institutions*, Higher Education Funding Council, Scottish Higher Education Funding Council, Higher Education Funding Council for Wales.

Department of Health (2002a), *NHS Hospital and Community Health Services: Total Employment by Sex at 30 September 2002*, www.performance.doh.gov.uk/HPSSS/TBL_D3.HTM, November 2005.

Department of Health (2002b), *Clinical Governance,* www.dh.gov.uk/PolicyAnd Guidance/HealthAndSocialCareTopics/ClinicalGovernance/ClinicalGovernance GeneralInformation/fs/en, November 2005.

Department of Health (2004a), *Staff in the NHS 2004*, London: Government Statistical Service.

Department of Health (2004b), *Modernising Medical Careers*, London: HMSO.

Department of Health (2004c), *Agenda for Change*, London: HMSO.

Department of Trade and Industry (2004), *Fairness for All*, London: HMSO.

Doherty, L. and Manfredi, S. (2005), 'Women's Progression in English Universities', Paper presented to the Fourth European Conference on Gender Equality in Higher Education, Oxford.

Edwards, C., McLaren, S., Robinson, O. and Whittock, M. (2000), *Part-Time Working in Nursing*, Kingston University, Survey Report.

Equality Act (2006), HMSO.

Federation of Royal Colleges of Physicians (2001), *Women in Hospital Medicine: Career Choices and Opportunities*, London: Federation of Royal Colleges of Physicians.

Glazer-Raymo, J. (1999), *Shattering the Myths: Women in Academe*, Baltimore: John Hopkins University Press.

Goode, J. and Bagilhole, B. (1998), 'Gendering the Management of Change in Higher Education: a Case Study', *Gender Work and Organization*, **5**(3), 148–64.

Halvorsen, E. (2002), 'Female Academics in a Knowledge Production Society', *Higher Education Quarterly*, **56**(4), 347–59.

Ham, C. (2005), *Health Policy in Britain: The Politics and Organization of The National Health Service*, Basingstoke: Palgrave Macmillan.

Harley, S. (2003), 'Research Selectivity and Female Academics in Universities: From Gentleman's Club and Barrack Yard to Smart Macho?', *Gender and Education*, **15**(4), 377–92.

Harvey, J.C. and Katz, C. (1983), *If I'm So Successful, Why Do I Feel Like a Fake?: Imposter Syndrome*, New York: St Martins Press.

Hearn, J. (1999) 'Men, Managers and Management: the Case of Higher Education', in S. Whitehead and R. Moodley (eds), *Transforming Managers: Gendering Change in the Public Sector*, London: UCL Press.

Heward, C. and Taylor, P. (1993), 'Effective and Ineffective Equal Opportunities Policies in Higher Education', *Critical Social Policy*, **37**, 75–94.

Heward, C. and Taylor, P. (1994), 'Women at the Top in Higher Education', *Policy and Politics*, **20**(1), 11–121.

Hewlett, S.A. and Luce, C.B. (2005), 'Off Ramps and on Ramps. Keeping Talented Women on the Road to Success', *Harvard Business Review*, March.

Hill, J. (2003), *Facing the Challenge in UK Higher Education*, London: Equalities Challenge Unit.

Inglis, L. (1999), 'Motives and Performance: Why Academics Research', Department of Management, Monash University, Working Paper 01/99.

ISD Scotland (2005), *NHS Scotland Workforce Statistics*, www.isdscotland.org, November.

Kanter, R. (1977), *Men and Women of the Corporation*, New York: Basic Books.

Kaulisch, M. and Enders, J. (2005), 'Career in Overlapping Institutional Contexts: The Case of Academe', *Career Development International*, **10**(2), 42–55.

Klein, R. (2000), *New Politics of the NHS*, London: Prentice Hall.

Knights, D. and Richards, W. (2003), 'Sex Discrimination in UK Academia', *Gender, Work and Organization*, **10**(2), 213–38.

Kooiman, J. (1993), *Modern Governance: Government-Society Interactions*, London: Sage.

Lane, N. (1999), 'Sources of Career Disadvantage in Nursing', *Journal of Management in Medicine*, **13**(6), 373–89.

Lewis, S. and Copeland, J. (1998), 'We're Tired of Talking about Women: Working with Men to Address the Culture of Male Dominated Work and Study Places', Paper presented at the Winds of Change: Women and the Culture of Universities International Conference, University of Technology, Sydney.

Martin, J. (2004), 'Treacherous Terrain: Equality and Equality at Work and at Home', Paper presented at the Senior Women Executives and the Cultures of Management Conference, ATNWEXDEV, www.uts.edu.au./oth/wexdev

McColl, P. and Isles, P. (2005), 'Exploring Career Satisfaction Among Academic Staff at a UK University – a Case of Grumpy Old Men and Grateful Girls?', Paper presented at the Fourth European Conference on Gender Equality in Higher Education, Oxford.

McTavish, D. (2005), *Website and Telephone Survey of Senior Management in Scottish Universities*, Glasgow Caledonian University, UK.

Miller, K. (2005), *Gender Balance in the Health Sector*, Glasgow: ESF, Scottish Leadership Foundation and Glasgow Caledonian Research Project.

Morley, L. (2005), 'Opportunity or Exploitation? Women and Quality Assurance in Higher Education', *Gender and Education*, **17**(4), 411–29.

Morley, L. and Walsh, V. (eds) (1995), *Feminist Academics*, London: Taylor and Francis.

Morley, L. and Walsh, V. (1996), 'Introduction', in L. Morley and V. Walsh (eds), *Breaking Boundaries: Women in Higher Education*, London: Taylor and Francis.

NATFHE (2002), 'The Price of Equality: Comprehensive Spending Review 2003/4 – 2005/6', *Higher Education Submission*, January, London: NATFHE.

Newman, J. (2001), *Modernising Governance. New Labour, Policy and Society*, London: Sage.

Newman, J. (2005), 'Regendering Governance', in J. Newman (ed.), *Remaking Governance. Peoples, Politics and the Public Sphere*, Bristol: The Policy Press.

NCSR (2000), *Who Applies for Research Funding?*, London: National Centre for Social Research.

NHS Executive (2000), *Women in the NHS – Opportunity 2000*, London: HMSO.

Ozga, J. and Deem, R. (2000), 'Colluded Selves, New Times and Engendered Organizational Cultures: the Experiences of Feminist Women-managers in UK Higher and Further Education', *Discourse*, **21**(2), 141–54.

Pierre, J. (2000), *Debating Governance*, Oxford: Oxford University Press.

Prime Minister (1999), *Modernising Government*, Cm. 4310, London: HMSO.

Probert, B. (2005), 'I Just Couldn't Fit It In: Gendered Outcomes in Academic Careers', *Gender Work and Organization*, **12**(1), 50–72.

Rendell, M. (1980), 'How Many Women Academics?' in R. Deem (ed.), *Schooling for Women's Work*, London: Routledge.

Rhodes, R.A.W. (1997), *Understanding Governance*, Buckingham: Open University Press.

Robbins, Lord (1963), *Committee on Higher Education Report*, Cm. 2145, London: HMSO.

Roberts, G.G. (2003), *Review of Research Assessment: Report by Sir Gareth Roberts to the UK Funding Bodies*, www.hefc.ac.uk

Saunderson, W. (2002), 'Women, Academia and Identity: Constructions of Equal Opportunities in the "New Managerialism" – a Case Study of Lipstick on the Gorilla?', *Higher Education Quarterly*, **56**(4), 376–406.

Scottish Executive (2003a), *Health Sector: Scottish Sector Profile 2003*, Edinburgh: Scottish Executive.

Scottish Executive (2003b), *Partnership for Care*, Edinburgh: Scottish Executive.

Scottish Executive (2004), *Health in Scotland*, Edinburgh: Scottish Executive.

Stoddart, J. and Probert, B. (2005), 'What Was the Question Again? Reflections on Research and Gender Equality Policies and Practice in a Changing Environment', Paper presented at the Fourth European Conference on Gender Equality in Higher Education, Oxford.

Thomas, T. and Davies, A. (2002), 'Gender and the New Public Management: Reconstituting Academic Subjectivities', *Gender Work and Organization*, **9**(4), 372–96.

Through the 'Glass Ceiling' (2005), *The First Fifteen Years – Into the Twenty First Century*, Through the 'Glass Ceiling'.

Vinnicombe, S. (2000), 'The Position of Men and Women in Management in Europe', in M.J. Davidson and R.J. Burke (eds), *Women in Management. Current Research Issues Vol 11*, London: Sage.

Wanless, D. (2002), *Securing our Future Health: Taking a Long-Term View*, London: HMSO.

Welsh Assembly (2005), *Health Statistics Wales 2005*, www.wales.gov.uk/keypubstatisticsforwales/content/publication/health/2004/hsw2005/hsw2005-ch14/hsw2005-ch14.htm, November 2005.

Whittock, M., Edwards, C., McLaren, S. and Robinson, O. (2002), '"The Tender Trap": Gender, Part-time Nursing and the Effects of "Family Friendly" Policies on Career Advancement', *Sociology of Health and Illness*, **24**(3), 305–26.

11. Gender and management in the European Commission

Ann Stevens and Roger Levy

INTRODUCTION

Over the last 30 years there has been not only an increasing feminist interest in feminist comparative politics, women and public policy, and feminist policy formation (Mazur 2002), but also an important, if still relatively small, body of work on women in organizations and in leadership, pioneered by Kanter (1977). She looked at organizations with bureaucratic structures, and linked the gender structures she observed there to power relations: 'A preference for male managers and superordinates is, insists Kanter, a preference for power, and power is something men possess' (Savage and Witz 1993: 15). Ferguson's influential theoretical work in the early 1980s (Ferguson 1984) argued on feminist grounds for a general rejection by women of bureaucratic modes of organization and the development of feminist alternatives. This leaves open the theoretical dilemma whether bureaucracies are so inherently gendered as masculine-dominated structures that women cannot – and possibly would not want to – have an appropriate place within them, or whether, as Maddock and Parkin, and Newman (Halford and Leonard 2001: 185) have suggested, public sector organizations are characterized by 'a complex mix of administrative, professional and gender discourses' within which 'possibilities may exist for individual women actively to modify, challenge or resist conforming to the dominant, traditional gender-power relations'.

The work of Stivers (1993) suggests that public administrations may be particularly marked by traditional gendered culture. She suggests that 'As long as we go on viewing the enterprise of administration as genderless, women will continue to face their current Hobson's choice, which is either to adopt a masculine administrative identity or accept marginalization in the bureaucratic hierarchy' (Stivers 1993: 10). Moreover, the 'new public management' approaches, with their emphasis on merit, may have changed managerial cultures, but women will need to demonstrate that they can, in a competitive environment, perform just like men. In Australia, some women have chosen to tackle these dilemmas by entering the administrative hierarchy but doing so with an explicitly feminist approach (Chappell 2002; Eisenstein 1996; Yeatman 1990). Eisenstein (1996) coined the term 'femocrat' to denominate 'a powerful woman within government administration with an ideological and political commitment to feminism'. Australian scholars have demonstrated the way in which these femocrats have used the 'political opportunity structures', open to them as a consequence of Australia's federal constitutional structure, its party system and the nature of the norms determining the scope for policy advocacy by individual officials, to advance policies desired by feminists.

Despite these theoretical debates, there has been relatively little empirical or qualitative research on women within state bureaucracies, two important exceptions being Martindale (1938) and Brimelow (1981) both referring to the UK civil service and the failure of women to advance to more senior posts. Bagilhole's work on a public service office provides strong pointers to patterns of relatively covert discrimination rife within the organization in the early 1990s (Bagilhole 1994). Marie Christine Kessler (2003) and Jeanne Siwek-Pouydesseau (2003) have studied senior women and middle- and junior-ranking women respectively in the French civil service. In the United Kingdom the Hansard Society sponsored a 'women at the top' study published as a pamphlet in 2000 (Ross 2000).

In the context of rather little research on women in public administrations the paucity of studies of the position of women within the European Commission is perhaps unremarkable. In his extensive study of the Commission and its staff Page (1997) has very little to say about gender, nor does gender appear as a variable in Liesbet Hooghe's exhaustive study of the attitudes of senior Commission officials (Hooghe 2001). Smith and Joana (2002) include two women amongst the eight Commissioners upon whom their research concentrated. However, neither in their extensive discussion of the origins of the Commissioners nor in their consideration of the composition of the Commissioners' personal staff (cabinets) are gender issues considered. Nevertheless, in an institution with as complex a melange of organizational cultures as the European Commission (Stevens and Stevens 2001), the relationship between the gender regime (Connell 1987) and the position of individual women may be particularly relevant. In the early 1990s Alison Woodward carried out a series of interviews with men and women in the Commission and observed that in a setting in which many aspects of national and professional culture and identity are challenged 'there may be a tendency to grasp at the few things that unite, including assumed beliefs about gender [roles]' (Woodward 1996: 184). Stevens and Stevens (2001) devote a few pages to the dearth of women in the organization at the end of the twentieth century and tentatively advance some explanations.

THE EUROPEAN UNION AND EQUAL OPPORTUNITIES

The Treaty of Rome contained within it an article (then Article 119) committing the member states of the European Economic Community (EEC) to equal pay for men and women. This article was one of those inserted to appease French concerns about the loss of their traditional protection against external commercial and industrial competition (Hoskyns 1996), given fears about competition from states which, unlike France, did not have formal equal pay and an undifferentiated minimum wage: it was originally allocated to a section on distortions to competition, and finally slipped into a section of the draft treaty that dealt with social policy (Hoskyns 1996: 56). Hoskyns argues (1996: 210) that the creative and imaginative use by women of 'legal channels and policy instruments' has resulted in the EU providing a considerable impetus to social change. The initial strategy was one of ensuring equal treatment. She demonstrates very clearly the extent to which the developments leading to the key directives of the 1970s involved 'policy-entrepreneur' (Cram 1997) advocacy by officials within the Commission, some of them women, for example Jacqueline Nonon, head of the Women's bureau in the Social Affairs Directorate General, in alliance with external groups (Hoskyns 1996: 100).

The outcome of advocacy within the commission and external pressures, both from the re-emergent women's movement of the early 1970s and from important judgments by the European Court of Justice, notably Defrenne 1, 2 and 3, was the equal pay and equal treatment directives of the mid-1970s. These included; 75/117 Equal Pay, 76/207 Equal Treatment (amended 2002 by 2002/73), and 79/7 Social Security. The Court and the Council between them in the 1970s and 1980s stretched the initial concepts a long way. But the Treaty was an essentially economic treaty, and women were of interest to it only insofar as they were workers. This approach can be described as the 'equal treatment' approach (Rees 1998 quoted in Pollack and Hafner-Burton 2000: 433) and is undoubtedly crucial. But it is also a limited one. However, in 1993 the Maastricht Treaty turned the EC into the EU and formally moved it away from being merely a strictly economic organization.

Theresa Rees identifies a shift in the 1980s to a 'positive action' stage of policy development. This shift was certainly furthered, after 1979, by the Committee on Women's Rights of the European Parliament. After the first direct elections in 1979, the Parliament saw the proportion of women members rise from 5 to 16 per cent, the election of a woman (Simone Weil) as its president, and the creation of an ad hoc parliamentary committee on women's rights (Hoskyns 1996: 127). The Commission's main vehicle for carrying positive action forward was a series of action programmes, approved by resolution in the Council of Ministers, commencing in 1982. The Fifth Action programme on Gender Equality ran until 2006.

The third stage of policy development identified by Rees is gender mainstreaming. The concept appeared in the EC's Third Action Programme on Equal Opportunities (1991–1996), with rather little impact (Pollack and Hafner-Burton 2000: 435), but was promoted as a general principle of action in 1995 as part of the preparation for the UN conference in women in Beijing, where it was incorporated into the Platform for Action. The year 1995 was also one of enlargement which included two countries with a strong commitment to gender equality (Finland and Sweden) and a new Commission with five female Commissioners. Moreover, strong pressure from the European Parliament obliged incoming Commission President Santer to commit the Commission to paying attention to equal opportunities (Pollack and Hafner-Burton 2000: 436). As a consequence the Fourth Medium Term Community Action Programme on Equal Opportunities for Men and Women strongly featured mainstreaming, and this was followed up by a communication (COM (1996) 67) setting out the guidelines for incorporating the promotion of gender equality in all EU programmes.

In 1997 the Amsterdam Treaty introduced Article 13 which allows discrimination against women as women, rather than women as workers, to be tackled by EU legislation. This provided a secure framework for gender mainstreaming which is now the approach to policy-making in this field embraced both by the European Commission (Mazey 1998; Bretherton 2001) and by some national governments (Squires and Wickham Jones 2004).

The notion of gender mainstreaming is a potentially radical one, since it implies the promotion of adaptation in the roles and behaviours of men as well as women (Bretherton 2001: 62). Unsurprisingly Pollack and Hafner-Burton (2000: 450) concluded from a study of five policy-areas that there has been substantial variation across policy issues in the acceptance and implementation of this new policy approach. In one case (the provision of development aid) where they judge mainstreaming policy to have made disappointing progress they identify 'the overwhelming dominance of male officials at the highest levels of the EU development bureaucracy' (Pollack and Hafner-Burton 2000: 466) as one of the specific obstacles. Similarly research policy was, until the advent of a female commissioner (Edith Cresson) in 1995, officially gender blind, but in fact 'the overwhelming dominance of men within the scientific community was reproduced in EU research policy, in which Commission officials, advisory committee members and recipients of EU research grants were overwhelmingly male' (Pollack and Hafner-Burton 2000: 448). Commissioner Cresson instigated a number of policy initiatives to remedy this situation. Since 1998, for example, partly as a result of the advocacy of a female official who in 2001 became the first head of a new unit in DG Research dealing with the issue, the promotion of 'women in science' has been a policy objective for the commission (interview 2005). It is clear that both in terms of structural factors and strategic agency, policy-making may be inflected by the presence of women as Commissioners and officials.

THE COMMISSION AS AN ORGANIZATION

The Commission has a number of distinctive characteristics. First, it is directly responsible for the implementation of very few policies – in most cases that is the responsibility of the Member States – and that is what generally requires large numbers of staff, particularly at the junior levels where the proportion of women is usually highest.

Second, its construction was influenced by the reflexes and instincts of the pioneers which were inevitably drawn from the habits of the systems to which they were accustomed in their home states. Page (1997: 7) has observed that '[t]he essence of a continental European bureaucracy was in its creation of a distinctive social class', and that social class was predominantly male, especially in the senior policy-making ranks. Page (1997: 8) adds that such bureaucracies 'are associated with formalism and hierarchy – the insistence that rules and procedures be observed'. Both these features demand a clear statutory definition in order to entrench them. These entrenched reflexes have in recent years been challenged by the growing influence of British and Scandinavian Commissioners and officials in the area of administration, and by movements for reform which take some of their inspiration from the new public management approaches which have flourished in the English speaking worlds. Whilst Scandinavian influence brings with it a strong orientation towards gender parity, new managerialism, as we have seen, is not necessarily women friendly.

Hence the Commission was, and still is, an organization in general regulated, rather than managed. A third characteristic of the Commmission's structures is the regulatory framework, a classically 'bureaucratic' and 'gender blind' system, highly dependent upon set and uniform procedures as a method of human resource management. For instance, although there was provision for unpaid leave on personal grounds which, when it was sought in order to allow an official (male or female) to bring up a dependent child, might extend to five years (Staff Regulations Article 30), provision for part-time working (Article 55) merely allowed for officials ('exceptionally' and on request) to be permitted to work half-time, and required that half the normal hours should be worked each month, thus, for example, prohibiting 'term-time only' working. It was not until the complete overhaul of the regulation in 2004 that parental leave was in fact available in the Commission. The so-called 'Kinnock reforms', whilst retaining the legal framework, have attempted to shift the balance towards a more flexible approach to human resource management, but have initially had rather little impact.

Fourth, in managerial terms the Commission does not resemble many bureaucracies which have a clearly pyramidal hierarchy. In 2004 very nearly half its established staff were graduate level administrators (Spence and Stevens 2005). Most of the implementation and delivery of EU policies falls to national governments. So a very high proportion of the work is policy-related desk work. Officials, working mostly on their own with little or no support, rather than in a team, generally handle files, not people, and career progression through promotion in which seniority continues to play a key role (Spence and Stevens 2005) can take an official to the normal career maximum (old Grade A4, new grade A* 12) without them ever managing any other person. It is possible that the lack of opportunity to experience management on a smaller scale before advancing to the more major responsibilities of Head of Unit post is one reason why potentially eligible women in the Commission are often reluctant to apply for such posts (interviews 2005).

EQUAL OPPORTUNITIES POLICY WITHIN THE COMMISSION OVER THREE DECADES

Despite the rather proactive role taken by the European Commission in the 1970s, its own record as an employer was far from exemplary, especially in relation to women in 'professional' or managerial posts. Progress was slow, but the Commission was not immune from the pressures that were slowly developing in this area. In 1984 the joint working party in the Commission was regularized into a standing joint Equal Opportunities Committee, known by its French acronym as COPEC, which later, in 1992, was recognized as a committee as provided for in the Staff Regulations (Article 9 paragraph 1a). It was assigned a specifically monitoring role: 'to monitor the implementation of the equal opportunities policy for staff in the Commission' (Women at the European Commission 1984–1994 1994: 11). It has continued to play a useful role as a consultative body, improving and refining the draft texts and documents presented to it, but it has not been able proactively to advance policies that would promote gender equality (interviews 2005).

Reflecting the mechanism utilized by the Social Affairs Directorate General to carry forward its general gender equality objectives, the mechanism of an Action Programme was adopted, and the first (of four between 1988 and the time of writing) such programme was approved for 1988–1990. Its objectives included increasing the number of women in categories where they were under-represented, and particularly in senior and scientific posts, and improving women's chances of promotion. The methods proposed were the standard nostrums – training, information, increased awareness, provision of facilities such as a crèche. However, the principle of 'giving priority to women in the event of equal qualifications and/or merits' (Women at the European Commission 1984–1994 1994) was specifically enunciated, a 'positive' principle, reiterated rather more visibly in 2000 in the Kinnock reform White Paper, from which many organizations might have shied away, and which, given the 'reserve list' system for appointment to administrative posts in the Commission (Spence and Stevens 2005), could potentially have had a substantive impact. Nevertheless the rise in the proportion of women was slow – in the A grades between 1984 and 1994 from 9.3 per cent to 13.5 per cent.

Sweden and Finland, which joined the EU in 1995, had a tradition of promoting gender equality, and indeed in 1995 the Swedish government consisted of equal numbers of men and women (Leijenaar 1997: 74). The new commissioner in charge of Personnel and Administration, Erkki Liikanen, was shocked at the imbalances he discovered (interview 1995), and attempted to push forward the Action Plans with greater vigour. Figures for the recruitment performance of each Directorate-General were produced, and precise targets were set. However, the position some ten years later is improving only slowly (see Table 11.1).

Table 11.1   European Commission – women in administrative and managerial grades

Grade	1994		1999		2002		2004[a]		2005[a]	
	N	%	N	%	N	%	N	%	N	%
A1/A16	1	1.9	2	4.1	4	6.6	3	5.5	3	5.5
A2/A15	4	2.5	20	12.0	24	12.4	34	17.4	35	15.4
A3/A14	29	7.0	57	11.0	67	10.5	83	15.3	90	14.2
A4/A12	90	9.2	154	12.8	233	13.3	403	23.8	519	23.3
A5/A11	118	14.4	175	17.1	357[b]	21.0	570	31.3	679	29.5
A6/A10	96	16.3	225	24.2	385	27.3	576	37.9	723	35.8
A7/A9	139	19.4	266	28.9	452	31.8	1	25.0	12	37.5
A8/A8	44	31.9	23	35.9	97	45.9	704	38.3	698	40.1
Total	521	13.5	922	18.9	1619	21.9	2374	31.0	2759	29.9

Notes:
[a] New grading system – top eight grades (A16-A8 excl. grade 13) only.
[b] No breakdown for UK-sourced A5s, so an average for all A5s has been assumed.

Sources: (Hoskyns 1996: 225 Table 5.3), (Stevens and Stevens 2001: table 5.2) Public Service Magazine, **5** (4) 4 May 2002, 37, European Commission, Directorate-General for Personnel and Administration, 2004B:7, Commission Européene, Direction générale du personnel et de l'administration, 2005B.

As the notion of gender mainstreaming, as opposed to segregating questions of equal opportunities and equal treatment into specialized action plans, took root, it was slowly extended to the Commission's policies on its own management and human resources. The 2000 reform White Paper (COM (2000) 200 final/2) contained a section on 'working environment and equal opportunities' within its human resources section. Within this section a rather inconspicuous phrase to the effect that 'gender mainstreaming must be central to the new integrated human resources policy' was added in between the initial draft communication produced in January (CG3 (2000) 1/17) and the final version in March. The Action Plan appended to the White Paper in its final (though not initial) version was more robust, noting under Action 47 that 'The principle of mainstreaming, that is the systematic consideration of gender issues in all policies and actions, must be a basic parameter for the reform of human resources policy'. Its proposals, discussed below, provided for an updated equal opportunities infrastructure, while 'softer' measures continued to be contained in the Action Programmes.

The Kinnock Reforms

The 2000 reform White Paper reiterated 'preference for women' as between 'candidates of equal merit' which should override the pressures for 'geographical balance' (COM (2000) 200 final, section IV 4). The action plan accompanying the paper contained commitments to the introduction of parental leave, better provision for flexible and part-time working and job-sharing (Action 53) and to the creation of a favourable environment for the recruitment, promotion and career development of women (Action 47).

The revised regulations contain a general commitment in Article 1(d) of Title 1 allow for positive actions in favour of the 'under-represented sex'. The same article also spells out the implications of the EU's own 'burden of proof' directive (Directive 97/80) by making it clear that where discrimination is alleged the 'onus shall be on the institution to prove that there has been no breach of the principle of equal treatment'. Maternity leave was increased, paternity leave (10 days) introduced, and six months' parental leave per child and parent, paid at a low flat rate, introduced. The circumstances under which part-time working would be allowed were extended and the possibility of half-time job sharing provided for. All these measures were certainly necessary to remove unwarranted obstacles to gender equality and bring the employment policies of the Commission into line with much contemporary practice. However, it may be argued that removal of obstacles was not likely in itself to permit the Commission to achieve its targets, and the new provision in Article 4 of Annex III of the Regulations, on recruitment competitions, that 'if a selection board consists of more than four members it shall include at least two members of each gender', may eventually be at least as significant.

CURRENT POSITION OF WOMEN IN COMMISSION POSTS

Hoskyns' study showed that women already accounted for over 44 per cent of Commission employees in 1977, with the corresponding figure for 1984 and 1994 being 45.4 per cent in both cases (Hoskyns 1996: appendix 5, 224). However, there were enormous disparities within these figures: in 1994, over 80 per cent of secretarial staff were female while 86.5 per cent of the highest managerial and administrative grades (A grades) were male, and there was a sharply tapering profile of females to males within the grading hierarchy. By 1999, there had been considerable progress at improving female representation at A2, A3, A6 and A7 grades principally as a result of the enlargement of 1995 which brought in Austria, Finland and Sweden to the EU. As Stevens with Stevens (2001) outline, the incoming Finnish Commissioner responsible for personnel and administration set targets for female recruitment and representation which were in many ways more ambitious than those which were to come later, although they were not met.

As can be seen from Table 11.1, there had been further improvement by 2002, but female participation in the administrative grades was still less than 22 per cent, and at the most senior level was only 6.6 per cent. Admittedly this is a huge improvement from the 1.9 per cent in 1994, but we are dealing with very small numbers at this level. The largest proportions of female administrative grade employees remained in the lower grades in 2002. Other than for grades A1 and A2, the rate of increase is roughly similar, and it may be argued that a 50 per cent improvement in female participation over eight years is quite impressive. On the other hand, this workforce had roughly doubled in size over the same period hence giving more opportunity for women to advance.

By 2004, the new grading system had come into operation and so it is difficult to make direct comparisons with the earlier data, as the 'A' grade has been extended from eight to 12 points. The total numbers of employees within the grade was roughly the same if the bottom three points (A7 to A5) are taken out and grade A13 is ignored (there was only one person in it in 2004). This leaves 7671 in 2004 compared with 7393 in 2002 in the eight grades compared. Overall, there was a 42 per cent improvement in the ratio of female to male employees (21.9 per cent to 31 per cent). In absolute numbers, there were 755 more women working in these grades compared with 2002. Given that there was a total increase of only 278 in all employees at these grades in 2004, meant that there were 477 fewer men in 2004 compared with 2002, certainly in part a result of early retirements encouraged by that part of the Kinnock managerial reforms.

The 2005 figures in Table 11.1 are not so encouraging. In a much bigger cohort (9237 compared with 7671) resulting from the influx of officials arriving from the ten new member states admitted to the EU in 2004, the total number of female employees was up from 2374 to 2759, but the percentage was down marginally at 29.9 per cent with small reductions in the most senior grades and increases in the two lowest grades of this population. As the Commission's 2005 survey acknowledges, the targets set for female participation for the end of 2004 were not met (Commission of the European Communities 2005: 13). Within the secretarial and manual grades there has been very little change since the 1970s.

The three targets for 2003 were to appoint five women at the old A1 and A2 grades, at least 25 per cent women at 'middle management' grades (Heads of Unit at A3–A5), and to maximize the recruitment of women from the reserve list for A6–A8; as of the end of 2003, five women had been appointed at A1/A2 (representing 19 per cent of those recruited at this level), 27.5 per cent of middle management appointees were women, and 33.3 per cent of reserve list candidates for A6–A8 posts were women (Commission of the European Communities 2004: 6). For 2004, the first target was increased from five to seven women (not met, five women only recruited), the second raised from 25 per cent to 27 per cent (not met, 24.5 per cent out-turn), and the third incorporated an overall target of 50 per cent (not met, out-turn 44 per cent) (Commission of the European Communities, 2005: 6–7). There were different targets again for 2005, these being a 20 per cent target for new recruits to senior management, a 30 per cent target for new recruits at middle management levels, and a 50 per cent target for other A grades so far as reserve lists allow (Commission of the European Communities, 2005: 13–14).

What is surprising is how modest most of these targets are given the scope for improved gender balance in recruitment. The 2005 report gives figures for the numbers of female and male applicants for posts at senior and middle management levels in 2004. While it is certainly the case that male applicants outnumber female applicants by seven to one and five to one respectively, there was no absolute shortage of female applicants. For the seven senior management positions targeted for women, there were 112 female applicants, and for the 23 middle management women appointees, there were 102 female applicants (Commission of the European Communities 2005: 5–6). There was scope therefore, to raise the targets.

EXPLANATIONS

A variety of inter-related structural and cultural explanations for female under-representation in management grades have been advanced. An explanation may be found in the gendered structure of the Commission, yet there is the key paradox of an organization overtly dedicated to advancing equal opportunities yet so manifestly deficient in achieving the aspirations it espouses for itself and others. A more nuanced approach will need to look at layers of explanation, taking account of individual cultural beliefs and assumptions (Cini 2001). And the deepest assumptions may include those related to gender. In the early 1990s Woodward observed that 'in multicultural situations with unclear rules, participants grasp for the stereotypical gender solutions and have strongly stereotypic expectations about gender ... since national chauvinism is taboo, gender chauvinism amongst men becomes more pronounced' (Woodward 1996: 174 and 176).

Until at least the 1980s, as we have seen, the traditional masculine values and solidarities, linked with power and historically intrinsic to bureaucratic structures, were unchallenged within the Commission. At the most basic level, this resulted in an initial preponderance of male managers which will perpetuate itself through the career progression process unless there is a sudden expansion of Commission staff numbers allowing the balance to be righted. While each enlargement has produced growth (as we have seen in the case of the most recent round), gender imbalance has not been corrected because of the greater or lesser preponderance of male officials who enter Commission service in the relevant grades from the incoming new member states.

As we have seen, it is also the case that in open competition for posts within the Commission, far fewer women apply than men. However, it is worth re-emphasizing that in 2004/5 there was no absolute shortage of well qualified female candidates (European Personnel Selection Office 2005).

Given these initial cohorts and the flow of suitably qualified female undergraduates through European universities over the past 20 years, it is simply inconceivable that a balance of suitable male and female candidates cannot be achieved, provided that the recruitment process is fair and appropriate. In the early 1990s this was not perceived to be the case, and the competitive examination process was characterized as having 'clearly discriminatory effects' (Woodward 1996: 181). However, the numbers in the lowest A grade categories for 2004 suggest that there is at least a rough balance, although there was a significant preponderance (63 per cent) of males in the higher (A6) grade (Commission of the European Communities 2005: 6 and 10).

This raises issues about the structure of the type of work and career progression subsequently, and why women are directly discriminated against or rule themselves out of consideration for it. Reporting in 1986, Monique Chalude and her colleagues identified a culture of sexual stereotyping (cited in Stevens and Stevens 2001: 112–113). Surveying the period from the Chalude report to 2001, Stevens with Stevens identified three main barriers to career progression for women including:

- The persistence of sexual stereotyping within the context of a male-dominated work environment which women felt pressure to conform to.
- The absence of informal support networks to cope with the practice of long working hours actively encouraged by some Commissioners as a prerequisite for career advancement.
- The importance of informal male-dominated patronage networks in the career advancement process.

The first of these barriers had already been identified by Woodward in the early 1990s. Woodward (1996: 176) noted that the gender dimension of the 'European' identity that was developing as a substitute for the national cultures which were less acceptable in a multinational organization 'assumes a subordinate position for women'. Since the second factor is a manifestation of organizational culture which may seem to lie at the most superficial level it has been most directly attacked by the various action programmes, and the recent Kinnock reforms have again emphasized measures to encourage more 'family friendly' structures and working practices. However, as Michelle Cini (2001) has argued in relation to general management reform in the Commission, there is a gulf between changes in structures and the cognitive changes in beliefs, assumptions and behaviours they are meant to induce. It is clear that both the resistance to part-time working and the unfriendly working hours identified by Woodward (1996: 183), and confirmed by interviewees in the later 1990s, persist. Indeed in 2005, Commissioner Kallas reported that 'a culture change is still necessary to effect a change in daily work practices, in particular late hours of meeting and work', and that further measures were needed in addition to the rather limited measures already taken in the revised Staff Regulations (Commission of the European Communities 2005: 8). Woodward (1996: 176) argues that professional cultures stemming from highly masculine professions – she cites law, economics and engineering – provide a shared, but male, language within the Commission which facilitates multinational networking and patronage, but excludes women.

The forms that patronage takes can be relatively veiled – a job description can, for example, be written to suit a particular candidate. It does not always work against women, and when a woman is the favoured candidate for a post it is of course helpful that her appointment can be claimed as a contribution to the equal opportunities targets. Moreover, the mentality which accepts patronage as well as hierarchy (Stevens and Stevens 2001) has other disadvantages for women. As one of the interviewees said:

> Around men of power ... I observe [an entourage] – the link with feudalism around men of power ... this I see much less around women of power ... It is as if men produce a sort of magnetic field where people like to be in – they like to follow a man. For a man to follow a woman – that they don't like. They much prefer to seduce women than to follow them. And that means that ... as a woman ... you have to [make] a much bigger effort ... and you are much more contested in your choices and decisions.

Despite widespread acknowledgement of some of these features over at least a decade it has proved extremely difficult to tackle them, not least because the problems included those of mentality as well as structures (Spence and Stevens 2005). Recent reforms have strengthened the meritocratic mechanisms, but the impact of these changes may well not be clear for another decade (Coull and Lewis 2003). As critics of the new public management have noted, ostensibly meritocratic systems do not necessarily treat women equally (see Chapter 10). It will take time to see whether the template of performance that would be applied will be so 'masculine' as to disadvantage women. Our interlocutors thought that would probably not be the case but it was clear that one problem has emerged in some instances. Women who have been on maternity leave have in some cases been disadvantaged when performance points which count towards promotion have been attributed in the appraisal rounds. They have been awarded a low number of points on the grounds that they have not been present to perform regardless of the merits of their performance when they were present.

CONCLUSION

The position and role of women in senior managerial posts in the European Commission is deeply influenced by the structures and culture within which they find themselves. And these are replete with paradoxes. The first paradox is the disjunction between the undoubted achievements of European policy-makers in advancing the cause of non-discrimination, equal opportunity and equal treatment in European Union policy, yet the halting progress made in these areas within the Commission itself. If the figures for the proportion of women in senior posts indicate this, another telling piece of evidence is that despite EU directives on parental leave it was not provided for in the Commission until the new statute came into force in 2004 (interview 2005). Procedures and plans are only a small part of the story, however, and the

Commission has had an equal opportunities programme since 1988. What has been crucially lacking is commitment, drive and political will from the highest levels and in a sustained way.

This is linked to a second crucial paradox between the rhetoric of equality and the practice of distinction. Within the Commission this takes two forms: first, the administration is a legally defined and regulated one. And this characteristic takes on an almost mythical aspect. In the European Commission the legally-protected rationality, equality and autonomy of the 'European civil servants' can be, and is, fiercely upheld as a guarantee of supranationality and a defence against the capture of the 'European project' by special interests. This framework of autonomy and equality can always be appealed to by those whose vested interests may seem to be threatened by reform or change, especially if it is suggested that there should be new ways of advancing the position of women. The paradox resides in the constant undermining of this equality and autonomy for other reasons through 'personal networking, political influence and parachutage' (Spence 1994: 98). Difference is accepted when the differing characteristic is nationality, and 'right to appropriate representation (geographical balance)' in senior positions is asserted (Commission of the European Communities 2002: 38). A number of insiders, including one of the smaller Commission staff unions (R&D – Renouveau et Democratie) (*European Voice* 27 May–2 June 2005 and interviews 2004), would like to see quotas for senior staff by gender introduced alongside those for the various nationalities. Short to medium term quotas are required, it is argued, because the current policy, which requires merely a preference for female candidates when all other qualities are equal, is not working in the absence of commitment and political will. But this is fiercely resisted on the basis that it will constitute unacceptable positive discrimination, militate against equality, and lead to promotion and appointment by gender not merit.

It is generally accepted that when entering the Commission, men and women start with the same qualifications and the same potential. They are not, however, achieving the same career positions. Our interviews suggest that the 'bonus' attached to being male is manifested in a number of ways. Just as in corporate life where Halford and Leonard (2001: 138) found 'women have to leap far more hurdles than men to become managers' so senior women felt that they had constantly to prove themselves, and ran the risk that their style of management, even if it actually resulted in, for example, fewer personnel problems and conflicts in their areas than in those managed by men, would be perceived as 'wimpish'. According to Halford and Leonard (ibid) in corporate life 'it is very difficult for women to gain access to those managerial positions where the greatest officially sanctioned organizational power is held. They are more likely to be given minority issues.' It is notable that there are very few women in the most highly esteemed Directorates-General such as

Competition or External Relations, although the recent appointments of women as Deputy Director General in the Legal Service and as Secretary General of the Commission may be the exceptions that prove the rule.

Our fieldwork provided some support for Ferguson's (1984) argument that bureaucracies are intrinsically masculine; the advancement of women, especially insofar as it may seem in some way to threaten a masculine solidarity, can be resisted by appeal to the absolute equality of individuals, but the model of the individual is masculine. In those circumstance the women who do succeed are often perceived as being 'female men' whose circumstances, styles and approaches conform most closely to male norms (see Chapter 4). This may render the prospect of moving up the hierarchy unattractive to a number of women, and there is strong anecdotal evidence that women at middle levels often decline to put themselves forward for managerial positions. This may also in part be because women tend to feel that they have to be 'perfect' to justify the occupation of a senior post. They may feel that the 'male bonus' discussed above would render it a wasted effort. Union spokeswoman Olga Profili told *European Voice* bluntly; 'Many women do not apply for senior Commission jobs because they know they are unlikely to get them' (*European Voice* 27 May–2 June 2004). It may also be that the measures, many introduced or strengthened by the recent reforms, which are supposed to assist women – maternity leave, possibilities of part-time working – in fact may be a hindrance, since they imply lack of commitment and availability and, at least while they are not utilized equally by men, emphasize difference not equality.

In the first years of the millennium the Commission's administration has faced considerable upheaval and reform, aimed at changing not only its structures but also its culture and ethos. Whilst the rhetoric of the reforms has stressed commitment to improving the position of women and developing family friendly structures, in practice these issues have been overshadowed by matters such as career structures, appointment procedures, pay and pensions, and the massive challenge of integrating ten new member states into all the structures and procedures of the union. Without assertive solid and collective commitment and political leadership from the top, progress will continue to be slow and the Commission will remain a regrettably poor example of a policy which it preaches but does not practice.

REFERENCES

Bagilhole, B. (1994), *Women, Work and Equal Opportunity: Underachievement in the Civil Service*, Aldershot: Avebury.

Bretherton, C. (2001), 'Gender Mainstreaming and EU Enlargement: Swimming Against the Tide', *Journal of European Public Policy*, **8**(1), 60–81.

Brimelow, E. (1981), 'Women in the Civil Service', *Public Administration*, **59**(3), 314–35.

Chappell, L.A. (2002), 'The "Femocrat" Strategy: Expanding the Repertoire of Feminist Activists', *Parliamentary Affairs*, **55**(1), 85–98.

Cini, M. (2001), 'Reforming the European Commission: an Organizational Culture Perspective. Review of Reviewed Item', *Queen's Papers on Europeanization*, (11), www.qub.ac.uk/schools/SchoolofPoliticsInternationalStudiesandPhilosophy/ FileStore/EuropeanisationFiles/Filetoupload,5285,en.pdf.

Commission of the European Communities (2000a), *Towards a Community Framework Strategy on Gender Equality (2001–2005)*, *COM (2000)355 Final*, Brussels: European Commission.

Commission of the European Communities (2000b), *Reforming the Commission: A White Paper – Part I: Communication from Mr Kinnock in Agreement with the President and Mrs Shreyer*, Brussels: European Commission.

Commission of the European Communities (2000c), *Reforming the Commission: A White Paper – Part II: Action Plan: Communication from Mr Kinnock in Agreement with the President and Mrs Shreyer*, Brussels: European Commission.

Commission of the European Communities (2002), *An Administration at the Service of Half a Billion Europeans: Staff Reforms at the European Commission: State of Play Spring 2002*, Brussels: European Commission.

Commission of the European Communities (2004), *Targets for the Recruitment and Appointment of Women, 2004: Operating and Research Budget. Memorandum from Mr Kinnock, C(2004)2048*, Brussels: European Commission.

Commission of the European Communities (2005), *Targets for the Recruitment and Appointment of Women to Management and Other A*/AD Level Posts in the Commission; Communication from Vice-president S. Kallas SEC(2005)784/4*, Brussels: European Commission.

Connell, R.W. (1987), *Gender and Power: Society, the Person and Sexual Politics*, Cambridge: Cambridge Polity in association with Blackwell.

Coull, J. and Lewis, C. (2003), 'The Impact Reform (sic) of the Staff Regulations in Making the Commission a More Modern and Efficient Organization: An Insider's Perspective. Review of Reviewed Item', *EIPASCOPE* (3), www.eipa.nl.

Cram, L. (1997), *Policy-making in the EU*, London: Routledge.

Diamantopolou, A. (2001), *Women at the Commission – Reform and Outlook for the 21st Century, Speech 01/149*, Brussels: European Commission.

Eisenstein, H. (1996), *Inside Agitators: Australian Femocrats and the State*, Philadelphia PA: Temple University Press.

European Personnel Selection Office (2005), *Press Releases 05/06*, 14 October 2005.

Ferguson, K.E. (1984), *The Feminist Case Against Bureaucracy*, Philadelphia PA: Temple University Press.

Halford, S. and Leonard, P. (2001), *Gender, Power and Organizations*, Basingstoke: Palgrave Macmillan.

Hooghe, L. (2001), *The European Commission and the Integration of Europe: Images of Governance*, Cambridge: Cambridge University Press.

Hoskyns, C. (1996), *Integrating Gender: Women, Law and Politics in the European Union*, London: Verso.

Kanter, R. (1977), *Men and Women of the Corporation*, New York: Basic Books.

Kassim, H. (2004), 'The Kinnock Reforms in Perspective: Why Reforming the Commission is a Heroic but Thankless Task', *Public Policy and Administration*, **19**(4), 25–41.

Kessler, M.C. (2003), 'Les femmes dans la haute fonction publique', *Revue administrative*, **56**(331), 71–86.

Leijenaar, M. (1997), *How to Create a Gender Balance in Political Decision-making*, Luxembourg: Office for Official Publications of the European Communities.

Martin, D. (1995), *What Future for the European Commission*, London: Philip Morris Institute for Public Policy Research.

Martindale, H. (1938), *Women Servants of the State 1870–1938: a History of Women in the Civil Service*, London George Allen & Unwin Ltd.

Mazey, S. (1998), 'The European Union and Women's Rights: from the Europeanization of National Agendas to the Nationalization of a European Agenda?', *Journal of European Public Policy*, **5**(1), 131–52.

Mazur, A.G. (2002), *Theorizing Feminist Policy*, Oxford: Oxford University Press.

Page, E. (1997), *People who Run Europe*, Oxford: Oxford University Press.

Pavan-Woolfe, L. (2005), *Why Women are Needed in Executive Positions in the EU*, Brussels: European Commission DG General Employment, Social Affairs and Equal Opportunities.

Pollack, M. and Hafner-Burton, E. (2000), 'Mainstreaming Gender in the European Union', *European Journal of Public Policy*, **7**, 432–56.

Rees, T. (1998), *Mainstreaming Equality in the European Union: Education, Training and Labour Market Policies*, London and New York: Routledge.

Ross, K. (2000), *Women at the Top 2000: Cracking the Public Sector 'Glass Ceiling'* King-Hall Papers, London: Hansard Society.

Savage, M. and Witz, A. (eds) (1993), *Gender and Bureaucracy*, Oxford: Blackwell.

Siwek-Pouydesseau, J. (2003), 'Les femmes dans la petite et moyenne fonction publique française', *Revue Administrative*, 87–93.

Smith, A. and Joana, J. (2002), '*Les commissaires européens: technocrates, diplomates ou politiques?*', Paris: Presses de Sciences Po.

Spence, D. (1994), 'Staff and Personnel Policy in the Commission', in G. Edwards and D. Spence (eds), *The European Commission*, London: Cartermill.

Spence, D. and Stevens, A. (2005), 'Staff and Personnel Policy in the Commission', in D. Spence (ed.), *The European Commission*, London: John Harper Publishers.

Squires, J. and M. Wickham Jones (2004), 'New Labour, Gender Mainstreaming and the Women and Equality Unit', *British Journal of Politics and International Relations*, **6**(1), 81–98.

Stevens, A. and Stevens, H. (2001), *Brussels Bureaucrats: the Administration of the European Union*, Basingstoke: Palgrave Macmillan.

Stevens, H. and Stevens, A. (2005), 'The Internal Reform of the Commission', in D. Spence (ed.), *The European Commission*, London: John Harper Publishers.

Stivers, C. (1993), *Gender Images in Public Administration*, Newbury Park, London: Sage.

Vianello, M. and Moore, G. (eds) (2000), *Gendering Elites: Economic and Political Leadership in Industrialized Societies*, Basingstoke: Macmillan.

Women at the European Commission 1984–1994 (1994), D.G.f.P.a. Administration (ed.), Commission of the European Communities.

Woodward, A.E. (1996), 'Multinational Masculinities and European Bureaucracy', in D. Collinson and J. Hearn (eds), *Men as Managers, Managers as Men*, London: Sage.

Yeatman, A. (1990), *Bureaucrats, Femocrats, Technocrats: Essays on the Contemporary Australian State*, Boston, MA: Allen and Unwin.

Conclusion   Key debates and responses: business, societal and policy contexts

Duncan McTavish

An analysis of women in leadership and management raises a series of interconnected issues on the wider societal, political and policy fronts as well as in the more obvious business sphere.

There is a clear business case for greater female representation. In overall business – economic terms, the potential value to be gained from increasing women's participation in the labour market is highly significant (see Introduction; Women and Work Commission 2006). Key skills gaps, including amongst managers and other organizational leaders, could be eased with greater proportional female participation in a wider variety of sectors and occupations than is currently the case. Attention must also be paid to the fact that advances can stall or indeed be reversed: in areas and sectors where women have been making career inroads, there is some evidence of personal disinvestment taking place, due to the unattractiveness or difficulty of further advance in traditional (male-oriented) gendered organizational cultures and spaces (see Chapter 10). Singh and Vinnicombe (Chapter 7) outline strong arguments for more females at the most senior levels in business: more diversity on boards gives a broader perspective, more aligned and consistent with the modern corporation's complexity of stakeholders; the good governance records of boards with existing female representation; evidence of positive correlation of boards with significant female representation and market capitalization; 'insurance' against headline discrimination litigation; symbolic roles for other females in the organization.

The book also captures a range of nuances in the gender in the management–business sphere. Much has been written elsewhere about the feminine side of management in positive terms, defining that as more collectivist/communal and transformative-values-based than its opposite, an agentic, masculine, transactional, often 'macho'-based, approach. Swan (Chapter 3) outlines a process which actually indicates that many of these 'feminine' practices are (re)constructed not as an alternative approach to the dominant paradigm, but to provide some legitimacy and add reinforcement to that approach in the context of coaching. The introductory chapter also highlights the contradictory demands this places on managers, particularly women. The progressive role which mentoring is thought to play in advancing women in leadership and management is questioned by Mavin (Chapter 4), given the context of senior females entering a male world of management, the persistence of traditional male and female attitudes, female misogyny and unrealistic expectations of senior women in organizations. One might ask, 'mentoring for what'?

There are though clearly positive messages and signs of some progress. Chapter 7 (Singh and Vinnicombe) presents some specific illustrations of company initiatives and indicates some good practice guidelines. Ogden and Maxwell (Chapter 8) and Fielden and Hunt (Chapter 9) show that the small business and entrepreneurial start-up sectors can provide spaces of real opportunity for women leaders and managers, although the barriers here are not underestimated and must be challenged. There is also a rich source of opportunity in female-initiated and -led networks and joint (solidarity-based) action as outlined in the chapter by Mavin, Bryans and Waring (Chapter 2) on the gendered nature of management and business education. This is part of a deep and long-standing feminist tradition, questioning the sole dependency of women on men and patriarchal organizations.

While the focus of this book was not to address the role of gender, women and society, the position of women in leadership and management cannot be seen without some awareness of relationships between gender, work and societal norms, expectations and perceptions. Many of the concerns in this book surround vertical occupational segregation and some of the issues surrounding the disproportionate numbers of women in management and leadership. There are other aspects of gender segregation in the workplace: there is vertical and horizontal segregation and an over-concentration of women in areas like caring, catering and cleaning. Interestingly, in response to this, the well researched report of the Women and Work Commission (2006) highlights the importance of encouraging girls and women into other (better paid) areas through the educational, training and careers guidance systems. Few would doubt the value of this response, but there is evidence that movement of women in significant numbers into occupations and sectors leads to a feminization and relative devaluation of remuneration and opportunities. This has been shown in areas of medicine in parts of eastern and central Europe; the growing numbers of females entering and graduating from medical schools in the UK (now the majority) has led senior figures in the medical profession here to voice similar fears. Such developments place the focus of attention on wider attitudes and values which society holds in relation to women in the workplace.

The 'traditional' public–private divide interprets the public world of work as a traditionally male-dominated domain and the private domestic world of female responsibility dominated by child rearing, child care and other family and home-centred responsibilities. Accordingly, the private domain has to be repressed for women to perform successfully in an organizational context. The traditional Parsonian work–family model (see Chapter 5) enshrined in the 1950s and 1960s is now difficult to sustain in the context of increased female participation in labour markets and other societal changes. Gatrell's interesting chapter (Chapter 5) challenges aspects of the notion of an accentuated 'home orientation' (see Hakim 2000) for female professionals and managers. In addition, although there continues to be gender disproportionate responsibility for domestic, child care, family and other out of work commitments, this is on its own an insufficient explanation for imbalances in gender in management. The structuring of opportunity is a clear inhibitor to greater gender balance. For example, only 7 per cent of managers and senior officials work part-time compared with 33 per cent of those in administrative and secretarial occupations (Women and Work Commission 2006: 34). Although there are a range of jobs (in both public and business sectors) difficult to organize on a share or part-time basis it is hardly credible to believe that the 7 per cent cited above represents a natural ceiling. Chapter 5 also reminds us that in twenty-first century Britain, negative, prejudicial attitudes hostile towards some women combining family, domestic life and career do get coverage in sections of the tabloid press and elsewhere, no doubt reflecting the views of some of its readers.

There is a political and policy context and undercurrent to women in leadership and management. A number of chapters outlined that 'new public management' had a tension, perhaps a contradiction, at its core. McTavish, Miller and Pyper (Chapter 10) indicate that in higher education the new public management had led to the growth of an externally referenced 'quality of learning and teaching' infrastructure along with increased transparency, thereby opening up career space for academic women, yet the agentic, target-based regime had regendering effects and a career dynamic far from gender neutral in its impact; the same chapter highlighted the gendered effect of new public management linked reforms in the NHS. The gap between policy rhetoric and reality was outlined in a number of chapters, perhaps most graphically by Levy and Stevens (Chapter 11). They identified Europe's evolution of approaches to equality and also noted a chasm between, on the one hand, the equality principles which the EU embeds in policy for the attention of its member states and, on the other, the lack of gender equality at middling and senior levels of management in the European Commission itself. This may be termed a 'credibility deficit'.

Political commitment and positive action were highlighted by a number of contributors. Affirmative action and quotas are options which have been used, most notably in the United States, to access under-represented groups into higher education (and in other sectors); there has also been the use of quotas internationally to increase the number of females in elected legislatures (Dahlerup and Freidenvall 2005) and as Collins and Singh highlight (Chapter 1) the largest party in the devolved Scottish Parliament used an affirmative action instrument (subsequently legally challenged) to increase female representation amongst its elected Members of the Scottish Parliament (MSPs). The legal basis of affirmative action in the UK is not secure. Collins and Singh also indicate that female leaders in their research indicated personal views on the undesirability of quotas or other affirmative measures (as distinct from positive action measures which they broadly supported). Norway has embarked on a legally enforceable approach to increasing the gender balance of corporate boards and an evaluation of this will be of interest.

The necessity of strong political commitment was highlighted. Improved opportunities for women in the European Commission were often the result of a strong drive from individual Commissioners (Levy and Stevens, Chapter 11). Policy intention for greater gender balance in the UK via government and service delivery modernization was outlined in Chapter 10 (McTavish, Miller and Pyper). There is also the use of governmental machinery and policy instruments like mainstreaming initiatives and Public Service Agreements (PSAs), currently in existence (Veitch 2005) – one such PSA is to target 45 per cent of large organizations having completed equal pay and management reviews by 2008. It is perhaps rather telling that the Trade and Industry Select Committee (2005) when reviewing progress on the gender equality PSAs stated: 'It is not clear to us whether the slowness of other departments in addressing the issues is a result of insufficient vigour in the lead department, the DTI, or a lack of co-operation from other departments'. Finally, the importance of political commitment is recognized by The Women and Work Commission (2006: 101) in its call for the establishment of a new Cabinet sub Committee of Ministers to implement a range of the Commission's recommendations across government.

REFERENCES

Dahlerup, D. and Freidenvall, L. (2005), 'Quotas as a "Fast Track" to Equal Representation for Women', *International Feminist Journal of Politics*, **7**(1), 26-48.
Hakim, C. (2000), *Work-lifestyle Choices in 21st Century: Preference Theory*, Oxford: Oxford University Press.
Trade and Industry Select Committee (2005), *Sixteenth Report, Jobs for the Girls: the Effect of Occupational Segregation on the Gender Pay Gap*, HC 300-1, 2004–05.
Veitch, J. (2005), 'Looking at Gender Mainstreaming in the UK Government', *International Feminist Journal of Politics*, **7**(4), 600–606.
Women and Work Commission (2006), *Shaping a Fairer Future*, London.

Index